SADLIER

VOCABULARY WORKSHOP®

TOOLS FOR EXCELLENCE

Level A

Jerome Shostak

Senior Series Consultant

Vicki A. Jacobs, Ed.D.
Adjunct Lecturer on Education
Harvard Graduate School of Education
Cambridge, Massachusetts

Series Consultants

Louis P. De Angelo, Ed.D.
Superintendent of Schools
Diocese of Wilmington
Wilmington, Delaware

John Heath, Ph.D.
Professor of Classics
Santa Clara University
Santa Clara, California

Sarah Ressler Wright
Head Librarian
Rutherford B. Hayes High School
Delaware, Ohio

Sadlier School

Reviewers

The publisher wishes to thank for their comments and suggestions the following educators who read portions of the series prior to publication.

Erica Backhurst
Dean of Students
Worthington Kilbourn High School
Worthington, OH

Melissa Elliot
Teacher, AP English
Martinsburg High School
Martinsburg, WV

Kristie Hofelich Ennis
English Instructor & Virtual Co-Teacher
Downers Grove North High School
Downers Grove, IL

Stephanie Fearn
Gifted, Reading, and Global Perspective Teacher, Department Head
Caloosa Middle School
Cape Coral, FL

Judith Hinds-Henry
Teacher, Language Arts
Coral Springs High School
Coral Springs, FL

Meghan Leach
Teacher, Language Arts
Harmony Science Academy — High
Houston, TX

Danielle Manock
Literacy Coach/Peer Collaborative Teacher
M.S. 137, America's School of Heroes
Ozone Park, NY

Cynthia Naroff
Teacher, Language Arts
Council Rock High School South
Holland, PA

Lisa Picardi
Assistant Coordinator of English
Council Rock High School South
Holland, PA

Susan Szafranski
Teacher, English and Journalism
Lemont High School
Lemont, IL

Charles Youngs, Ed.D.
Curriculum Facilitator, English Language Arts
Bethel Park High School
Bethel Park, PA

Cover Series Design: Silver Linings Studios; Cover pencil: Shutterstock.com/VikaSuh.

Photo Credits: akg-images/Collection Jean-Pierre Verney, Paris: 71 *bottom*; Universal Images Group/Father Browne: 32, 33 *bottom*. Alamy Stock Photo/A.F. Archive: 69; Allstar Picture Library: 107; Archive Images: 141; Classic Image: 19; Entertainment Pictures / SNAP: 79; Everett Collection Inc.: 93, 169; INTERFOTO: 17; LatitudeStock: 27; Lebrecht Music and Arts: 75, 179; National Geographic Image Collection/Edward Herbert Miner: 184; Photo 12: 97; Pictorial Press Ltd: 127 *top*, 135; Wild Places Photography/Chris Howes: 55; World History Archive: 155. Art Resource, NY/Alinari: 51 *bottom*; HIP: 99. Bridgeman Images: 31, 71 *top*.; Jonathan Barry: 145; Lebrecht Authors: 193; Lebrecht Authors/Harold Copping: 65; Look and Learn: 41; Peter Newark American Pictures: 50. Digital Vision Ltd: 60 *bottom*, 60–61 *background*. Fotolia.com/highwaystarz: 10. Getty Images/Archive Photos: 165 *left*; Bettmann: 131, 189; Corbis Historical: 61 *bottom*; De Agostini/DEA/F. Galardi: 137; Dorling Kindersley: 164 *left*; Hulton Deutsch: 59; Michael Ochs Archives/BMI: 126; Moviepix/Paramount Pictures: 89 *top*; New York Daily News Archive/Jim Mooney: 175 *top*; The LIFE Picture Collection/Joseph Scherschel: 113; Paul Towne: 151; VCG/Tim Davis: 165 *right*. Granger/ullstein bild: 108. TopPhoto/Mary Evans Picture Library: 51 *top*; ArenaPAL/Marilyn Kingwill: 183. Tim Flach Photography Ltd: 185 *top*. Library of Congress/Prints and Photographs Division, LC-DIG-ggbain-35698: 33 *left*. Mary Evans Picture Library/ONSLOW AUCTIONS LIMITED: 70. Media Bakery/Frans Lanting: 185 *bottom*. NASA: 60 *top*; 89 *bottom*, 109 *bottom*. National Portrait Gallery, London: 98. NativeStock/Marilyn Angel Wynn: 88. Photodisc: 175 *top*. Picture Press/Detlev van Ravenswaay: 61 *top*. Punchstock/Blend Images: 22 *center*. Science & Society Picture Library/Universal Images Group/Father Browne: 33 *top*. Science Source: 37. Shutterstock.com/alphaspirit: 60—61 *inset*; Marc Dietrich: 51 *top*; emo_O: 99 *inset*; Fotokor77: 108–109 *background*; Iwona Grodzka: 126 *background*; Kobal/RKO: 117; Taras Kompaniets: 146–147 *background*; Ice-Storm: 32–33 *background*; Olivier Le Moal: 22 *bottom left*; Lina_S: 146 *bottom*, 147 *background*; MaxyM: 70–71 *background*; Jeff Metzger: 98; More Trendy Design Here: 60–61 *inset*; Moviestore Collection: 173; Pola36: 127 *inset*; Thirteen: 164 *left*, 165 *left*; Valentyn Volkov: 88–89 *background*. Smithsonian Institution/National Museum of African American History and Culture: 175 *bottom*. SuperStock: 127 *bottom*; All Canada Photos/Wayne Lynch: 136 *bottom*; Peter Bennett: 22 *bottom*; Science Faction/Steven Kazlowski: 164 *right*; Stockbroker/Purestock: 23 *top*. The British Library: 103. U.S. Postal Service: 174. Wikimedia Commons: 109 *top*; freeworldmaps.net/Daniel Feher: 136 *top*.

Illustration Credits: Sally Wern Comport: 12. Tim Haggerty: 46, 84, 122, 161, 198. Britt Spencer: 146, 147.

Address inquiries to Permissions Department,
William H. Sadlier, Inc.,
25 Broadway, New York, NY 10004-1010.

Printed in the United States of America.
ISBN: 978-1-4217-1806-4
4 5 6 7 8 9 10 CWR 27 26 25 24

CONTENTS

iWords Audio Program is available at **SadlierConnect.com**.

PROGRAM FEATURES

For more than six decades, **VOCABULARY WORKSHOP** has proven to be a highly successful tool for vocabulary growth and the development of vocabulary skills. It has also been shown to help students prepare for standardized tests.

Each level of **VOCABULARY WORKSHOP** introduces and provides practice with 300 vocabulary words and contains features such as reading passages, writing prompts, vocabulary in context, evidence-based questions, and word study that will help you to master these new vocabulary words and succeed in using skills to comprehend unfamiliar words.

Each Unit in **VOCABULARY WORKSHOP** consists of the following sections: an introductory **Reading Passage** that shows how vocabulary words are used in context; **Definitions** that include sentences that give examples of how to use the words; **Choosing the Right Word**; **Synonyms**; **Antonyms**; **Completing the Sentence**; and **Vocabulary in Context** that provide practice with the vocabulary words. Each introductory **Reading Passage** includes most of the vocabulary words from the Unit to which it belongs.

Look for the QR codes on the **Reading Passage** and **Vocabulary in Context** pages. The code can be read with a smartphone camera. To read the QR code, download any free QR code application. Snap the code with a smartphone camera to go directly to the iWords for the Unit or an interactive quiz.

The five Review sections contain all 60 words from their corresponding Units. **Vocabulary for Comprehension** is modeled on the reading sections of college entrance exams. It presents reading comprehension questions, including vocabulary-related items and evidence-based items that are based on the reading passages.

Word Study sections that contain activities on **Idioms**, **Proverbs**, **Adages**, **Denotation and Connotation**, and **Classical Roots** follow the Review. These sections will help you develop your understanding of figurative language and practice skills that will help you to determine the meaning of new and unfamiliar vocabulary.

The Final Mastery Test assesses a selection of words from the year and allows you to see the growth you have made in acquiring new vocabulary words and in mastering the comprehension skills you need to understand unfamiliar words.

DIGITAL RESOURCES

SadlierConnect.com

Go to **SadlierConnect.com** to find iWords, an audio program that provides pronunciations, definitions, and examples of usage for all of the vocabulary words presented in this level of **VOCABULARY WORKSHOP**. You can listen to the entire **Reading Passage** and the 20 Unit vocabulary words.

At **SadlierConnect.com** you will also find vocabulary quizzes, flash cards, and activities that will help reinforce and enrich your understanding of the vocabulary words presented in this level of **VOCABULARY WORKSHOP**.

VOCABULARY IN CONTEXT

The context of a word is the printed text of which that word is a part. By studying a word's context, we may find clues to its meaning. We might find a clue in the immediate or adjoining sentence or phrase in which the word appears; in the topic or subject matter of the passage; or in the physical features—such as photographs, illustrations, charts, graphs, captions, and headings—of a page itself.

The **Reading Passages** as well as the **Choosing the Right Word**, **Completing the Sentence**, **Vocabulary in Context**, and **Vocabulary for Comprehension** exercises that appear in the Units, the Reviews, and the Final Mastery Test provide practice in using context to decode and to determine the meaning of unfamiliar words.

Three types of context clues appear in the exercises in this book.

A **restatement clue** consists of a synonym for or a definition of the missing word. For example:

Faithfully reading a weekly newsmagazine not only broadens my knowledge of current events and world or national affairs but also ______________ my vocabulary.

a. decreases **b.** fragments **c.** increases **d.** contains

In this sentence, *broadens* is a synonym of the missing word, *increases*, and acts as a restatement clue for it.

A **contrast clue** consists of an antonym for or a phase that means the opposite of the missing word. For example:

"My view of the situation may be far too rosy," I admitted. "On the other hand, yours may be a bit (**optimistic, bleak**)."

In this sentence, *rosy* is an antonym of the missing word, *bleak*. This relationship is confirmed by the presence of the phrase *on the other hand*, which indicates that the answer must be the opposite of *rosy*.

An **inference clue** implies but does not directly state the meaning of the missing word or words. For example:

"A treat for all ages," the review read, "this wonderful novel combines the ______________ of a scholar with the skill and artistry of an expert ______________."

a. ignorance . . . painter **c.** wealth . . . surgeon

b. wisdom . . . beginner **d.** knowledge . . . storyteller

In this sentence, there are several inference clues: (a) the word *scholar* suggests knowledge; (b) the words *novel*, *artistry*, and *skill* suggest the word *storyteller*. These words are inference clues because they suggest or imply, but do not directly state, the missing word or words.

VOCABULARY AND READING

There is a strong connection between vocabulary knowledge and reading comprehension. Although comprehension is much more than recognizing words and knowing their meanings, comprehension is nearly impossible if you do not know an adequate number of words in the text you are reading or have the vocabulary skills to figure out their meaning.

The **Reading Passages** in this level provide extra practice with vocabulary words. Vocabulary words are in boldface to draw your attention to their uses and contexts. Context clues embedded in the passages encourage you to figure out the meanings of words before you read the definitions provided after the passages.

Test Prep

Your knowledge of word meanings and your ability to think carefully about what you read will help you succeed in school and on standardized tests, including the SAT® and ACT® exams.

The **Vocabulary for Comprehension** exercises in each Review consist of a reading passage followed by comprehension questions. The passages and questions are similar to those that you are likely to find on standardized tests.

Types of Questions

You are likely to encounter the following types of questions in VOCABULARY WORKSHOP and on standardized tests.

Main Idea Questions generally ask what the passage as a whole is about. Often, the main idea is stated in the first paragraph of the passage. You may also be asked the main idea of a specific paragraph.

- The primary or main purpose of the passage is . . .
- The author's primary or main purpose in the passage is to . . .
- Which of the following statements most nearly paraphrases the author's main idea in the ninth paragraph (lines 77–88)?
- The main purpose of the fourth paragraph (lines 16–25) is to . . .

Detail Questions focus on important information that is explicitly stated in the passage. Often, however, the correct answer choices do not use the exact language of the passage. They are instead restatements, or paraphrases, of the text.

Vocabulary in Context Questions check your ability to use context to identify a word's meaning.

- As it is used in the second paragraph, "adherents" most nearly means . . .

Use the word's context in a passage to select the best answer, particularly when the vocabulary word has more than one meaning. The answer choices may contain two (or more) correct meanings of the word in question. Choose the meaning that best fits the context.

Inference Questions ask you to make inferences or draw conclusions from the passage.

- It can be most reasonably inferred from the information in the fifth paragraph (lines 53–69) that . . .
- The passage clearly implies that . . .

Your answer must be based on the information in the passage. Using the facts from the passage and your own knowledge and reasoning helps you understand what is implied and reach logical conclusions.

Evidence-Based Questions ask you to provide evidence from the passage that will support the answer you provided to a previous question.

- Which choice provides the best evidence for the answer to the previous question?
- Which statement is the best evidence for the answer to the previous question?

Questions About Tone show your understanding of the author's attitude toward the topic of the passage. To determine the tone, pay attention to the author's word choice. The author's attitude may be positive (respectful), negative (scornful), or neutral (distant).

- The author's primary purpose in the passage is to . . .
- Which word best describes the author's tone?

Questions About Author's Technique focus on the way a text is organized and the language the author uses. These questions ask you to think about structure and function.

- In the context of the passage, the primary function of the fourth paragraph (lines 30–37) is to . . .
- The organizational structure of the passage is best described as . . .

To answer the questions, you must demonstrate an understanding of the way the author presents information and develops ideas.

VOCABULARY AND WRITING

The **Writing: Words in Action** writing prompts require a response to the **Reading Passage** and provide practice in writing for standardized tests.

WORD STUDY

Word Study helps build word knowledge with strategies to help you look closely at words for meanings. Word Study instruction and practice include **Idioms**, **Proverbs**, **Adages**, **Denotation and Connotation**, and **Classical Roots**.

Idioms, Proverbs, and Adages

Word Study sections feature instruction on and practice with idioms, proverbs, and adages. Developing a clear understanding of idioms, proverbs, and adages will help you better understand the figurative language that authors use in their writing.

Denotation and Connotation

Instruction in **Denotation and Connotation** and practice with connotations is included in the Word Study sections. Understanding a word's connotation will develop your skills as a reader, writer, and speaker.

Understanding the difference between denotation and connotation is important to understanding definitions and how concepts are used, as well as in choosing the right word. In these exercises, practice choosing the correct word by determining the emotional association of the word.

Classical Roots

Each Word Study includes a **Classical Roots** exercise that provides instruction in and practice with Greek and Latin roots. Developing a useful, transferable technique to make sense out of unfamiliar words through Greek and Latin roots will help you unlock the meanings of thousands of words. An example word drawn from the vocabulary words in the previous Units is referenced at the top of the page and serves as a guide to help you complete the exercise.

PRONUNCIATION KEY

The pronunciation is indicated for every basic word in this book. The pronunciation symbols used are similar to those used in most recent standard dictionaries. The author has primarily consulted *Webster's Third New International Dictionary* and *The Random House Dictionary of the English Language (Unabridged)*. Many English words have multiple accepted pronunciations. The author has given one pronunciation when such words occur in this book except when the pronunciation changes according to the part of speech. For example, the verb *project* is pronounced **prə jekt'**, and the noun form is pronounced **präj' ekt**.

Vowels	ā	l*a*ke	e	str*e*ss	ü	l*oo*t, n*ew*
	a	m*a*t	ī	kn*i*fe	u̇	f*oo*t, p*u*ll
	â	c*a*re	i	s*i*t	ə	j*u*mp, brok*e*n
	ä	b*a*rk, b*o*ttle	ō	fl*ow*	ər	b*ir*d, bett*er*
	au̇	d*ou*bt	ô	*a*ll, c*o*rd		
	ē	b*ea*t, word*y*	oi	*oi*l		

Consonants	ch	*ch*ild, lec*t*ure	s	*c*ellar	wh	*wh*at
	g	*g*ive	sh	*sh*un	y	*y*earn
	j	*g*entle, bri*dg*e	th	*th*ank	z	i*s*
	ŋ	si*ng*	t̶h̶	*th*ose	zh	mea*s*ure

All other consonants are sounded as in the alphabet.

Stress The accent mark follows the syllable receiving the major stress: en rich'.

Abbreviations	*adj.*	adjective	*n.*	noun	*prep.*	preposition
	adv.	adverb	*part.*	participle	*v.*	verb
	int.	interjection	*pl.*	plural		

---

*Read the following passage, taking note of the **boldface** words and their contexts. These words are among those you will be studying in Unit 1. As you complete the exercises in this unit, it may help to refer to the way the words are used below.*

City of Gold

<First-Person Narrative>

Long ago in western Africa, bands of traders traveled to the city of Timbuktu to buy goods in exchange for gold. The following account is given by a boy describing his first trip to the famous city. He is with a group of friends in the year 1450.

My father has been carrying gold from our land to sell in Timbuktu since he was young. His father was a gold trader before him, and now I've joined him and my brothers. We joined other travelers with their goods and camels in a caravan. We brought gold to Timbuktu to sell, and now I've come home. I'll tell you about that city of gold, because soon you'll be old enough to go there with your fathers, too. I'm **famished**—I haven't eaten since morning. Let's enjoy this small **repast** together while I talk.

I'll start at the end: What a **gainful** expedition! You saw the great load of goods we brought home. **Immense** packages of salt, some **expressly** for our own use, but most for trade here and to the south. We brought back kola nuts to chew on, some palm oil for cooking, and fine cloth for clothing. We profited more than usual, because the buyers of gold wanted more than was available. One man even offered to lend my father gold at interest so we could trade more before having to leave. Father refused, saying, "Lend your money and lose a friend."

Before the journey, I had imagined that we would take our bags to Timbuktu and trade a handful here and there. What an **inept** trader I would become, if not for the wisdom of my father! My father is an **ingenious** man who knows his way

around the world. Before we even entered the city, we stopped to rest by the river. We washed and set up a cooking fire. My father left and returned with a wealthy merchant and his men. They brought us much salt in exchange for our gold. My father and this merchant, who's a big man in Taghaza up north, chewed kola nuts and spoke like old friends. Then, the merchant **dispatched** his men, ordering them back to their camp. Their compliance was **instantaneous**, and I watched them **recede** into the distance, carrying gold this time instead of salt. **Irked** by my idling, my father told me to stop gawking like an **oaf** and start packing the salt.

We ate a quick meal and **doused** the fires. At last, I entered the city of Timbuktu. There are people in Timbuktu of every shape, size, and color; and they come from everywhere, wearing all sorts of **apparel** and speaking many languages. Many speak Arabic, and many speak Mande, like us. There are thousands of people in that city. It's a busy place, but exciting, with massive mosques and palaces and markets.

We exchanged the rest of our gold in the marketplaces. Because there was so much happening, our time in the city went quickly. Now that I am home, I confess that I had some **misgivings** before I went. I feared thieves would attack our caravan. I wondered if the city might be raided or **besieged** while we were there. But everything went smoothly on my first visit. What a place, that busy city—I can hardly wait till we return!

Audio

For iWords and audio passages, snap the code, or go to **SadlierConnect.com**.

Definitions

Note the spelling, pronunciation, part(s) of speech, and definition(s) of each of the following words. Then write the word in the blank spaces in the illustrative sentence(s) following. Finally, study the lists of synonyms and antonyms.

1. apparel (ə par′ əl)

(*n.*) clothing, that which serves as dress or decoration; (*v.*) to put clothes on, dress up

Winter ____________________ should be warm and cozy.

Let's ____________________ our cats for the party.

SYNONYMS: (*n.*) attire, garments; (*v.*) deck out
ANTONYMS: (*v.*) undress, unclothe, strip, denude

2. besiege (bi sēj′)

(*v.*) to attack by surrounding with military forces; to cause worry or trouble

If troops ____________________ their stronghold, the rebel forces may be forced to surrender.

SYNONYMS: blockade, encircle, pressure, hound

3. compress (*v.*, kəm pres′, *n.*, käm′ pres)

(*v.*) to press together; to reduce in size or volume; (*n.*) a folded cloth or pad applied to an injury

The editor helped ____________________ my rambling 25-page mystery into an 8-page thriller.

A cold ____________________ may soothe headache pain.

SYNONYMS: (*v.*) condense, shrink, shorten
ANTONYMS: (*v.*) enlarge, swell

4. denounce (di naůns′)

(*v.*) to condemn openly; to accuse formally

The United Nations decided to publicly ____________________ the tyrant's crimes.

SYNONYMS: criticize, censure
ANTONYMS: hail, acclaim

5. dispatch (dis pach′)

(*v.*) to send off or out for a purpose; to kill; (*n.*) an official message; promptness, speed; the act of killing

We'll ____________________ a repair crew right away.

He approved the request with ____________________.

SYNONYMS: (*v.*) slay; (*n.*) report, communication
ANTONYMS: (*v.*) recall, withhold

6. douse (daůs)

(*v.*) to plunge into a liquid, drench; to put out quickly, extinguish

I'll ____________________ the flames with the hose.

SYNONYMS: submerge, soak, dunk, immerse
ANTONYMS: dry out, dehydrate, kindle, ignite

7. expressly (ek spres′ lē)

(*adv.*) plainly, in so many words; for a particular purpose

At the meeting, parents ____________________ stated their approval of students wearing school uniforms.

SYNONYMS: pointedly, explicitly
ANTONYMS: implicitly, accidentally

8. famished (fam′ isht)

(*adj., part.*) suffering severely from hunger or from a lack of something

The Vietnamese immigrants, new to a strange American city, were ____________________ for news of home.

SYNONYMS: hungry, starving, ravenous
ANTONYMS: well fed, full, satisfied, satiated

9. forsake (fôr sāk′)

(*v.*) to give up, renounce; to leave, abandon

I will never ____________________ my children, no matter what they do or say.

SYNONYMS: desert, disown
ANTONYMS: keep, hold on to, stand by

10. gainful (gān′ fəl)

(*adj.*) profitable; bringing in money or some special advantage

I hope to find ____________________ employment that is pleasing to me.

SYNONYMS: moneymaking, paying
ANTONYMS: unprofitable, unrewarding, nonpaying

11. immense (i mens′)

(*adj.*) very large or great; beyond ordinary means of measurement

Alaska enjoys ____________________ natural resources, but its severe climate makes those resources difficult to use.

SYNONYMS: vast, immeasurable, gigantic
ANTONYMS: small, tiny, minute, infinitesimal

12. inept (in ept′)

(*adj.*) totally without skill or appropriateness

The scientist is brilliant in the research laboratory but is ____________________ at dealing with people.

SYNONYMS: clumsy, unskilled, incompetent
ANTONYMS: skillful, accomplished, adroit

13. ingenious (in jēn′ yəs)

(*adj.*) showing remarkable originality, inventiveness, or resourcefulness; clever

The students found an ____________________ solution to the math problem.

SYNONYMS: imaginative, resourceful
ANTONYMS: unimaginative, unoriginal, uninventive

14. instantaneous (in stən tā′ nē əs)

(*adj.*) done in an instant; immediate

Most computer software is designed so that users can obtain nearly ________________ responses.

SYNONYMS: prompt, quick, speedy
ANTONYMS: delayed, slow, gradual

15. irk (ərk)

(*v.*) to annoy, trouble, make weary

Questions that show a student's lack of attention ________________ the teacher.

SYNONYMS: bother, irritate, vex
ANTONYMS: please, delight, cheer

16. libel (lī′ bəl)

(*n.*) a written statement that unfairly or falsely harms the reputation of the person about whom it is made; (*v.*) to write or publish such a statement

The young celebrity accused her unauthorized biographer of ________________.

The writer was careful not to ________________ the people she interviewed for her report on the event.

SYNONYMS: (*n.*) slur; (*v.*) smear, defame

17. misgiving (mis giv′ iŋ)

(*n.*) a feeling of fear, doubt, or uncertainty

They had ________________ about joining the chorus because of its demanding schedule.

SYNONYMS: worry, qualm, hesitation
ANTONYMS: feeling of confidence, assurance

18. oaf (ōf)

(*n.*) a big, clumsy, slow individual

He generally moved like an ________________, so I was surprised to see how graceful he was on the dance floor.

SYNONYMS: clod, lout

19. recede (ri sēd′)

(*v.*) to go or move backward; to become more distant

The town residents must wait for the flood waters to ________________ before they can deal with the terrible mess left behind.

SYNONYMS: retreat, go back, back up
ANTONYMS: advance, come closer

20. repast (ri past′)

(*n.*) a meal, food

Let's get together after the show at Callie's Café for a late-night ________________.

SYNONYM: victuals

Choosing the Right Word

*Select the **boldface** word that better completes each sentence. You might refer to the unit selection to see how most of these words are used in context.*

In the fifteenth century, da Vinci drew a design for the first armored tank, which had guns and was powered by men turning crankshafts.

1. His notebooks show that Leonardo da Vinci was not only a masterful artist but an (**inept, ingenious**) inventor as well.

2. We can (**compress, besiege**) the message of the sermon into one short sentence: "Do unto others as you would have others do unto you."

3. He may claim that we have (**libeled, doused**) him, but we have facts to back up every statement made in the column about him.

4. The beauty of the Grand Canyon is so (**immense, instantaneous**) that it is absolutely impossible to capture its grandeur on film.

5. Which job would you take—one that is more (**ingenious, gainful**) right now or one that pays a small salary but offers a chance for valuable training?

6. Her conscience forced her to (**denounce, libel**) the conspirators to the authorities.

7. Tom may not be as polished and clever as some of the other boys, but I think it is unfair of you to call him an (**apparel, oaf**).

8. The story I am reading features a(n) (**inept, doused**) detective who cannot solve a case and continually loses things.

9. We were pleasantly surprised to see that she completed the difficult task we had given her with neatness and (**irk, dispatch**).

10. As soon as she took over the office of Mayor, she was (**besieged, dispatched**) by dozens of people eager to get city jobs.

11. (**Famished, Compressed**) for a chance to see her work in print, the young writer begged the magazine editor to publish her story.

12. His conceit is so (**immense, gainful**) that he cannot imagine anyone voting against him in the election for class president.

13. I will never (**recede, forsake**) the people who helped me in my hour of need!

14. After all the bad things he has done, I feel no (**dispatches, misgivings**) about telling him that I don't want him to be my "friend" anymore.

15. My sister is learning French, taking cooking classes, and participating in other (**inept, gainful**) pursuits that will allow her to become a master chef.

16. You may criticize the roads and the lights, but the fact is that (**inept, immense**) drivers are the cause of most car accidents.

17. I always feel sad at the end of the autumn, when the trees lose their beautiful (**repast, apparel**) of leaves.

18. As soon as he began his long, boring speech, our excitement died down, as though we had been (**denounced, doused**) with cold water.

19. Our puppy's paws and legs are much larger than her body, but she looks adorable as she lumbers around the yard like a huge (**libel, oaf**).

20. Where did he ever get the curious idea that we set up this volleyball court (**expressly, instantaneously**) for him and his friends?

21. We are working hard to improve conditions in our community, but we cannot expect (**famished, instantaneous**) results.

22. Each day, after she finishes her homework, she enjoys a light (**repast, misgiving**) of the detective stories she loves so well.

23. Instead of feeling (**forsaken, irked**) because you did poorly on the exam, why don't you make up your mind to study harder in the future?

24. When I realized that I was thoroughly prepared for the final exams, my fears quickly (**receded, irked**).

25. Hold the (**repast, compress**) on your ankle until the swelling goes down.

Synonyms

Choose the word from this Unit that is the same or most nearly the same in meaning as the ***boldface*** *word or expression in the phrase. Write that word on the line. Use a dictionary if necessary.*

1. compelled to **ditch** the leaky boat ____________________

2. had to fire the **bungling** carpenter ____________________

3. thought the article **tarnished** her reputation ____________________

4. **inventive** use for lumber scraps ____________________

5. using a machine to **squash** the cans ____________________

6. fashionable hand-me-down **outfits** ____________________

7. waiting until the crowds **ebb** ____________________

8. **bad feelings** about the leading candidate ____________________

9. is **clearly** forbidden for use by minors ____________________

10. **expressed disapproval of** the protestors' actions ____________________

Antonyms

Choose the word from this Unit that is most nearly opposite in meaning to the ***boldface*** *word or expression in the phrase. Write that word on the line. Use a dictionary if necessary.*

1. writes a **compliment** ____________
2. likes to **support** all causes ____________
3. **expand** the bundle to fit ____________
4. was certain to **gladden** the passengers ____________
5. reasons to **validate** the winner ____________

Completing the Sentence

From the words in this Unit, choose the one that best completes each of the following sentences. Write the correct word form in the space provided.

1. How can we hope to ____________ a city that is surrounded by such strong walls and has ample supplies of everything it needs?

2. Don't allow yourself to be ____________ by every small trouble that may arise during the day.

3. Let's make certain to ____________ the fire before leaving camp.

4. Some of life's rewards are ____________; others are a long time in coming.

5. Some people hailed the man as a genius; others ____________ him as a quack.

6. You had no right to call me a clumsy ____________ just because I spilled some water on you.

7. As it was well past their lunchtime by the time we arrived home, the children were ____________ and demanding food.

8. You will be able to get everything into a single suitcase if you ____________ all the items as much as possible.

9. On my first baby-sitting job, I found that one must have ____________ patience to take care of young children.

10. When you play tennis for the first time, you are going to find that your attempts to hit the ball are very ____________.

11. As an inexperienced sailor, I had more than a few ____________________ about taking out the small boat in such rough weather.

12. The laws of this land do not shield public figures from just criticism, but they do protect them against ____________________.

13. A(n) ____________________ will be sent to all our representatives in Latin America advising them how to handle the problem.

14. While all true vegetarians ____________________ animal meats, some do eat dairy products, such as milk and yogurt.

15. Far away on the horizon, we saw the tiny figures of a lonely traveler and his mule ____________________ into the sunset.

16. None of us could figure out how the ____________________ magician had managed to escape from the trunk submerged in the tank of water.

17. When you are really hungry, even the simplest foods, such as a slice of buttered bread, will be a delicious ____________________.

18. Your ____________________ can be neat and attractive without being expensive.

19. Because I have reached an age at which I am unwilling to depend on my parents, I am out to find a(n) ____________________ occupation.

20. The terms of our agreement ____________________ forbade us to take any of the goods for our own use.

Writing: Words in Action

1. Look back at "City of Gold" (pages 12–13). Suppose you will be traveling soon with the traders. You wonder what your trip will be like when you arrive in Timbuktu. Write a journal entry, describing what excites you about the trip and what worries you. Use at least two details from the passage and three Unit words.

2. Like the traders from the 1400s, countries continue to trade gold, salt, clothing, and other goods in the world market. How is trading in the 1400s different from how people trade in modern times? What goods are most valued today? Write a brief essay in which you support your observations with specific examples, studies, and the reading (refer to pages 12–13). Write at least three paragraphs, and use three or more words from this Unit.

Vocabulary in Context

Literary Text

The following excerpts are from the novel The Swiss Family Robinson *by Johann David Wyss. Some of the words you have studied in this unit appear in* ***boldface*** *type. Complete each statement below the excerpt by circling the letter of the correct answer.*

1. I found Ernest busily engaged in weaving a basket in which to catch fish: he had devised it **ingeniously**, with a funnel-shaped entrance; through which the fish passing would not easily find their way out.

When something is created **ingeniously**, it requires

a. feelings
b. payment
c. imagination
d. patience

2. On her work-table [were] fishing-lines of all sorts, and knives and other tools.

These latter she told me were, with a chest of wearing **apparel**, almost the only things washed ashore after the wreck.

A chest packed with **apparel** is filled with

a. clothing
b. books
c. jewels
d. food

The classic novel *The Swiss Family Robinson* tells of the adventures of a family that becomes shipwrecked on a deserted island.

3. We found the whole family in a state of the greatest excitement, and I felt it necessary to calm them down as much as possible, for neither could I answer the questions with which I was **besieged,** nor could I conceal the fact that the visit of the vessel might not prove so advantageous as they expected.

Someone who is **besieged** with questions feels

a. angry
b. overwhelmed
c. pleased
d. calm

4. By this time the sun was sinking beneath the horizon, and the poultry, which had been straying to some little distance, gathered round us, and began to pick up the crumbs of biscuit which had fallen during our **repast**. My wife hereupon drew from her mysterious bag some handfuls of oats, peas, and other grain, and with them began to feed the poultry.

A **repast** is a

a. meal
b. gathering
c. hike
d. bucket

5. I heard [Ernest] loudly calling: "Father, father! I've caught a fish! An **immense** fellow he is. I can scarcely hold him, he drags the line so!"

A fish that is **immense** is NOT

a. massive
b. significant
c. large
d. small

Interactive Quiz

Snap the code, or go to **SadlierConnect.com**.

Read the following passage, taking note of the ***boldface*** *words and their contexts. These words are among those you will be studying in Unit 2. As you complete the exercises in this unit, it may help to refer to the way the words are used below.*

West End School Has Comestible Curriculum

<Interview>

The Scrumptious Schoolyard is a grassroots program that transforms concrete playgrounds into functional farmland. Part of the Scrumptious Schoolyard Project, it is the brainchild of **contemporary** food-education pioneer Clarissa Z. Ochoa. Students explore the connection between what they eat and where it comes from through hands-on organic gardening and cooking classes. The "comestible curriculum" **encompasses** math, science, history, geography, social studies, and more.

Interviewer: **Rosa, you're a sixth grade student gardener in the Scrumptious Schoolyard at T.R. Middle School in West End. Have you tried growing anything before?**

Rosa: No, this is my first time, and now I have a green thumb. I might become a farmer or a chef, or both!

Interviewer: **I heard that the Scrumptious Schoolyard concept was somewhat controversial in the beginning.**

Rosa: It **ruffled** a few feathers. Some people were **disinterested**, while others were suspicious, **depicting** it as playing instead of learning. I think their complaints are **groundless**, and they really don't know what they're missing. It's amazing to watch something grow from a tiny seed. It takes a lot of **stamina** and enthusiasm to keep the gardens growing, but everyone works together.

Interviewer: **What are some favorite experiences and things you've learned?**

Rosa: I was excited when the blossoms on the squashes and pumpkins appeared. We made pumpkin pancakes and sauteed zucchini blossoms, so I actually cooked and ate a flower! Rule number one for gardeners is smart planning, and we need to get **maximum** use from our plot. Have you heard of companion planting? Plants are like people—some exist together better than others, so we **manipulate** the plants, materials, and space to get the best harvest. We also extend the natural growing seasons by **mimicking** Mother Nature with grow lights and mini-greenhouses.

Scrumptious Schoolyard student gardeners plant, tend, harvest, cook, and eat what they grow.

Interviewer: **Have you encountered any stumbling blocks so far?**

Rosa: We develop tools and strategies for overcoming **adverse** conditions. Our climate isn't extremely **arid**, but sometimes it's pretty dry, so we practice water conservation by using rain barrels. Also, the first time we tried to make compost, it was unbelievably smelly. You have to get the ingredients and layers right. The second time, it turned out great. One of our teachers calls compost "black gold."

One of the best parts of the Scrumptious Schoolyard program is eating what you've grown.

Interviewer: **Do you have a secret for attracting butterflies and bees to the garden?**

Rosa: We grow flowers that draw beneficial insects. Honeybees pollinate our plants, but the bees are in trouble because of Colony Collapse Disorder, so we try to do our part. Since our gardens are organic, we would be **hypocrites** if we used pesticides, so we're studying all-natural pest control. One raised bed has a *koinobori*, a Japanese fish kite that **billows** in the breeze and scares off scavengers.

Interviewer: **What would you say to other schools or kids interested in the program?**

Rosa: **Confront** obstacles and go for it! You may think one kid can't do much to help the environment or change how people eat, but working in the Scrumptious Schoolyard has made me believe we *can* make a big difference.

Interviewer: **Finally, I have to ask—do you really eat *all* the vegetables you're growing? I thought kids were supposed to hate vegetables.**

Rosa: There's no way I'm going to eat turnips. But it's good to try new things, according to my science teacher. We're still waiting to see *him* try turnips!

Audio

For iWords and audio passages, snap the code, or go to **SadlierConnect.com**.

Definitions

Note the spelling, pronunciation, part(s) of speech, and definition(s) of each of the following words. Then write the word in the blank spaces in the illustrative sentence(s) following. Finally, study the lists of synonyms and antonyms.

1. adverse (ad vərs′)

(*adj.*) unfavorable, negative; working against, hostile

Some people suffer an ____________ reaction if they eat peanut butter or anything with peanuts.

SYNONYMS: difficult, trying
ANTONYMS: favorable, positive, helpful, beneficial

2. arid (ar′ id)

(*adj.*) extremely dry; uninteresting, dull

Although California leads the nation in farming, crops won't grow in its most ____________ regions.

SYNONYMS: waterless, parched, boring, unimaginative
ANTONYMS: waterlogged, soggy, fertile, lush

3. assailant (ə sa′ lənt)

(*n.*) a person who attacks violently (with blows or words)

The jogger was injured by an unknown ____________, who left him immobile at the side of the road.

SYNONYMS: assaulter, mugger
ANTONYMS: victim, prey

4. billow (bil′ o)

(*n.*) a large wave; (*v.*) to rise or swell like a wave

The ocean ____________ rose and fell, attracting the most daring surfers.

Fans cheered enthusiastically when they saw their team's flags ____________ over the stadium.

SYNONYMS: (*n.*) breaker; (*v.*) surge, bulge, balloon
ANTONYMS: (*n.*) trough; (*v.*) deflate, collapse

5. confront (kən frənt′)

(*v.*) to meet face-to-face, especially as a challenge; come to grips with

In court, defendants can ____________ their accusers in a controlled setting.

SYNONYMS: face, encounter
ANTONYMS: avoid, evade, sidestep

6. constrain (kən strān′)

(*v.*) to force, compel; to restrain, hold back

You can't ____________ me against my will.

SYNONYMS: pressure, confine, limit
ANTONYMS: loosen, liberate, unfetter, relax

7. contemporary (kən tem′ pə rer ē) (*adj.*) belonging to the same period of time as oneself; (*n.*) a person of the same time

His novel used a ____________________ style but had a historical setting.

Rather than ask parents for help, teens often turn to a ____________________ for advice.

SYNONYMS: (*adj.*) present-day, modern, current; (*n.*) peer
ANTONYMS: (*adj.*) ancient, prehistoric, antique, antiquated

8. depict (di pikt′) (*v.*) to portray; to represent or show in the form of a picture

The painter chose to ____________________ a plain prairie landscape using bold colors and shadows.

SYNONYMS: sketch, draw, picture, illustrate

9. disinterested (dis in′ trəst id) (*adj.*) fair-minded, free from selfish motives; indifferent

A judge must remain ____________________ in order to render an evenhanded and logical decision.

SYNONYMS: impartial, unbiased, apathetic
ANTONYMS: partial, biased, prejudiced

10. encompass (en kəm′ pəs) (*v.*) to encircle, go or reach around; to enclose; to include with a certain group or class

Oceans ____________________ about three-fourths of the surface of our planet.

SYNONYMS: surround, envelop, comprise
ANTONYMS: leave out, omit, exclude

11. groundless (grau̇nd′ ləs) (*adj.*) without any good reason or cause, unjustified

Kate's ____________________ fear of hurting herself during exercise has left her weak and out of shape.

SYNONYMS: baseless, unsupported
ANTONYMS: well-founded, reasonable, justified

12. hypocrite (hip′ ə krit) (*n.*) a person who pretends to be what he or she is not or better than he or she really is; a two-faced person

The speaker who said one thing but did something else entirely was regarded as a ____________________.

SYNONYMS: phony, charlatan, fraud

13. incomprehensible (in käm pri hen′ sə bəl) (*adj.*) impossible to understand

Our school's intercom system is so old that this morning's announcements were almost ____________________.

SYNONYMS: baffling, confusing, bewildering
ANTONYMS: understandable, plain, intelligible

14. manipulate (mə nip′ yə lāt)

(*v.*) to handle or use skillfully; to manage or control for personal gain or advantage

Scientists should not ____________________ data.

SYNONYMS: work, maneuver, exploit, influence

15. maximum (mak′ sə məm)

(*n.*) the greatest possible amount or degree; (*adj.*) reaching the greatest possible amount or degree

This postage scale can weigh a ____________________ of only five pounds.

To ease the patient's suffering, the doctor prescribed the ____________________ dosage of painkillers.

SYNONYMS: (*adj.*) highest, (*n. adj.*) utmost
ANTONYMS: (*n.*, *adj.*) least, minimum, (*adj.*) lowest, smallest

16. mimic (mim′ ik)

(*n.*) a person who does imitations; (*v.*) to imitate; to make fun of

The comedy troupe needs to hire a ____________________.

Troy can ____________________ any accent he hears.

SYNONYMS: (*n.*) copycat, impersonator; (*v.*) parrot, impersonate

17. ruffle (rəf′ əl)

(*v.*) to wrinkle, make uneven; to annoy, upset; to flip through; (*n.*) material used for trimming edges; a ripple; a low drumbeat

His wisecracks always ____________________ my feelings.

My favorite pillow has a velvet ____________________.

SYNONYMS: (*v.*) disturb; (*n.*) frill
ANTONYMS: (*v.*) smooth out, soothe

18. serene (sə rēn′)

(*adj.*) peaceful, calm; free of emotional upset; clear and free of storm; majestic, grand

She stayed ____________________ in the face of chaos.

SYNONYMS: composed, fair, august
ANTONYMS: agitated, troubled, inclement

19. sheepish (shēp′ ish)

(*adj.*) embarrassed; resembling a sheep in meekness, timid

His ____________________ grin made the crowds cheer all the more for his unlikely victory.

SYNONYMS: shamefaced, meek
ANTONYMS: bold, saucy, brazen

20. stamina (stam′ ə nə)

(*n.*) the strength needed to keep going or overcome physical or mental strain; staying power

Marathon runners need a great deal of ____________________ to cover the many miles.

SYNONYM: endurance

Choosing the Right Word

*Select the **boldface** word that better completes each sentence. You might refer to the unit selection to see how most of these words are used in context.*

1. After many stormy years in the service of his country, George Washington retired to the (**serene, adverse**) life of his beloved Mount Vernon.

George Washington's home, Mount Vernon

2. His decision not to accept our sincere offer of assistance is completely (**disinterested, incomprehensible**) to me.

3. We expected the lecture on the energy crisis to be exciting, but it turned out to be a(n) (**ruffled, arid**) rundown of well-known facts and figures.

4. After giving a few (**sheepish, serene**) excuses, the swimmers packed up and left the private beach.

5. Anyone who has ever sailed a small boat knows how thrilling it is to feel the spray in your face while the sails (**billow, encompass**) overhead.

6. After the storm, residents were (**constrained, depicted**) to stay in their homes, as all roads were impassable.

7. The big-league shortstop (**manipulates, constrains**) his glove like a magician, snaring every ball hit within reach.

8. After living for many years in that roomy old farmhouse, I felt awfully (**arid, constrained**) in that small apartment.

9. While some find her smile comical, I have always found the Mona Lisa's smile to be (**serene, sheepish**) and mysterious.

10. If you (**billow, confront**) your problems honestly and openly, instead of trying to hide them, you will have a better chance of solving them.

11. Do you think it would be a good idea to set a (**maximum, contemporary**) figure for the amount of homework any teacher is allowed to assign?

12. A good scientist must have a keen mind, an unquenchable curiosity, and a (**groundless, disinterested**) desire to discover the truth.

13. She has gained success as a writer who knows how to (**confront, depict**) in a lifelike way the hopes, fears, and problems of young people today.

14. She has many interesting ideas, but she seems to lack the physical and mental (**stamina, assailant**) to make good use of them.

15. The man was trying to (**depict, manipulate**) the young woman as a troublemaker, simply because she had dyed her hair purple and dressed in an unusual manner.

16. My idea of a(n) (**assailant, hypocrite**) is a person who gives advice that he or she is not willing to follow.

17. The (**adverse, sheepish**) publicity that he received during the investigation was probably the cause of his defeat in the next election.

18. Instead of working so hard to (**mimic, ruffle**) popular TV stars, why don't you try to develop an acting style of your own?

19. It was (**groundless, incomprehensible**) to think that our grandparents had to spend sweltering summers without air-conditioning.

20. The science program in our school (**depicts, encompasses**) biology, chemistry, physics, earth science, and other related courses.

21. I didn't want to (**ruffle, manipulate**) the feelings of the hotel manager, but I felt that I had to complain about the miserable service.

22. Despite the fact that she was in shock, the victim gave a clear description of her (**hypocrite, assailant**).

23. Martin Luther King, Jr. and Robert F. Kennedy were (**contemporaries, mimics**), born within a few years of each other.

24. What a relief to learn that my parents had been delayed by a storm, and that all my fears about an accident were (**groundless, maximum**)!

25. Report any (**sheepish, adverse**) side effects to your doctor immediately.

Synonyms

Choose the word from this Unit that is the same or most nearly the same in meaning as the ***boldface*** *word or expression in the phrase. Write that word on the line. Use a dictionary if necessary.*

1. possesses **determination** for the walkathon ____________
2. the **largest** quantity available ____________
3. always remembered the **attacker's** voice ____________
4. able to **replicate** a bird's call ____________
5. ran away with a **humiliated** look ____________
6. confused by the child's **puzzling** behavior ____________
7. mistrustful of that **impostor** ____________
8. a **tranquil** expanse of clear blue sky ____________
9. tried to **restrict** the patient ____________
10. to serve as a **neutral** witness ____________

Antonyms

*Choose the word from this Unit that is most nearly opposite in meaning to the **boldface** word or expression in the phrase. Write that word on the line. Use a dictionary if necessary.*

1. exhibits a **confident** attitude ______________________
2. hopes to **release** the prisoner soon ______________________
3. trying to control his **stormy** emotions ______________________
4. protecting the **injured party** ______________________
5. rules that are quite **clear** ______________________

Completing the Sentence

From the words in this Unit, choose the one that best completes each of the following sentences. Write the correct word form in the space provided.

1. As you become a more skillful driver, you will be able to ______________________ all the controls of the car while keeping your eyes on the road.

2. This basic textbook ______________________ all the information you will have to master for the entrance examination.

3. The jury found the defendant "not guilty" because they were convinced that the charges against her were ______________________.

4. You and Lucy will never settle your quarrel unless you ______________________ each other directly and listen to what the other person has to say.

5. The brisk breeze caused the sheets on the line to ______________________ like the sails on a yacht that is running with the wind.

6. Under the law, the ______________________ number of people who may ride in this bus is seventy-five.

7. For a long time, I thought that he was a good and sincere person, but I finally saw that he was no more than a(n) ______________________.

8. I was so embarrassed by my blunder that I could do nothing but grin in a(n) ______________________ and self-conscious way.

9. The hot, ______________________ climate of Arizona is favorable for many people suffering from various diseases, such as arthritis.

10. Since Tom is both smart and ______________________, I think he is just the person to decide which of us is right in this long and bitter quarrel.

11. The skyscraper is one of the best-known and widely admired forms of ______________________ architecture.

12. A breeze sprang up and began to ______________________ the smooth and tranquil surface of the water.

13. You talk so fast and in such a low tone of voice that you are going to be completely ______________________ to most people.

14. Although I may hurt your feelings, my conscience ______________________ me to tell you exactly what is on my mind.

15. Held back by ______________________ winds, the plane arrived at the airport two hours late.

16. Fortunately, I was able to fight off my ______________________, even though his attack took me by complete surprise.

17. Parrots and a few other kinds of birds can ______________________ sounds, particularly human speech.

18. The ______________________ expression on her face showed that she was totally undisturbed by the confusion and turmoil around her.

19. Using the entire east wall of the new post office building, the painter tried to ______________________ the founding of our city.

20. Very few starting pitchers have the ______________________ to pitch consistently well for nine innings.

Writing: Words in Action

1. Look back at "West End School Has Comestible Curriculum" (pages 22–23). Suppose you have been asked to speak to your classmates about starting a similar program at your school. You have to persuade them that a Scrumptious Schoolyard is a great idea. Write a speech using at least two details from the passage and three Unit words to support your position.

2. There is much discussion these days about eating healthy, organic foods. Some people associate healthy and organic diets with bland-tasting, expensive food and preparation that is too complicated and time-consuming. Can healthy foods be tasty? Do you think a healthy diet requires too much effort? Write a brief essay in which you support your opinion with specific examples, personal experience, and, if relevant, the reading (refer to pages 22–23). Write at least three paragraphs, and use three or more words from this Unit.

Vocabulary in Context

Literary Text

The following excerpts are from Leaves of Grass, *a collection of poems by Walt Whitman. Some of the words you have studied in this unit appear in* **boldface** *type. Complete each statement below the excerpt by circling the letter of the correct answer.*

1. Thou ever-darting Globe! through Space and Air!
Thou waters that **encompass** us!
Thou that in all the life and death of us, in action or in sleep!
Thou laws invisible that permeate them and all,
Thou that in all, and over all, and through and under all, incessant!

Waters that **encompass** the Globe

a. cover it
b. expose it
c. widen it
d. seep into it

2. Those that look carelessly in the faces of Presidents and governors, as to say Who are you?
Those of earth-born passion, simple, never **constrain'd**, never obedient,
Those of inland America.

Someone who is NOT **constrained** is

a. controlled
b. restricted
c. free
d. loyal

Whitman, an American poet, wrote in a free-verse style that has influenced modern poetry.

3. The mocking-bird, the American **mimic**, singing all the forenoon,
singing through the moon-lit night. . .

A bird that is a **mimic** is a(n)

a. originator
b. traitor
c. creator
d. imitator

4. Far, far at sea,
After the night's fierce drifts have strewn the shore with wrecks,
With re-appearing day as now so happy and **serene**,
The rosy and elastic dawn, the flashing sun....

A **serene** day is one that is

a. blistering
b. soothing
c. humid
d. noisy

5. ....O to be self-balanced for contingencies,
To **confront** night, storms, hunger, ridicule, accidents, rebuffs, as the trees and animals do.

To **confront** something is to

a. ignore it
b. alert it
c. tackle it
d. support it

Interactive Quiz

Snap the code, or go to **SadlierConnect.com**.

*Read the following passage, taking note of the **boldface** words and their contexts. These words are among those you will be studying in Unit 3. As you complete the exercises in this unit, it may help to refer to the way the words are used below.*

This Day in 1923: The *Olympic*'s the Thing!

<Archived Newspaper Article>

Before planes whisked people around the world in a day, travelers sailed to their destinations on large ocean liners. Shipping companies such as the Cunard Line and the White Star Line competed with each other to build the largest, most luxurious ships. Today the Times *archives presents a 1923 feature article about one of the most glamorous of all sea-going vessels, the* Olympic.

London, June 24, 1923—As the White Star Liner *Olympic* shoved off from New York last Monday, I stood on its giant deck and gazed at the open sea. I've traveled on big ships before, but never one quite so big. I felt small on its sprawling decks and a bit in awe of the vessel's size. I stood quietly. The **enigma** of the ocean and the equally mysterious grandeur of this gigantic boat surrounded me.

For a time the *Olympic* was the largest ocean liner in the world. She was matched once by her sister ship, the doomed *Titanic*. The *Olympic* has been plying the seas since her maiden voyage in 1910. In World War I she entered military service. She transported troops about the Atlantic. Incredibly, the *Olympic* was the only merchant vessel to sink an enemy warship during the war. She rammed a German submarine, the U-103, and sent it underwater for good. That was five years ago, in the spring of 1918.

Today on the *Olympic*, the war is ancient history. Happy passengers wander the ship. Linger in one spot, and you might be **waylaid** by a passenger who wants a partner for a game of that great racquet sport, squash, or for shuffleboard. And the dining rooms are full of good eating. There's a great **diversity** of food, with English, French, and American cuisine on the menu. A variety of beverages is also available for guests to **slake** their summer thirsts. Open-air settings provide the **illusion** of relaxing at a Mediterranean café. At every turn, there's another surprise, another lounge, another entertainment. I've made several trips between the library and the swimming pool. And I've **vowed** to visit the gym before we get to England. I'm sure I will—just as soon as that **infuriating**

Tug boats push the *Olympic* out of the New York Harbor in 1912.

The fabulous promenade deck

Passengers enjoy the open air on deck.

fellow with the squash racquet stops irritating me and sits down for a bite to eat. Perhaps he'll trot off somewhere to **gloat** about his latest score.

The Turkish baths are a favorite stop for many guests. This area has rooms of the most fantastic decoration. They are decked out from top to bottom. The floors and walls are dressed in colorful tiles. The decoration is so fine and abundant that any more would have been gilding the lily. What **sage** was it who knew to stop at this perfection? Each day I am **motivated** to return to the baths. All cares seem to **wither** away under the **barrage** of care and attention the attendants shower upon visitors there.

If I could make it my **vocation** to wander the earth on ships like this, I'd **queue** up for the job without a moment's hesitation. But obligation **restricts** the choices we make. My life's work lies ashore. Tomorrow we'll arrive in Southampton, England. I'll attend to my business there and look forward to the return trip to New York. Then it's back to the usual routine. For the time being, I'm happy to report, the sun is setting, the squash racquets are tucked away, and all's well on the *Olympic*.

Definitions

Note the spelling, pronunciation, part(s) of speech, and definition(s) of each of the following words. Then write the word in the blank spaces in the illustrative sentence(s) following. Finally, study the lists of synonyms and antonyms.

1. barrage (bə räzh′)
(*n.*) a rapid, large-scale outpouring of something

The governor faced a ____________________ of questions about possible budget cuts.

SYNONYMS: bombardment, shelling, volley, blast

2. bigot (big′ ət)
(*n.*) an intolerant, prejudiced, or biased person

When you speak in that narrow-minded way, you sound like a ____________________.

SYNONYM: racist

3. designate (dez′ ig nāt)
(*v.*) to indicate, point out; to appoint; (*adj.*) selected but not yet installed

Will you please tell me when the coach will ____________________ a team leader?

The new student council ____________________ is looking forward to making many changes to the student government.

SYNONYMS: (*v.*) name, signify, denote, nominate

4. diversity (di vər′ sə tē)
(*n.*) difference, variety; a condition of having many different types or forms

Our science teacher has a ____________________ of interests, including an appreciation of Russian literature.

SYNONYM: dissimilarity
ANTONYMS: similarity, sameness, uniformity

5. enigma (i nig′ mə)
(*n.*) someone or something that is extremely puzzling; that which cannot be understood or explained

Critics complained that the plot twists in the new mystery movie make it an ____________________.

SYNONYMS: riddle, mystery, puzzle, conundrum

6. gloat (glōt)
(*v.*) to look at or think about with great intensity and satisfaction; to take great personal joy in

I will try not to ____________________ about winning a scholarship to music camp.

SYNONYMS: relish, revel in, crow over
ANTONYMS: regret, bemoan, mourn, feel chagrined

7. global
(glō′ bəl)

(*adj.*) of, relating to, or involving the entire world; comprehensive

E-mail and the Internet have linked the entire world into a ________________ village.

SYNONYMS: worldwide, universal, widespread
ANTONYMS: regional, provincial

8. illusion
(i lü′ zhən)

(*n.*) a false idea; something that one seems to see or to be aware of that really does not exist

Magicians use optical ________________ to amaze their audiences.

SYNONYMS: delusion, fantasy
ANTONYMS: reality, truth, actuality

9. infuriate
(in fyu̇r′ ē āt)

(*v.*) to make very angry, enrage

It ________________ most parents when their children refuse to listen to them and treat them with disrespect.

SYNONYMS: provoke, incense, madden
ANTONYMS: calm, soothe, pacify, please

10. motivate
(mō′ tə vāt)

(*v.*) to provide with a reason for doing; to push on to some goal

How can we ________________ the students to undertake more challenging work?

SYNONYMS: spur on, encourage, prompt, goad
ANTONYMS: discourage, dissuade, disincline

11. pacifist
(pas′ ə fist)

(*n.*) one who is against war or the use of violence;
(*adj.*) opposing war or violence

Martin Luther King, Jr., was a ________________ who influenced the civil rights movement.

________________ students protested the war.

SYNONYMS: (*n.*) peacemaker, dove; ANTONYM: (*n.*) warmonger

12. queue
(kyü)

(*n.*) a line of people waiting for something (such as a bus);
(*v.*) to form such a line

A long ________________ formed at the bus stop.

Eager fans ________________ up for the best seats.

SYNONYMS: (*n.*) column, file, row, line
ANTONYM: (*n.*) disorganized crowd

13. restrict
(ri strikt′)

(*v.*) to keep within set limits; to confine

Doctors often advise patients to ________________ their intake of fatty or salty foods.

SYNONYMS: hold back, limit; ANTONYMS: open up, enlarge, expand

14. sage (sāj)

(*adj.*) wise; (*n.*) a very wise person

My aunt always gives me ____________________ advice.

Let's ask the ____________________ for guidance.

SYNONYMS: (*adj.*) sagacious; (*n.*) philosopher, Solomon
ANTONYMS: (*adj.*) foolish, unwise; (*n.*) fool, dunce

15. slake (slāk)

(*v.*) to satisfy, relieve, or bring to an end

Nothing can ____________________ thirst better than water.

SYNONYMS: gratify, sate, ease, assuage
ANTONYMS: increase, intensify, aggravate

16. terrain (tə rān′)

(*n.*) the landscape, especially its physical features or fitness for some use; a field of knowledge

Mountain bikes are designed to withstand even the most rugged ____________________.

SYNONYMS: ground, topography, territory

17. vocation (vō kā′ shən)

(*n.*) any trade, profession, or occupation; a sense of fitness or special calling for one's work

After many years of searching, she found her true ____________________ as a horse trainer.

SYNONYMS: career, pursuit
ANTONYMS: hobby, pastime, avocation

18. vow (vau̇)

(*n.*) a solemn or sacred promise or pledge; (*v.*) to declare or promise in a solemn way

Prince Hamlet made a solemn ____________________ to avenge his father's murder.

A bride and groom ____________________ to love each other throughout their marriage.

SYNONYMS: (*n.*) word of honor; (*v.*) pledge

19. waylay (wā′ lā)

(*v.*) to lie in wait for and attack, ambush

Thugs will often choose to ____________________ weary travelers as they make their way home.

SYNONYMS: entrap, ensnare

20. wither (wit͟h′ ər)

(*v.*) to dry up, wilt, sag; to cause someone to feel ashamed, humiliated, or very small

Despite people's best efforts to remain young looking, skin will eventually ____________________ with age.

SYNONYMS: shrivel, droop, shame, abash
ANTONYMS: bloom, flower, flourish, burgeon

Choosing the Right Word

*Select the **boldface** word that better completes each sentence. You might refer to the unit selection to see how most of these words are used in context.*

1. Jane Addams was an outspoken (**pacifist, enigma**), yet her views about war were not embraced by everyone.

2. No matter what it may cost me to carry out, I will never break my sacred (**vow, illusion**).

3. Just how and why two people fall in love is a(n) (**queue, enigma**) that no scientist has ever been able to explain.

4. A good loser doesn't sulk over defeat; a good winner doesn't (**gloat, vow**) after victory.

5. A great teacher not only makes the material of the course understandable but also (**infuriates, motivates**) the students to want to learn more.

6. The applicants for the job will have to (**queue, slake**) up in an orderly way and wait their turns to be interviewed.

Jane Addams was a social reformer whose work earned her a Nobel Peace Prize in 1931.

7. The United States has laws that (**restrict, waylay**) the numbers and kinds of immigrants allowed to enter this country.

8. She is never bored because she has a great (**enigma, diversity**) of interests, ranging from folk dancing to mathematics.

9. Her analysis of what is wrong with our city government seems to me remarkably (**sage, global**) and helpful.

10. Because Sam is so good at stealing bases, he has become the (**slake, designated**) runner for our baseball team.

11. By the time you are old enough to enter the workforce, many (**sages, vocations**) that are important today may not even exist anymore.

12. Many view Shakespeare as the timeless (**illusion, sage**) and constantly use his words to give advice.

13. The children who are admitted free to the ball game will be allowed to sit only in certain (**motivated, designated**) parts of the stands.

14. President Jefferson sent Lewis and Clark to survey water routes, animals, plant life, and the (**terrain, waylay**) of the Louisiana Territory.

15. As the defense attorney left the courtroom, he was (**waylaid, designated**) by a group of eager reporters trying to get a statement from him.

16. Entangled in the trapper's net, the (**infuriated, withered**) lion thrashed at the ropes and roared in helpless anger.

17. With the other team ten points ahead and only a few minutes left to play, our hopes of victory began to (**gloat, wither**).

18. As you have so many prejudices of your own, you should think twice before you accuse other people of being (**enigmas, bigots**).

19. Because I am convinced that violence always creates more problems than it solves, I have become a (**pacifist, bigot**).

20. To (**slake, restrict**) our curiosity, you will have to tell us everything that happened during that strange trip.

21. Before we begin our backpacking trip, we should have a good idea of the (**terrain, vocation**) we are going to cover.

22. Has it ever occurred to you that your belief that you are a superior person and a natural leader may be no more than a(n) (**barrage, illusion**)?

23. World War II was a truly (**global, pacifist**) struggle, fought in all parts of the world by people of every race and background.

24. When the speaker asked for opinions from the audience, he was greeted with a (**terrain, barrage**) of critical remarks and angry questions.

25. Lilies are delicate and will (**wither, vow**) quickly if not protected from the hot sun.

Synonyms

Choose the word from this Unit that is the same or most nearly the same in meaning as the ***boldface*** *word or expression in the phrase. Write that word on the line. Use a dictionary if necessary.*

1. offering trades on the **international** market ________________

2. **quench** their cravings for a refreshing drink ________________

3. a plot to **trap** unsuspecting victims ________________

4. close-ups of the **land** of Mars ________________

5. must **assure** to tell the truth ________________

6. ignore the ravings of **prejudiced people** ________________

7. the magician's most unique **deception** ________________

8. was once a **conscientious objector** ________________

9. trying to **irritate** the manager ________________

10. **choose** it as the team's new logo ________________

Antonyms

*Choose the word from this Unit that is most nearly opposite in meaning to the **boldface** word or expression in the phrase. Write that word on the line. Use a dictionary if necessary.*

1. wants to **withdraw** his name as candidate ____________________
2. finding particles of pollen in the **atmosphere** ____________________
3. tries to be a **fair-minded person** ____________________
4. speeches given by a notable **hawk** ____________________
5. part of a **local** charity fund ____________________

Completing the Sentence

From the words in this Unit, choose the one that best completes each of the following sentences. Write the correct word form in the space provided.

1. A person can usually tell how popular a new movie is by the length of the ____________________ in front of the box office.

2. Even before the new president took office, he ____________________ the men and women who were to serve in his cabinet.

3. Because the show is scheduled to end after midnight, the management will ____________________ admission to people over sixteen years old.

4. For better or for worse, as you become older and more experienced, you will lose many of the comforting ____________________ of youth.

5. Nothing ____________________ my boss more than an employee who is late for work and then offers a foolish excuse for not arriving on time.

6. Our hike was not very long, but the ____________________ was so rocky and hilly that we were exhausted by the time we reached our goal.

7. As he greatly enjoys woodworking and also makes a living from it, his hobby and his ____________________ are one and the same.

8. I came to regard my grandmother as a(n) ____________________ whose wisdom helped solve many family problems.

9. The pollution problem, far from being limited to the United States, is truly ____________________ in scope.

10. As she was sworn in, she made a(n) ____________________ that she would never use the powers of her office for selfish or unworthy purposes.

11. On the way to his hotel room the celebrity was ______________________ by reporters eager for an interview.

12. No decent or kind person will ______________________ over someone else's failures or misfortunes.

13. The desire to be the world's top tennis player ______________________ the young woman to spend hours every day improving her game.

14. Is it possible to be a(n) ______________________ in a world where so many people are using force to take unfair advantage of others?

15. The deadly ______________________ of shells from our guns pinned down the enemy troops on the narrow beach where they had landed.

16. The animals in the drought area traveled for many miles to reach a body of water where they could ______________________ their thirst.

17. The rich ______________________ of plant and animal life in a tropical rain forest never ceases to amaze me.

18. How sad it is to see such beautiful flowers ______________________ and die!

19. I don't understand what he is aiming at or why he behaves as he does; in fact, his whole personality is a(n) ______________________ to me.

20. Like a typical ______________________, he believes that any customs different from his own are "wrong" and "uncivilized."

Writing: Words in Action

1. Look back at "This Day in 1923: The *Olympic's* the Thing!" (pages 32–33). Suppose your job is to write a radio announcement that persuades people to take a cruise on the *Olympic*. Write an advertisement, using at least two details from the passage and three Unit words.

2. *"Experience, travel—these are an education in themselves."—Euripides*

   Travel not only provides people with unique and memorable experiences, but it also gives them opportunities to learn about new cultures and consider different outlooks. Think about the quotation from Euripides shown above. Do you agree with this outlook? In what ways can experience and travel be educational? Write a brief essay in which you support your opinion with specific examples, personal experience, your studies, and the reading (refer to pages 32–33). Write at least two paragraphs, and use three or more words from this Unit.

Vocabulary in Context

Literary Text

The following excerpts are from Twenty Thousand Leagues Under the Sea *by Jules Verne. Some of the words you have studied in this unit appear in* **boldface** *type. Complete each statement below the excerpt by circling the letter of the correct answer.*

1. Commander Farragut was a good seaman, worthy of the frigate he commanded. His ship and he were one. He was its very soul. On the *cetacean* [whale] question no doubts arose in his mind, and he didn't allow the animal's existence to be disputed aboard his vessel.... The monster existed, and he had **vowed** to rid the seas of it.

If a person has **vowed**, he or she has

a. questioned **c.** promised
b. judged **d.** waited

2. Three seconds after reading this letter from the honorable Secretary of the Navy, I understood at last that my true **vocation**, my sole purpose in life, was to hunt down this disturbing monster and rid the world of it.

A **vocation** is a(n)

a. occupation **c.** enemy
b. command **d.** hobby

3. Science has defined the **global** paths of five chief currents: one in the north Atlantic, a second in the south Atlantic, a third in the north Pacific, a fourth in the south Pacific, and a fifth in the southern Indian Ocean.

Something that is **global** is

a. limited **c.** worldwide
b. native **d.** confined

4. This chase dragged on for about three-quarters of an hour.... At this rate, it was obvious that we would never catch up with it.

Infuriated, Commander Farragut kept twisting the thick tuft of hair that flourished below his chin.

Someone who is **infuriated** is definitely NOT

a. furious **c.** upset
b. irate **d.** serene

5. I wanted to preserve a few specimens of these delicate zoophytes, but they were merely clouds, shadows, **illusions**, melting and evaporating outside their native element.

Illusions are

a. fantasies **c.** challenges
b. studies **d.** secrets

In Jules Verne's novel, Captain Nemo and his crew confronted many "monsters" of the sea.

Interactive Quiz

Snap the code, or go to **SadlierConnect.com**.

Vocabulary for Comprehension
Part 1

Read "A Winter Playground," which contains words in ***boldface*** *that appear in Units 1–3. Then answer the questions.*

A Winter Playground

Picture a vast castle, or imagine an oversized cartoon figure. Now try to imagine each of them made of snow and ice. That sight is what you might see if you attend the Sapporo Snow Festival, a weeklong event held each year in northern Japan, on the island of Hokkaido.

Sapporo is the capital of Hokkaido. Unlike other cities in Japan, Sapporo is fairly young. It has no ancient temples. Its streets are unusually wide and straight. Sapporo is known for its cold winters and heavy snowfall. The average annual snowfall in the city is around 19 feet.

The climate of Sapporo makes it an ideal place for winter festivities and a popular destination for winter sports. In fact, the city hosted the 1972 Winter Olympic Games. Skiing is even part of the school curriculum for many children in Sapporo.

The Sapporo Snow Festival takes place every February. The event draws both young and old into its wintry wonderland fantasies. Most people familiar with winter festivals **designate** the Sapporo Snow Festival as the most famous of its kind. The city plans ahead for months. It is impossible for visitors to get hotel rooms without **expressly** reserving them far in advance.

The Sapporo Snow Festival had modest beginnings. In 1950, high school students made six snow sculptures in a **serene** park in the center of town. What began as fun for creative teenagers has grown into an event that has **global** appeal. Odori Park, the location of those first snow sculptures, continues to be one of the three main festival sites.

Since the early days, much of the work to mount the festival has been done by the Self-Defense Forces. This branch of the Japanese military **dispatches** hundreds of soldiers in army trucks to haul snow from nearby mountains into the city. This peacetime work serves the public and keeps festival costs down.

Visitors to the Snow Festival today might see gigantic sculptures that **depict** prehistoric animals, Viking warriors, famous people, and even cartoon characters! Bands play music from atop huge sound stages built of snow. Daredevils can zoom down elaborate ice and snow slides at a sports venue called the Tsudome, one of the festival sites. Here, a snow rafting attraction also treats visitors to rides on rafts towed by snowmobiles. Every year at the Sapporo Snow Festival, one young woman is crowned "Queen of the Ice." Nightly fireworks, colored lights, and other special sound and lighting effects add extra excitement. The festival has earned a worldwide reputation as a winter playground.

1. **Part A**
   Based on the evidence in the passage, what is **most likely** the author's purpose in "A Winter Playground"?
   A) to praise the Japanese Self-Defense Force
   B) to describe traditional Japanese customs
   C) to inform the reader about the Sapporo Snow Festival
   D) to describe traditional Japanese customs

   Part B
   Which line from the text **best** supports the answer to Part A?
   A) "Picture a vast castle, or imagine an oversized cartoon figure." (lines 1–2)
   B) "the Sapporo Snow Festival, a weeklong event held each year in northern Japan" (lines 5–7)
   C) "Sapporo is the capital of Hokkaido." (line 9)
   D) "known for its cold winters and heavy snowfall" (lines 13–14)

2. What does the word **designate** mean as it is used in line 29?
   A) avoid
   B) attend
   C) deny
   D) name

3. Which word means the opposite of **expressly** in line 33?
   A) unintentionally
   B) explicitly
   C) purposely
   D) pointedly

4. What is the author's **most likely** reason for including lines 39–41 in "A Winter Playground"?
   A) to explain the Sapporo Snow Festival's rules
   B) to introduce the festival's artists
   C) to demonstrate the festival's popularity
   D) to describe the history of the festival

5. What does the word **serene** mean as it is used in line 38?
   A) tranquil
   B) enormous
   C) popular
   D) pretty

6. As it is used in line 41, what does the word **global** suggest about the festival?
   A) It is held in many different countries.
   B) Its popularity is widespread.
   C) It has regional appeal.
   D) It is a mysterious event.

7. Why does the author **most likely** refer to the sights and sounds of the festival in lines 54–71?
   A) to make generalizations about the festival
   B) to describe the festival through exaggerations
   C) to provide statistics about the festival
   D) to use sensory details to make the festival come alive

8. What is **most likely** the purpose of the last two paragraphs?
   A) to analyze athletic events in Japan
   B) to promote attendance at the festival
   C) to caution visitors about dangers
   D) to suggest festival improvements

Vocabulary for Comprehension

Part 2

*Read this passage, which contains words in **boldface** that appear in Units 1–3. Then choose the best answer to each question based on what is stated or implied in the passage. You may refer to the passage as often as necessary.*

Questions 1–8 are based on the following passage.

Among the most famous words of the American Revolution is the exclamation, "Give me liberty or give me death!" This was the **vow** of Patrick Henry in his address to the Second Virginia Convention in March of 1775. As a member of the House of Burgesses, the lower house of the legislature, Henry was well known as a brilliant orator and a radical opponent of the British government. In 1765, for example, he had spoken out vehemently against the Stamp Act. Some of his adversaries branded Henry's views as treason.

In 1775, Henry's goal was to persuade the convention to raise a militia. He felt that war with Britain was inevitable. His opponents, to whom he refers ironically in his speech as "very worthy gentlemen," advocated caution and patience. Early in the speech, Henry **ingeniously** turns the accusation of treason on its head. He defiantly declares, "Should I keep back my opinions at such a time, through fear of giving offence, I should consider myself as guilty of treason towards my country . . . ." Henry solemnly warns his fellow legislators that the issue they are debating is "nothing less than a question of freedom or slavery."

Two arguments lie at the heart of the speech. In the first, Henry invokes the "lamp of experience" to show that the conduct of the British over the past ten years has been both treacherous and menacing. The buildup in British forces, he says, can have only one objective: to **douse** resistance and force the colonists into submission. Every petition, argument, and entreaty the colonists have presented has been rejected or has **withered** away. Addressing the presiding officer of the convention, Henry declares, "Let us not, I beseech you sir, deceive ourselves. . . . There is no longer any room for hope. If we wish to be free . . . we must fight! I repeat it, sir, we must fight!" Plainly, Henry found his opponents' hesitation **incomprehensible**. For Henry, serene coexistence with Britain had proved impossible. Any other view amounted to an **illusion**. Henry implied, in fact, that the British were **gloating** over the prospect of reducing the colonies to servitude to the Crown.

In his second major argument, Patrick Henry refutes the claim that the colonists are weak. On the contrary, Henry argues, the passage of time will only allow the British to diminish the colonists' strength. In a remarkably accurate prediction, Henry proudly emphasizes the size of the American population and the geographical advantages of the colonists' **terrain**. "Three millions of people, armed in the holy cause of liberty, and in such a country as that which we possess, are invincible by any force which our enemy can send against us."

Henry concludes with **maximum** emotional force in his call to arms. "Our brethren are already in the field.

Why stand we here idle? What is it that gentlemen wish? . . . Is life so dear, or peace so sweet, as to be purchased at the price of chains and slavery? . . . I know not what course others may take, but as for me, give me liberty or give me death!" Barely four weeks later, the first shots of the Revolution were fired at Lexington and Concord, Massachusetts.

1. According to the passage, Patrick Henry was well known in Virginia for his
A) brilliant public speaking.
B) wealth and influence.
C) writing ability.
D) tact and diplomacy.

2. Which choice provides the best evidence for the answer to the previous question?
A) Lines 1–4 ("Among the . . . death!'")
B) Lines 4–7 ("This was . . . 1775")
C) Lines 7–11 ("As a member . . . government")
D) Lines 16–19 ("In 1775 . . . inevitable")

3. As it is used in line 4, "vow" most nearly means
A) threat.
B) pledge.
C) distress.
D) hint.

4. The author includes Henry's description of his opponents as "very worthy gentlemen" (line 21) in order to
A) give an example of how subtle and sensitive Henry was.
B) show that Henry was loyal to England.
C) give an example of a speech that is rambling and incoherent.
D) show that Henry was scornful and unafraid.

5. As it is used in line 23, "ingeniously" most nearly means
A) hopelessly.
B) resourcefully.
C) arrogantly.
D) proudly.

6. In his speech, Patrick Henry emphasizes which of the following ideas?
A) The passage of time will make the colonists stronger.
B) British strength is an illusion.
C) The colonists are stronger than they realize.
D) The colonial population is growing at a slow rate.

7. As it is used in line 72, "terrain" most nearly means
A) ground.
B) coastline.
C) mountain ranges.
D) road network.

8. Which of the following best identifies the primary purpose of the passage?
A) to refute the claim that Patrick Henry was guilty of treason
B) to provide a brief biographical sketch of Patrick Henry
C) to explain how Patrick Henry became a prominent politician
D) to offer a brief survey of Patrick Henry's most famous speech

Denotation and Connotation

Words have a literal meaning that you can look up in a dictionary. The literal meaning of a word is its **denotation**, which has a neutral tone.

Many words also have emotional associations beyond the literal meaning, called **connotations.** Connotations can be positive or negative.

Consider these synonyms for the verb *prompt*:

motivate   *encourage*   *goad*   *pressure*

Goad and *pressure* have negative connotations. *Motivate* and *encourage* have positive connotations.

> **Think:** People do not want to feel that they are being goaded or pressured to do something, but they welcome being motivated or encouraged to accomplish something.

Look at these examples of words. Notice how the connotation of each word varies.

NEUTRAL	POSITIVE	NEGATIVE
recede	**ebb**	**recoil**
meet	**challenge**	**confront**
mimic	**imitate**	**impersonate**

Writers choose their words carefully in order to express a particular tone or point of view. The most precise word helps readers understand exactly what the writer is trying to say. If a writer wants the reader to view a character as a private, thoughtful person, the writer might use a word like *discreet* to describe him or her. But if the writer wants us to see the character as secretive, he or she might use words like *guarded* or *wary*.

Shades of Meaning

Write a plus sign (+) in the box if the word has a positive connotation. Write a minus sign (–) if the word has a negative connotation. Put a zero (0) if the word is neutral.

1. famished ☐	**2.** stamina ☐	**3.** douse ☐	**4.** terrain ☐
5. vocation ☐	**6.** assailant ☐	**7.** wither ☐	**8.** serene ☐
9. ingenious ☐	**10.** restrict ☐	**11.** pacifist ☐	**12.** hypocrite ☐
13. waylay ☐	**14.** sheepish ☐	**15.** repast ☐	**16.** gainful ☐

Expressing the Connotation

Read each sentence. Select the word in parentheses that better expresses the connotation (positive, negative, or neutral) given at the beginning of the sentence.

neutral	**1.**	If you're shopping for sports (**duds, apparel**), I recommend the athletic supply store on Midway Drive.
positive	**2.**	Does anyone actually enjoy the sound of Sandra (**gloating, rejoicing**) over her tennis victories?
negative	**3.**	It (**infuriates, bothers**) me when I have to wait in a slow-moving line at the grocery store.
neutral	**4.**	In the novel, the hero vows to never (**renounce, forsake**) the girl he has loved since childhood.
negative	**5.**	I think it is wrong to (**constrain, imprison**) wild animals.
negative	**6.**	The (**inept, untrained**) gardener had trouble keeping even the hardiest plants alive.
neutral	**7.**	My sister always shares her opinions, but she is (**indifferent to, disinterested in**) other people's reactions to her ideas.
positive	**8.**	Marisa seemed to truly appreciate the (**outpouring, barrage**) of good will from her friends and neighbors after her long illness.

Challenge: Using Connotation

Choose vocabulary words from Units 1–3 to replace the highlighted words in the sentences below. Then explain how the connotation of the replacement word changes the tone of the sentence.

immense	**dispatched**	**contemporary**
besieged	**enigma**	**mimic**

1. When we visited the state park, I was amazed at the **large** ________________ canyons and beautiful rock structures.

____

____

2. Although Hannah loves the theater, she was not impressed with this **updated** ________________ version of *Romeo and Juliet.*

____

____

3. Daniel thought he would have time during spring break to relax; instead, he was **occupied** ________________ with chores.

____

____

Idioms

In the passage about the luxury liner, the *Olympic* (see pages 32–33), the narrator describes the decorations in the Turkish baths and mentions that adding more would have been "gilding the lily."

"Gilding the lily" is an idiom that means "adding extra adornments to something that is already beautiful." An **idiom** is a figure of speech or an informal expression that is not meant literally. When you say that someone is "gilding the lily," you are saying that the person is adding additional and probably unnecessary decoration to something that does not need it. You learn idioms by hearing them used in daily conversation. Idioms can be fun to use in writing and in conversations, but you should use them sparingly and in mostly informal situations.

Choosing the Right Idiom

Read each sentence. Use context clues to figure out the meaning of each idiom in ***boldface*** *print. Then write the letter of the definition for the idiom in the sentence.*

1. The amount of money she paid for that smartphone is **small potatoes** compared to what her fancy computer cost. ________
2. After yelling and cheering at last night's football game, I woke up with **a frog in my throat**. ________
3. We spent all afternoon praising Mom's great apple pie, so her **ears must be burning**. ________
4. Don't you think Mark is a little **long in the tooth** to be taking on the role of a young superhero? ________
5. I always have to **ride shotgun**; I get carsick when I sit in the backseat. ________
6. That hot chocolate sure **hit the spot** after a long hike in the snow! ________
7. It sure seems as if **time is flying** when we get together and play games. ________
8. The suspect, exhausted from the reporters' constant questioning at the courthouse, begged them to **call off the dogs**. ________
9. My brother always has to **put in his two cents' worth** when it comes to my choice of music. ________
10. Evan should stop the **monkey business** and just finish his project. ________

a. old

b. a certain period passes quickly

c. not very big in comparison

d. stop criticizing or harassing

e. make a comment or give an opinion

f. fooling around

g. a feeling of hoarseness in the throat

h. was refreshing and satisfying

i. sit in the front seat of a car

j. awareness that one is being talked about

Classical Roots

de—down; away from; completely; not

The Latin root *de* appears in **denounce** (page 14), **depict** (page 25), and **designate** (page 34). The root signifies separation or undoing. Some other words based on the same root are listed below.

debunk	**default**	**demerit**	**desperate**
decapitate	**defraud**	**depression**	**devolve**

From the list of words above, choose the one that corresponds to each of the brief definitions below. Write the word in the blank space in the illustrative sentence below the definition. Use a dictionary if necessary.

1. to cut off the head, behead

   Experienced chefs know how to gut, scale, and ____________________ a fish before cooking it.

2. an area that is sunk below its surroundings; a period of severe economic decline; a mood of dejection or sadness.

   Slapstick comedy films were popular during the Great ____________________ of the 1930s.

3. to expose the falseness of unsound or exaggerated claims

   New evidence allows us to ____________________ a time-honored legend.

4. a mark against, usually involving the loss of some privilege or right; a fault, defect

   Bad behavior at school earned him many ____________________.

5. to pass on (*"a duty or task"*) to someone else; to be passed on to; to be conferred on

   When the mayor's powers ____________________ upon her successor, little will change at City Hall.

6. to fail to perform a task or fulfill an obligation; the failure to do something required by law or duty

   Because the challenger failed to show up, the defender won the match by ____________________.

7. driven to take any risk; hopeless; extreme

   Lack of water led homesteaders to take ____________________ measures.

8. to cheat, take away from, or deprive of by deceit or trickery

   The corrupt attorney tried to ____________________ the heirs of their rightful inheritance and fortune.

*Read the following passage, taking note of the **boldface** words and their contexts. These words are among those you will be studying in Unit 4. As you complete the exercises in this unit, it may help to refer to the way the words are used below.*

The Art and Science of Traditional Healing

<Expository Essay>

Advances in science provide modern man with cures and treatments undreamed of by his prehistoric counterparts. But how did early humans deal with disease? Serious illnesses could **devastate** whole families or clans. What remedies were available? In olden times, folk medicine **generated** relief or cures. A thorough **scan** of the long history of medicine reveals some similar **strands** woven throughout the history of healing.

Plants were one source of medicine for early humans. Some vegetables or herbs were **deemed** especially effective for minor illnesses, and botanics are the source of many modern medicines. In ancient times, though, major disorders were likely to have **mortal** results. These deadly diseases needed more intensive treatment than the herbal remedies offered.

To fight these killer illnesses, early medicine men turned to magic and ritual. In many parts of the world, healers were called shamans. Although precise definitions of shamanism are **elusive**, it is likely that these shamans resembled what other societies called magicians or sorcerers. It is easy now, from a modern perspective, to dismiss them as quacks. But most shamans seem to have **acquitted** themselves honorably. Indeed, the specialized knowledge of shamans often caused society to **idolize** and revere them.

Shamans lived in different societies around the world and can still be found today. Some North American Indian nations and people in areas such as modern Siberia, Mongolia, and South America practiced shamanism. Wherever they were found, shamans revealed some common qualities. They often experienced periods of deep trance. Trances were not just **reveries** or daydreams; they were altered states of consciousness. The shaman's soul was believed to roam on journeys through the upper and lower worlds. A shaman's contact with spirits, both good and evil, was no **petty** talent. On the contrary, it was a key

A Mandan Indian medicine man during ceremonial dance

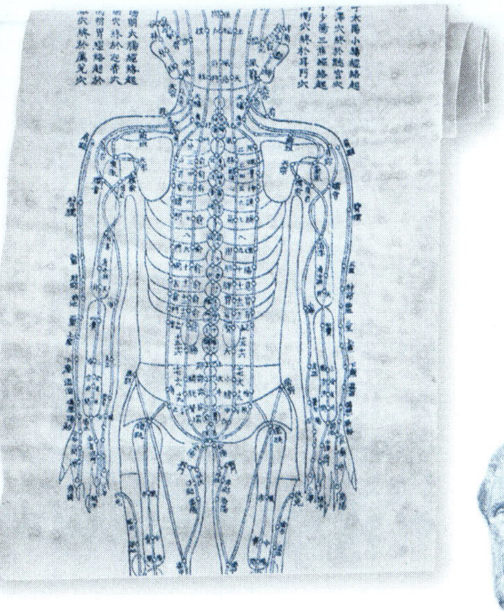

The Chinese practice of acupuncture is based on the idea that stimulating certain pressure points in the body can correct imbalances.

element in the healer's ability to rescue ailing patients from their wretched **plights**.

The early historical period had many medical traditions. In China, a typical healer's goal was to control the proportions of various elements in the body. Water therapy and acupuncture came from the Chinese tradition. Such treatments are still practiced today. In India, the classic writings on disease and treatment date back several thousand years. In both India and China, though, religious beliefs hindered efforts to learn more about anatomy. Cutting the bodies of the dead was considered a breach of the law and a source of **discredit**.

Despite their successes, early healers could not have hoped to cure all the sick. As the Arabic saying goes, "When fate arrives, the physician becomes a fool." If a healer lived in ancient Babylon, the price of failure could be steep. In the Law Code of Hammurabi around 1750 BCE, for example, doctors were warned that their hands would be cut off if a patient died from certain treatments.

In early Greek medicine, the outstanding figure was Hippocrates. Born around 460 BCE, probably on the island of Cos, he insisted that disease was a natural rather than a supernatural phenomenon. His written works began to **topple** magic from its commanding position in medicine. Perhaps his most enduring **keepsake** for the modern world is the Hippocratic Oath; this solemn promise "to do no harm" is still subscribed to by physicians today.

Hippocrates is known as the father of Western medicine.

Definitions

Note the spelling, pronunciation, part(s) of speech, and definition(s) of each of the following words. Then write the word in the blank spaces in the illustrative sentence(s) following. Finally, study the lists of synonyms and antonyms.

1. acquit (ə kwit′)

(*v.*) to declare not guilty, free from blame, discharge completely; to conduct or behave oneself

Now that we have proof of their innocence, we can ____________ them of all charges.

SYNONYMS: exonerate, dismiss
ANTONYMS: convict, declare guilty

2. deem (dēm)

(*v.*) to think, believe; to consider, have an opinion

Most people ____________ it a wise plan to set aside savings for the future.

SYNONYMS: judge, regard

3. devastate (dev′ ə stāt)

(*v.*) to destroy, lay waste, leave in ruins

Failure or harsh criticism can ____________ a person who has shaky self-esteem.

SYNONYMS: wreck, desolate
ANTONYMS: develop, improve

4. discredit (dis kred′ it)

(*v.*) to throw doubt upon, cause to be distrusted; to damage in reputation; (*n.*) a loss or lack of belief, confidence, or reputation

We have gathered a considerable amount of evidence to ____________ her story.

Both parents and students felt strongly that the cheating scandal was a ____________ to the school.

SYNONYM: (*v.*) disparage
ANTONYMS: (*v.*) confirm, corroborate, bolster

5. elusive (ē lü′ siv)

(*adj.*) difficult to catch or to hold; hard to explain or understand

According to legend, Zorro, the heroic Mexican character, was too ____________ for local police to capture.

SYNONYMS: slippery, wily, fleeting, puzzling, baffling

6. generate (jen′ ə rāt)

(*v.*) to bring into existence; to be the cause of

Solar power uses the energy of the sun to ____________ electricity.

SYNONYMS: create, produce, beget, cause
ANTONYMS: end, terminate, extinguish, stifle

7. idolize (ī′ dəl īz)

(*v.*) to worship as an idol, make an idol of; to love very much

Teens who ____________ a movie star may repeatedly see the same movie featuring that actor or actress.

SYNONYMS: adore, revere
ANTONYMS: despise, scorn, disdain, detest

8. ingratitude (in grat′ ə tüd)

(*n.*) a lack of thankfulness

Hosts who make every effort to please their guests are apt to be hurt by ____________.

SYNONYMS: thanklessness, ungratefulness
ANTONYMS: thankfulness, gratefulness, recognition

9. keepsake (kēp′ sāk)

(*n.*) something kept in memory of the giver; a souvenir

Before my grandmother died, she made me a special quilt as a ____________ of her love.

SYNONYMS: reminder, memento

10. mortal (môr′ təl)

(*n.*) a being that must eventually die; (*adj.*) of or relating to such a being; causing death, fatal; possible, conceivable

In the mythology of many cultures, a heavenly god can come down to Earth and act as a ____________.

The soldier was the only one in her battalion to suffer a ____________ injury.

SYNONYMS: (*n.*) human; (*adj.*) fleeting, extreme
ANTONYMS: (*n.*) a god; (*adj.*) undying, everlasting, eternal, divine

11. ovation (ō vā′ shən)

(*n.*) an enthusiastic public welcome, an outburst of applause

The audience gave the dancer a standing ____________ after his impressive performance.

SYNONYMS: bravos, hurrahs; ANTONYMS: boos, jeers

12. petty (pet′ ē)

(*adj.*) unimportant, trivial; narrow-minded; secondary in rank, minor

You say my complaint is ____________, but to me it is an issue of great importance.

SYNONYMS: insignificant, piddling
ANTONYMS: important, major, significant, weighty

13. plight (plīt)

(*n.*) a sorry condition or state; (*v.*) to pledge, promise solemnly

The ____________ of the homeless upsets many concerned citizens.

Wedding guests watched the bride and groom ____________ their undying love.

SYNONYMS: (*n.*) predicament, quandary

14. repent (ri pent′)

(*v.*) to feel sorry for what one has done or has failed to do

As people grow older and gain more maturity, some of them come to ____________________ their youthful mistakes.

SYNONYM: regret; ANTONYM: rejoice over

15. reverie (rev′ ə rē)

(*n.*) a daydream; the condition of being lost in thought

My boss interrupted my pleasant ____________________ by reminding me about our deadline.

SYNONYMS: fantasy, meditation

16. revocation (rev ə kā′ shən)

(*n.*) an act or instance of calling back, an annulment, cancellation

His failure to complete the job according to schedule led to a ____________________ of his contract.

SYNONYMS: repeal, withdrawal
ANTONYMS: ratification, confirmation

17. scan (skan)

(*v.*) to examine closely; to look over quickly but thoroughly; to analyze the rhythm of a poem; (*n.*) an examination

Let's ____________________ the list to see the finishing times of each marathon runner.

The doctor did a bone ____________________ to discover the location of each fracture.

SYNONYMS: (*v.*) study, glance at, skim; (*v., n.*) survey

18. strand (strand)

(*n.*) a beach or shore; a string of wire, hair, etc.; (*v.*) to drive or run aground; to leave in a hopeless position

We asked the waiter to take back the soup when we discovered a ____________________ of hair in it.

I don't want to be the third out in the inning and ____________________ the two base runners.

SYNONYMS: (*n.*) fiber, thread; (*v.*) abandon, maroon
ANTONYMS: (*v.*) rescue, save

19. strife (strīf)

(*n.*) bitter disagreement; fighting, struggle

The experienced senator from South Carolina was a veteran of political ____________________.

SYNONYMS: conflict, discord, turmoil
ANTONYMS: peace, calm, agreement

20. topple (täp′ əl)

(*v.*) to fall forward; to overturn, bring about the downfall of

The trains that rumble past our apartment often cause books to ____________________ from the shelves.

SYNONYMS: unseat, upset, tumble
ANTONYMS: remain upright, establish, set up

Choosing the Right Word

*Select the **boldface** word that better completes each sentence. You might refer to the unit selection to see how most of these words are used in context.*

1. During several of Heracles's labors, Athena noticed the (**ovation, plight**) the hero was in and offered her assistance.

2. Our supervisor (**topples, scans**) the newspaper each morning for items that may serve as leads for the sales force.

3. Once order had been restored, the leaders of the opposition called for the (**revocation, keepsake**) of martial law.

4. By reelecting him to Congress, the court of public opinion has forever (**generated, acquitted**) him of the charges of neglecting his duties.

The great Greek hero Heracles had to accomplish twelve labors, or difficult tasks, to atone for the deaths of his sons. One task was to wrestle and subdue the powerful Cretan bull.

5. In Shakespeare's *A Midsummer Night's Dream*, which character speaks the line, "Lord, what fools these (**mortals, keepsakes**) be"?

6. Imagine his (**plight, ingratitude**)—penniless, unemployed, and with a large family to support!

7. A team of filmmakers spent a year in the rain forests of South America, searching for the (**elusive, toppled**) harpy eagle.

8. Since you are the only one of us who has had experience with this kind of problem, we shall do whatever you (**deem, scan**) necessary.

9. The children stood on the southern (**reverie, strand**) and waved at the boats sailing into the harbor.

10. Are we going to allow (**elusive, petty**) quarrels to destroy a friendship that has endured for so many years?

11. While the actors were busy rehearsing, the manager ran away with all the money and left them (**stranded, plighted**) in a strange town.

12. After so many years of (**strife, ovation**)—in business, politics, and the family—he wants only to retire to the peace and quiet of his ranch.

13. A special edition of poems by the noted writer was presented as a (**reverie, keepsake**) to all who attended her eightieth birthday party.

14. In my composition, I tried to give a definition of "humor," but I found the idea too (**petty, elusive**) to pin down.

15. At times we all enjoy a(n) (**ovation, reverie**) about "what might have been," but before long we must return to "the way things are."

16. It was upsetting to see that his best friend was trying to (**discredit, scan**) his record as the best receiver on the team.

17. I knew that she was wrapped up in herself, but I never dreamed that even she could be guilty of such (**revocation, ingratitude**).

18. Many diseases that have disappeared in the United States continue to (**devastate, idolize**) countries in other parts of the world.

19. At times it is quite natural to feel afraid, and it is certainly no (**discredit, mortal**) to anyone to admit it.

20. We will never allow such vicious, unfounded rumors to (**deem, generate**) discord and conflict in our school!

21. What a(n) (**ovation, reverie**) he received when he trotted back to the bench after scoring the winning touchdown!

22. Our business is barely managing to pay its bills; one bad break will be enough to (**acquit, topple**) it into bankruptcy.

23. Our father often says that he has never stopped (**repenting, devastating**) the decision he made many years ago to give up the study of medicine.

24. We should respect our national leaders, but we should not (**idolize, discredit**) them and assume that they can do no wrong.

25. Katie purchased a (**revocation, keepsake**) box to store letters and photographs.

Synonyms

Choose the word from this Unit that is the same or most nearly the same in meaning as the ***boldface*** *word or expression in the phrase. Write that word on the line. Use a dictionary if necessary.*

1. asked for a **retraction** of the news column ____________________
2. pitied her for the **difficult situation** she was in ____________________
3. too much **friction** to remain partners ____________________
4. to **desert** them on a dangerous island ____________________
5. may never **apologize for** his wrongdoing ____________________
6. power to **demolish** an entire community ____________________
7. waved his cap to acknowledge the **cheers** ____________________
8. **search** the night sky for shooting stars ____________________
9. immersed in **contemplation** ____________________
10. a **lack of appreciation** that was uncalled for ____________________

Antonyms

*Choose the word from this Unit that is most nearly opposite in meaning to the **boldface** word or expression in the phrase. Write that word on the line. Use a dictionary if necessary.*

1. **heckling** that was not appreciated ____________________
2. to **boast** about a crime ____________________
3. show our **appreciation** for your kindness ____________________
4. cooperation that produces **harmony** ____________________
5. giving the nominee our **approval** ____________________

Completing the Sentence

From the words in this Unit, choose the one that best completes each of the following sentences. Write the correct word form in the space provided.

1. Why argue about such ____________________ matters when there are so many important problems to deal with?
2. The sudden racket produced by a noisy car radio jolted me out of my deep and peaceful ____________________.
3. Tom is not a very fast runner, but he is so ____________________ that he is extremely hard to tackle on the football field.
4. Though that actress's name and face are all but forgotten today, she used to be ____________________ by adoring fans all over the world.
5. I don't have the time to read every word of that long newspaper article, but I'll ____________________ it quickly to get the main idea.
6. Instead of telling us how much you ____________________ your outrageous conduct, why don't you sincerely try to reform?
7. We learned that even unfavorable reviews of a new book may help to ____________________ a certain amount of public interest in it.
8. Regardless of what you might think proper, I do not ____________________ it necessary for someone of your age to wear an evening gown to the dance.
9. The famous Leaning Tower of Pisa looks as though it might ____________________ over any minute.
10. The evidence against the accused man proved to be so weak that the jury had no choice but to ____________________ him.

11. As it is clear that his only interest is to make money for himself, his plan for building a new highway has been completely ____________________.

12. Because the members of my family disagree on so many matters, the dinner table is often the scene of much verbal ____________________.

13. The wound at first did not appear to be too serious, but to our great grief it proved to be ____________________.

14. The TV program made us keenly aware of the ____________________ of retired people trying to live solely on Social Security payments.

15. The defendant was warned that another speeding ticket would result in the ____________________ of her driver's license.

16. The rope is made of many ____________________ of fiber woven together.

17. The hurricane so ____________________ a large section of the coast that the president declared it a disaster area.

18. As I sincerely appreciate all my parents have done for me, how can you accuse me of ____________________?

19. She richly deserved the audience's ____________________ for her brilliant performance of Lady Macbeth.

20. I plan to save this old notebook as a(n) ____________________ of one of the best and most enjoyable classes I have ever had.

Writing: Words in Action

1. Look back at "The Art and Science of Traditional Healing" (pages 50–51). How is the traditional approach to disease and healing similar to or different from contemporary approaches? Write a brief essay comparing traditional healing to modern-day healing. Support your comparison using at least two details from the passage and three Unit words.

2. Modern medicine has made tremendous scientific advances. Yet today, many physicians and patients embrace holistic approaches. Holistic, or alternative, medicine considers the emotional and spiritual as well as the physical aspects of illness. Holistic approaches may include the use of herbs, massage, acupuncture, and practices such as yoga and meditation. Do you think a holistic approach to medicine makes sense in today's world? Write a brief essay in which you support your opinion with specific examples, personal experience, your studies, and the reading (refer to pages 50–51). Write at least three paragraphs, and use three or more words from this Unit.

Vocabulary in Context

Literary Text

The following excerpts are from A Princess of Mars *by Edgar Rice Burroughs. Some of the words you have studied in this Unit appear in* **boldface** *type. Complete each statement below the excerpt by circling the letter of the correct answer.*

1. I have never told this story, nor shall **mortal** man see this manuscript until after I have passed over for eternity. I know that the average human mind will not believe what it cannot grasp, and so I do not purpose being pilloried by the public, the pulpit, and the press, and held up as a colossal liar when I am but telling the simple truths which some day science will substantiate.

One who is **mortal**

a. will live forever
b. has a strong sense of duty
c. will die one day
d. has trouble believing the truth

2. "Cannot the war be ended at once?" spoke Sab Than. "It requires but the word of Than Kosis to bring peace. Say it, my father, say the word that will hasten my happiness, and end this unpopular **strife**."

Strife is a(n)

a. reign
b. war
c. peace
d. conversation

Edgar Rice Burroughs set many of his adventure stories on the planet Mars, but he became famous for his tales of Tarzan.

3. When Woola had finished his meal I again took up my weary and seemingly endless wandering in quest of the **elusive** waterway.

A waterway that is **elusive** is

a. very large
b. hard to find
c. difficult to navigate
d. rough and choppy

4. On the seventh day following the battle with the air craft we again took up the march toward Thark, all probability of another attack being **deemed** remote by Lorquas Ptomel.

Something that is **deemed** is

a. ignored
b. described
c. approved
d. considered

5. "Good-bye, my princess," I whispered, "we may meet in Helium yet. I have escaped from worse **plights** than this," and I tried to smile as I lied.

"What," she cried, "are you not coming with us?"

A **plight** is NOT a(n)

a. great difficulty
b. easy circumstance
c. dangerous situation
d. serious vow

Interactive Quiz

Snap the code, or go to **SadlierConnect.com**.

UNIT 5

*Read the following passage, taking note of the **boldface** words and their contexts. These words are among those you will be studying in Unit 5. As you complete the exercises in this unit, it may help to refer to the way the words are used below.*

Continue Space Exploration, Now!

<Persuasive Speech>

The United States should continue to support an active program of space exploration. Opponents of such a policy have **blustered** that space exploration is a waste of resources. Why spend money on rockets, they argue, when desperate needs here on Earth are so **acute**? Billions of the planet's **inhabitants** struggle from day to day. The **numbing** curses of war, famine, and poverty cry out for attention and relief.

For all but the most stubborn and **headstrong**, however, this argument can be convincingly **refuted**. For the entire **duration** of the space program's existence—a little more than half a century—the budget of the National Aeronautics and Space Administration (NASA) has averaged under one percent of total federal annual expenditures. One must keep these numbers in perspective. In a country where appetites are often **ravenous**, Americans spend nearly twenty times more money at restaurants every year than the government spends on NASA! Even a brief **synopsis** of costs and budgets shows that space exploration does not account for major outlays.

Apollo 15 astronaut on the moon, 1971

But how about astronaut safety? Opponents in the **fray** over space policy point to the risks of human spaceflight. They argue that these risks justify an end to space exploration. It is true that the space shuttle disasters of 1986 and 2003 marked major **setbacks** for NASA. In over 50 years, however, only 18 people worldwide have died in spaceflights. This one **facet** of the debate over future policy certainly elicits strong emotions. Yet the vast majority of astronauts undergo rigorous training. To **pacify** the critics, some have suggested that spaceflights should depend on robotics, which are

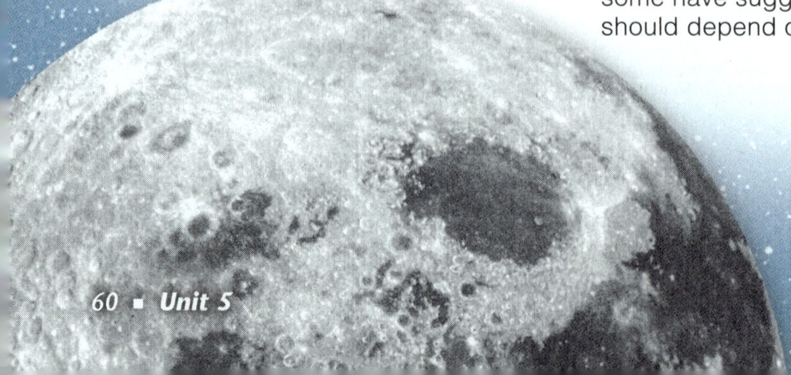

less costly and risky than manned flights. It may well be cheaper and safer to organize unmanned missions into space. Human intelligence and flexibility, though, will still be invaluable for many purposes. Astronauts, moreover, have served as powerful role models for generations of young people.

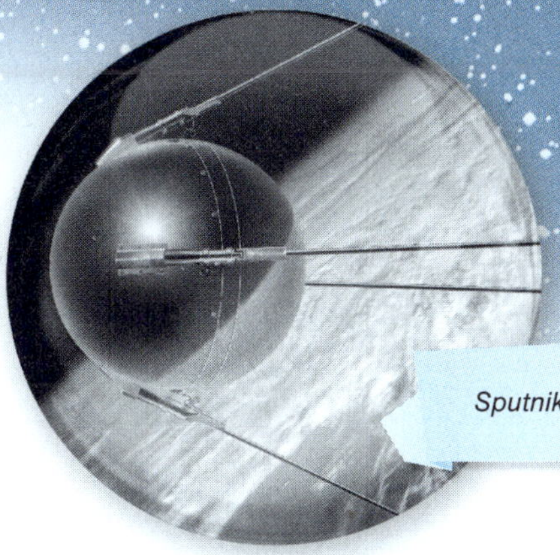

Sputnik 1, orbit

Fidelity to balance and fairness demands an evaluation of the numerous benefits derived from the space program so far. These include many advances in technology. What are some of these breakthroughs? Among them are satellites, microchips, and fuel cells. Take just one example. Satellites have vastly improved global communications. Better weather forecasts from satellites save lives. More accurate data make research on climate change possible. The demands and challenges of space exploration have meant that scientists and inventors can't risk being complacent. Ever bolder objectives in space require ever more ingenious responses.

Finally, the most important reason to press on in space is psychological, not material. The writer and inventor Arthur C. Clarke won fame for his achievements in science and science fiction. In one essay, Clarke offered this insightful **commentary** on human nature. He said that civilization cannot exist without new frontiers and that people have a physical and spiritual need for them. Clarke was right. The fascination with the *Apollo 11* moon landing of July 1969 swept the world. Humanity should continue to press forward in space. This effort is not so much to explore space's **eerie** depths but rather to explore the soul and timeless aspirations of humans themselves.

Space Shuttle *Discovery* launch, Kennedy Space Center, September 9, 1994

Audio

For iWords and audio passages, snap the code, or go to **SadlierConnect.com**.

Definitions

Note the spelling, pronunciation, part(s) of speech, and definition(s) of each of the following words. Then write the word in the blank spaces in the illustrative sentence(s) following. Finally, study the lists of synonyms and antonyms.

1. acute (ə kyüt′)

(*adj.*) with a sharp point; keen and alert; sharp and severe; rising quickly to a high point and lasting for a short time

One who is an ______________ observer of human nature may notice subtle changes in people's behavior.

SYNONYMS: clever, penetrating
ANTONYMS: blunted, mild, stupid, obtuse

2. bluster (bləs′ tər)

(*v.*) to talk or act in a noisy and threatening way; to blow in stormy gusts; (*n.*) speech that is loud and threatening

When we saw harsh winds ______________ around our tent, we decided to change our plans for the weekend.

Dad's manner is all ______________, but beneath it all, he's really a kind-hearted man.

SYNONYMS: (*v.*) spout, rant, brag, swagger; (*n.*) bravado

3. bungle (bəŋ′ gəl)

(*v.*) to act or work clumsily and awkwardly; to ruin something through clumsiness

If we ______________ this project, we may never get another chance to prove ourselves as a worthy team.

SYNONYMS: blunder, mess up

4. commentary (käm′ ən ter ē)

(*n.*) a series of notes clarifying or explaining something; an expression of opinion

Our spiritual leader gave us a ______________ on the true meaning of charity.

SYNONYMS: explanation, narration, description, account, review, analysis

5. duration (dů rā′ shən)

(*n.*) the length of time that something continues or lasts

Even though the story was hard to follow, my friends decided to stay for the ______________ of the opera.

6. eerie (ē′ rē)

(*adj.*) causing fear because of strangeness; weird, mysterious

It is a lot of fun to tell ______________ ghost stories around a campfire.

SYNONYMS: frightening, spooky, creepy

7. facet (fas′ ət)

(*n.*) one aspect or side of a subject or problem; one of the cut surfaces of a gem

One important ____________________ of problem solving is to recognize when a solution makes no sense.

SYNONYMS: angle, characteristic, factor, element

8. fidelity (fi del′ ə tē)

(*n.*) the state of being faithful; accuracy in details, exactness

The ____________________ of scratchy old records can't match the clarity of CDs.

SYNONYMS: loyalty, faithfulness; ANTONYMS: disloyalty, treachery

9. fray (frā)

(*n.*) a brawl, a noisy quarrel; (*v.*) to wear away by rubbing; make ragged or worn; to strain, irritate

After the two loudest students began arguing, the whole class jumped into the ____________________.

A faucet that drips continuously can ____________________ anyone's nerves.

SYNONYMS: (*n.*) scuffle; (*v.*) unravel

10. headstrong (hed′ strôŋ)

(*adj.*) willful, stubborn

Even the most patient caregiver may feel challenged when faced with a ____________________ child.

SYNONYMS: obstinate, mulish, unruly
ANTONYMS: obedient, docile, submissive

11. inhabitant (in hab′ ə tənt)

(*n.*) one living permanently in a given place

Although she enjoys traveling to exotic places, she's a lifelong ____________________ of this small town.

SYNONYMS: resident, native, tenant
ANTONYMS: stranger, outsider, visitor

12. numb (nəm)

(*adj.*) having lost the power of feeling or movement; (*v.*) to dull the feelings of; to cause to lose feeling

Bitter cold may leave your toes ____________________.

This injection will ____________________ the area so that the doctor can stitch the cut painlessly.

SYNONYMS: (*adj.*) unfeeling, insensible; (*v.*) deaden
ANTONYMS: (*adj.*) sensitive, alert

13. pacify (pas′ ə fī)

(*v.*) to make peaceful or calm; to soothe

The factory owners hope to ____________________ the angry protesters with promises of higher wages.

SYNONYMS: mollify, placate
ANTONYMS: anger, arouse, stir up, foment, ignite

14. ravenous (rav′ ə nəs)

(*adj.*) greedy; very hungry; eager for satisfaction

Exercising vigorously for several hours gives me a ______________________ appetite.

SYNONYMS: starved, voracious, wolfish
ANTONYMS: not hungry, well-fed, satisfied

15. refute (ri fyüt′)

(*v.*) to prove incorrect

After analyzing the situation, I now know a foolproof way to ______________________ the original claim.

SYNONYMS: disprove, rebut
ANTONYMS: prove, confirm, corroborate

16. remorse (ri mors′)

(*n.*) deep and painful regret for one's past misdeeds; pangs of conscience

When the driver realized what a terrible accident he had caused, he was overcome with ______________________.

SYNONYM: guilt
ANTONYMS: clear conscience, guiltlessness

17. setback (set′ bak)

(*n.*) something that interferes with progress; a disappointment, unexpected loss or defeat; a step-like recession in a wall

A broken toe can be a major ______________________ for a skater who hopes to qualify for the Olympics.

SYNONYMS: failure, reversal
ANTONYMS: advance, gain, progress, triumph

18. smug (sməg)

(*adj.*) overly self-satisfied, self-righteous

Just because he got the lead in the school play doesn't justify his irritating air of ______________________ superiority.

SYNONYMS: conceited, complacent
ANTONYMS: discontented, disgruntled

19. synopsis (si näp′ sis)

(*n.*) a brief statement giving a general view of some subject, book, etc.; a summary

The teacher's guide gives a ______________________ of the plot of each story in the collection.

SYNONYMS: outline, digest, abstract

20. tarry (tar′ ē)

(*v.*) to delay leaving; to linger, wait; to remain or stay for a while

He will be tempted to ______________________ longer if he thinks that this might be their last visit together.

SYNONYMS: dawdle, dally
ANTONYMS: rush, hasten, leave, depart

Choosing the Right Word

*Select the **boldface** word that better completes each sentence. You might refer to the unit selection to see how most of these words are used in context.*

1. The character Scrooge in Charles Dickens's *A Christmas Carol* starts out as a(n) (**acute, ravenous**) miser, but he undergoes a great change of heart.

2. The bloodhound's (**numb, acute**) sense of smell led the trackers to the bank robber's hideout in record time.

3. When I realized how deeply I had hurt my dear friend with my careless insult, I suffered a terrible pang of (**remorse, duration**).

4. With a winter storm (**blustering, bungling**) outside, what could be more welcome than a warm room, a good meal, and my favorite TV program?

5. Since it had seemed that winter would (**tarry, pacify**) forever, we were all heartily glad when it finally quit dragging its heels and departed.

Ebenezer Scrooge, the holiday-hating miser, is one of the most famous characters in fiction.

6. His (**headstrong, acute**) analysis of the housing problem in our town gave us a clear idea of what we would have to overcome.

7. Although I don't agree with all her ideas, I must admire her unshakable (**fidelity, synopsis**) to them.

8. We cannot assume that all the people one sees on the streets of a large city are actually (**facets, inhabitants**) of the place.

9. When the plane encountered turbulence, we had to remain seated with our seat belts fastened for the (**duration, synopsis**) of the flight.

10. The idea that most people usually behave in a calm and reasonable way is (**refuted, numbed**) by all the facts of history.

11. On the camping trip out West, some of the children were frightened when they first heard the (**smug, eerie**) howls of coyotes at night.

12. The victims of the disaster were so (**numbed, tarried**) by the scope of the tragedy that they scarcely showed any emotion at all.

13. I keep telling you things for your own good, but you're just too (**eerie, headstrong**) to listen.

14. Have you ever wondered if there is life on other planets and, if so, what the (**frays, inhabitants**) might look like?

15. We know that we are going through a period of economic instability, but there is no way of telling what its (**duration, remorse**) will be.

16. Maria's illness, after she had been chosen for the leading role in the class show, was a serious (**setback, commentary**) to our plans.

17. The lost hikers, having endured several days in the blistering sun, became discouraged after sighting (**headstrong, ravenous**) vultures circling overhead.

18. If you read no more than a(n) (**inhabitant, synopsis**) of the plot of any one of Shakespeare's plays, you will get very little idea of what it is all about.

19. "It's your job to help (**pacify, fray**) the conquered area," the general said, "not to add fuel to an already explosive situation."

20. There is so much wear and tear on the ropes in this pulley system that they become (**frayed, refuted**) in only a few days.

21. The fact that so many people are still living in poverty is indeed a sad (**fidelity, commentary**) on our civilization.

22. Each time she answered a question correctly, she rewarded herself with a (**smug, ravenous**) little smile of self-congratulation.

23. The strength of this book lies in the author's ability to describe and explain different (**setbacks, facets**) of human experience.

24. After the way you (**bungled, blustered**) the job of arranging the class trip, I can never again trust you with anything important.

25. My lawyer prepared to (**bungle, refute**) the outrageous accusations against me.

Synonyms

*Choose the word from this Unit that is the same or most nearly the same in meaning as the **boldface** word or expression in the phrase. Write that word on the line. Use a dictionary if necessary.*

1. reflected off the **cuts** of the diamond ____________________
2. shock that left them **dazed** and speechless ____________________
3. lip-smacking sounds of the **famished** eaters ____________________
4. to expect yet another **holdup** ____________________
5. should not **loiter** in the hall ____________________
6. after they **botched** the paint job ____________________
7. offer a brief **summation** of the movie ____________________
8. flashing that **haughty** grin of hers ____________________
9. tried to **contradict** her argument ____________________
10. no sense of **shame** for what happened ____________________

Antonyms

*Choose the word from this Unit that is most nearly opposite in meaning to the **boldface** word or expression in the phrase. Write that word on the line. Use a dictionary if necessary.*

1. needs to **hurry** to get ready ______________
2. could never **support** their opinion ______________
3. presenting a **modest** outlook ______________
4. hopes to **succeed at** her job ______________
5. maintains **peace of mind** despite his actions ______________

Completing the Sentence

From the words in this Unit, choose the one that best completes each of the following sentences. Write the correct word form in the space provided.

1. I had a(n) ______________ feeling that we were being followed and that something bad might happen.
2. Although the rain was heavy, it was of such short ______________ that it didn't interfere with our plans.
3. Because I ______________ at the book fair, I was ten minutes late for my piano lesson.
4. Warmth and understanding are two outstanding ______________ of her memorable personality.
5. His ______________ expression showed how highly he valued his own opinions and scorned the views of others.
6. The program contained a(n) ______________ of the opera, so we were able to follow the action even though the singing was in Italian.
7. Is it true that the ______________ of Maine are often called "Mainiacs"?
8. No one can question her complete ______________ to basic American ideas and ideals.
9. After the dentist gave me an injection of novocaine, the whole side of my jaw and face became ______________.
10. Some children are as docile as sheep; others are as ______________ as mules.

11. By ____________________ in a loud, confident voice, he tried to convince us that he had nothing to do with the accident.

12. Our team suffered a tough ____________________ when our best player was hurt in the first few minutes of play.

13. Anyone who has never had a sprained ankle will find it hard to imagine how ____________________ the pain is.

14. Because of our inexperience and haste, we ____________________ the little repair job so badly that it became necessary to replace the entire motor.

15. We had eaten only a light breakfast before hiking for hours in the crisp mountain air, so you can imagine how ____________________ we were by lunchtime.

16. The newscaster on my favorite TV program not only tells the facts of the news but also offers a(n) ____________________ that helps us to understand it.

17. Do you think it is a good idea to try to ____________________ the weeping child by giving her a lollipop?

18. When my two sisters began their bitter quarrel, only Mother had enough nerve to enter the ____________________ and tell them to stop.

19. Since the convicted felon had shown no ____________________ for his crimes, the judge sentenced him to the maximum prison term allowed.

20. The accused person must be given every chance to ____________________ the charges against him or her.

Writing: Words in Action

1. Look back at "Continue Space Exploration, Now!" (pages 60–61). What is your position on funding space exploration? Should the United States continue to spend federal money to support NASA? Write an editorial persuading your audience either to support or oppose funding space travel. Clearly state your position and use at least two details from the passage and three Unit words to support your claim.

2. A current argument states that privately held aerospace businesses, and not government agencies like NASA, should invest in and develop the spacecraft and new technologies that will transport people into space. What are the pros and cons of leaving space program development in the hands of private entrepreneurs and non-government-affiliated aerospace companies? Consider issues such as inspecting for safety, training, sharing of knowledge, and profit. Write a brief essay in which you support your opinion with specific examples, your studies, and the reading (refer to pages 60–61). Write at least three paragraphs, and use three or more words from this Unit.

Vocabulary in Context

Literary Text

The following excerpts are from The First Men in the Moon *by H.G. Wells. Some of the words you have studied in this Unit appear in* ***boldface*** *type. Complete each statement below the excerpt by circling the letter of the correct answer.*

1. There were several amazing forms, with heads reduced to microscopic proportions and blobby bodies . . . And oddest of all, as it seemed to me for the moment, two or three of these weird **inhabitants** of a subterranean world, a world sheltered by innumerable miles of rock from sun or rain, *carried umbrellas* in their tentaculate hands—real terrestrial-looking umbrellas!

Inhabitants are best described as

a. invaders **c.** exiles
b. creatures **d.** dwellers

2. He reminded me of mountain sickness, and of the bleeding that often afflicts aeronauts who have ascended too swiftly, and he spent some time in the preparation of a sickly tasting drink which he insisted on my sharing. It made me feel a little **numb**, but otherwise had no effect on me.

If someone's senses are **numb**, they are

a. deadened **c.** delicate
b. heightened **d.** clear

3. We ate and presently drank like tramps in a soup kitchen. Never before nor since have I been hungry to the **ravenous** pitch, and save that I have had this very experience I could never have believed that . . . it would be possible for me to eat in utter forgetfulness of all these things.

A person who is **ravenous** is definitely NOT

a. famished **c.** satiated
b. eager **d.** alert

In the movie based on the H.G. Wells novel, astronauts discover they are not the first to land on the moon!

4. One imagines him about the moon with the **remorse** of this fatal indiscretion growing in his mind. During a certain time I am inclined to guess the Grand Lunar was deliberating the new situation.

To have **remorse** is to feel

a. demands **c.** enthusiasm
b. regrets **d.** irresponsibility

5. The outline of things had gained in character, had grown **acute** and varied; save for a shadowed space of white substance here and there . . . the arctic appearance had gone altogether.

Something that appears **acute** is

a. dull **c.** sharp
b. peaceful **d.** unruly

Interactive Quiz

Snap the code, or go to **SadlierConnect.com**.

*Read the following passage, taking note of the **boldface** words and their contexts. These words are among those you will be studying in Unit 6. As you complete the exercises in this unit, it may help to refer to the way the words are used below.*

The Fine Art of War: WWI Propaganda Images

<Textbook Entry>

The Great War Begins

Austrian Archduke Franz Ferdinand was assassinated in Sarajevo, Bosnia, in 1914 by a Serbian **partisan**. This event was the spark that ignited the tinderbox. Long-simmering international resentments and a complex and **befuddling maze** of military alliances erupted into the world's first global conflict: World War I (1914–1918).

The United States was neutral for the first three years. President Woodrow Wilson tried to play peacemaker. But by 1917, events like the torpedoing of passenger ships by German U-boats (submarines), which took a **gross** toll of civilian lives, convinced Wilson to declare war. Now the United States was one of the Allies (along with France, Great Britain, Russia, Italy, and Japan).

The War at Home

When World War I began, propaganda campaigns were waged on all sides. Propaganda aimed to win the hearts and minds of citizens and discourage the enemy. The United States entered the war in 1917. Its publicity machine went into overdrive to **induce** public support. In a speech to the nation, President Wilson said, "The world must be made safe for democracy." With that **clarity** of vision, Wilson **debuted** the new Committee on Public Information (CPI), which, along with other government agencies such as the U.S. Food Administration, mobilized support for the war effort. Journalist George Creel, a **boisterous** supporter of America's entry into the war, led the CPI.

Creel hired 150,000 writers, actors, artists, and others to help drum up American support for the war. CPI planned a clear **agenda**. It had plenty of freedom and **leeway** in its efforts. It presented pro-war speeches, articles, pamphlets, books, and films.

Division of Pictorial Publicity

The CPI writers, directors, actors, and speechmakers were successful in getting the message out. But there were still Americans out of reach. So Creel created the Division of Pictorial Publicity within the CPI. It is said that a bad cause requires many words. Creel needed few words for

U-boat attacks spurred the U.S. into WWI. The public was urged to help defeat the U-boat.

7. compliant (kəm plī′ ənt)

(*adj.*) willing to do what someone else wants; obedient

A ____________________ child is easy to discipline, even when in an unfamiliar environment.

SYNONYMS: meek, docile, submissive
ANTONYMS: disobedient, obstinate, rebellious, perverse

8. conserve (kən sərv′)

(*v.*) to preserve; to keep from being damaged, lost, or wasted; to save

Responsible citizens try to ____________________ our precious natural resources.

SYNONYMS: guard, care for; ANTONYMS: waste, squander, dissipate

9. debut (dā′ byü)

(*n.*) a first public appearance; a formal entrance into society; (*v.*) to make a first appearance

The talented flute player in the marching band finally made her ____________________ as a soloist today.

Many theaters will ____________________ the film tonight.

SYNONYM: (*n.*) coming-out; ANTONYMS: (*n.*) retirement, departure

10. gory (gôr′ ē)

(*adj.*) marked by bloodshed, slaughter, or violence

The Civil War battle of Antietam is, to this day, the most ____________________ one-day fight in our history.

SYNONYMS: bloody, gruesome; ANTONYM: bloodless

11. gross (grōs)

(*adj.*) coarse, vulgar; very noticeable; total; (*n.*) an overall total (without deductions); twelve dozen; (*v.*) to earn

They responded to the ____________________ injustice in an unsatisfactory manner.

A ____________________ of pencils lasts all year.

She expects to ____________________ $3,000 in tips.

SYNONYMS: (*adj.*) sheer, utter, flagrant
ANTONYMS: (*adj.*) delicate, fine, partial; (*n., v.*) net

12. induce (in düs′)

(*v.*) to cause, bring about; to persuade

Can drinking warm milk ____________________ sleep?

SYNONYMS: prevail upon, influence
ANTONYMS: prevent, deter, hinder

13. leeway (lē′ wā)

(*n.*) extra space for moving along a certain route; allowance for mistakes or inaccuracies; margin of error

Experienced planners allow ____________________ of a week or so in case a project runs into snags or delays.

SYNONYMS: latitude, elbow room

14. limber (lim′ bər)

(*adj.*) flexible; (*v.*) to cause to become flexible

Serious dancers develop ____________________ bodies.

Runners ____________________ up before a race.

SYNONYMS: (*adj.*) supple, pliable; (*v.*) stretch
ANTONYMS: (*adj.*) stiff, wooden; (*v.*) stiffen

15. maze (māz)

(*n.*) a network of paths through which it is hard to find one's way; something very mixed-up and confusing

Ancient Rome was a ____________________ of narrow streets and winding alleys.

SYNONYMS: labyrinth, puzzle, tangle

16. oracle (ôr′ ə kəl)

(*n.*) someone or something that can predict the future; someone who gives astute answers or advice that seems authoritative

According to Greek legend, people sought prophecy at the great ____________________ at Delphi.

SYNONYMS: prophet, seer, sibyl

17. partisan (pärt′ ə zən)

(*n.*) a strong supporter of a person, party, or cause; one whose support is unreasoning; a resistance fighter, guerrilla; (*adj.*) strongly supporting one side only

That candidate is a ____________________ of term limits.

____________________ hometown fans can be hostile to those from out of town.

SYNONYMS: (*n.*) fan, booster; (*adj.*) partial, biased
ANTONYMS: (*n.*) critic, foe; (*adj.*) impartial, neutral

18. reimburse (rē im bərs′)

(*v.*) to pay back; to give payment for

When you go on business trips, the company will ____________________ all your traveling expenses.

SYNONYMS: repay, refund, compensate

19. vacate (vā′ kāt)

(*v.*) to go away from, leave empty; to make empty; to void, annul

We have a lot of cleaning up to do before we ____________________ the apartment for good.

SYNONYMS: depart, abandon; ANTONYMS: occupy, keep, hold

20. vagabond (vag′ ə bänd)

(*n.*) an idle wanderer; a tramp; (*adj.*) wandering; irresponsible

The ____________________ carried his few belongings in a shabby cardboard suitcase.

The ____________________ life interests some people, but it doesn't appeal to me.

SYNONYMS: (*n.*) vagrant; (*adj.*) unsettled, footloose
ANTONYMS: (*n.*) homebody, resident; (*adj.*) settled

Choosing the Right Word

*Select the **boldface** word that better completes each sentence. You might refer to the unit selection to see how most of these words are used in context.*

Victor Hugo, the French Romantic author, wrote plays, poems, and novels.

1. My sister made her (**agenda, debut**) in the Broadway production of *Les Misérables*, a musical based on Victor Hugo's novel.
2. Over the years, so many of the columnist's predictions have come true that he is now looked on as something of a(n) (**debut, oracle**).
3. One of the biggest problems facing the United States today is how to stop the (**blight, agenda**) that is creeping over large parts of our great cities.
4. Until we were in (**compliance, conservation**) with the neighborhood regulations, we could not build a tree house.
5. An experienced backpacker can give you many useful suggestions for (**befuddling, conserving**) energy on a long, tough hike.
6. After all the deductions had been made from my (**gross, limber**) salary, the sum that remained seemed pitifully small.
7. Students must take many required courses, but they also have a little (**oracle, leeway**) to choose courses that they find especially interesting.
8. What I thought was going to be a(n) (**amiable, vagabond**) little chat with my boss soon turned into a real argument.
9. Don't let the (**clarity, leeway**) of the water fool you into supposing that it's safe for drinking.
10. To become a good all-around athlete, you not only need a strong and (**induce, limber**) body, but also a quick, disciplined mind.
11. Because she is usually so (**compliant, partisan**), we were all surprised when she said that she didn't like our plans and wouldn't accept them.
12. Poland was at the top of Adolf Hitler's (**maze, agenda**) of military conquests in the fall of 1939.
13. If you want to get a clear picture of just what went wrong, you must not (**befuddle, induce**) your mind with all kinds of wild rumors.
14. As we moved higher up the mountain, I was overcome by dizziness and fatigue (**induced, grossed**) by the thin air.
15. This video game is not appropriate for children or minors due to its violent and (**amiable, gory**) content.

16. Because he is an expert gymnast and works out every day, his body has remained as (**limber, gory**) as that of a boy.

17. Many a student dreams about spending a (**vagabond, partisan**) year idly hiking through Europe.

18. In her graphic description of the most gruesome scenes in the horror film, Maria left out none of the (**amiable, gory**) details.

19. At the end of the long series of discussions and arguments, we felt that we were trapped in a (**maze, blight**) of conflicting ideas and plans.

20. The landlord ordered all tenants to (**vacate, reimburse**) the premises by noon.

21. This matter is so important to all the people of the community that we must forget (**boisterous, partisan**) politics and work together.

22. I will feel fully (**reimbursed, conserved**) for all that I have done for her if I can see her in good health again.

23. The disc jockey promised to (**vacate, debut**) the band's long-awaited new song as soon as it was released by the recording company.

24. Mr. Roth, our school librarian, may seem mild and easygoing, but he cracks down hard on (**compliant, boisterous**) students.

25. One of the items on the council's (**agenda, partisan**) is the proposal of a curfew.

Synonyms

*Choose the word from this Unit that is the same or most nearly the same in meaning as the **boldface** word or expression in the phrase. Write that word on the line. Use a dictionary if necessary.*

1. acrobats who are quite **agile** ____________________
2. **encourage** them to speak softly ____________________
3. an **affliction** hidden from society's view ____________________
4. when he saw the **horrific** spectacle ____________________
5. can't rely on their **one-sided** viewpoint ____________________
6. had never consulted the **visionary** before ____________________
7. seemed like a **delightful** fellow ____________________
8. enough **breathing space** for a beginner to succeed ____________________
9. no choice but to **desert** the cabin ____________________
10. a **hobo** who hopped freight trains ____________________

Antonyms

*Choose the word from this Unit that is most nearly opposite in meaning to the **boldface** word or expression in the phrase. Write that word on the line. Use a dictionary if necessary.*

1. rains that will **restore** the vegetation ______________________
2. a long-term **occupant** of this apartment ______________________
3. the guitar player's **rigid** fingers ______________________
4. try to avoid an **uninformed fool** ______________________
5. socializing with our **gruff** neighbors ______________________

Completing the Sentence

From the words in this Unit, choose the one that best completes each of the following sentences. Write the correct word form in the space provided.

1. Before the game starts, the players ______________________ up by doing a few deep knee bends, sit-ups, and other exercises.
2. How can a mind ______________________ by distractions make the type of snap decisions needed to drive safely in heavy traffic?
3. We cannot allow the lives of millions of people to be ______________________ by poverty.
4. You certainly have a right to cheer for your team, but try not to become too ______________________ and unruly.
5. Because of her outgoing and ______________________ personality, she is liked by nearly everyone at school.
6. The crowd is so ______________________ that the umpire is booed every time he makes a decision against the home team.
7. The high standard of excellence that the woman had set for herself left her no ______________________ for mistakes.
8. For years, his restless spirit led him to wander the highways and byways of this great land like any other footloose ______________________.
9. Because you are working with older and more experienced people, you should be ______________________ with their requests and advice.
10. None of us could possibly overlook the ______________________ error that the waiter had made in adding up our check.

11. If you would be kind enough to buy a loose-leaf notebook for me while you are in the stationery store, I'll ______________ you immediately.

12. If the superintendent of schools should ______________ his position by resigning, the mayor has the right to name someone else to the job.

13. Trying to untangle a badly snarled fishing line is like trying to find one's way through a(n) ______________.

14. Ms. Fillmer explained with such ______________ how to go about changing a tire that I felt that even someone as clumsy as I could do it.

15. Because our energy resources are limited, the American people must try to do everything possible to ______________ fuel.

16. No matter what you may say, you cannot ______________ me to do something that I know is wrong.

17. The high point of the social season was the formal ______________ of young ladies at the annual Society Ball.

18. Each of the items on the ______________ for our meeting today will probably require a good deal of discussion.

19. I was not prepared for the ______________ sight that met my eyes at the scene of that horrible massacre.

20. Why do you always ask me what's going to happen? I'm no ______________!

Writing: Words in Action

1. Look back at "The Fine Art of War: WWI Propaganda Images" (pages 70–71). Study the posters that became popular during World War I. Using the passage and posters, write a short essay that explains why these images were so effective in persuading Americans to support the war effort. Use at least two details from the passage and three Unit words to support your claim.

2. Advertisements are all around us, from billboards and television commercials to newspaper ads and pop-ups on the Internet. The messages and images of a clever advertising campaign can be powerful and persuasive. Would it ever be appropriate today for the government to use slick advertising tactics to get the American public to support a particular cause, such as a war? At some point might such "advertising" become propaganda—one-sided and even false support of a cause? Write a brief essay in which you support your opinion with specific examples, your studies, and the reading (refer to pages 70–71). Write at least three paragraphs, and use three or more words from this Unit.

Vocabulary in Context

Literary Text

The following excerpts are from the novel The Prince and The Pauper *and the short story "The Celebrated Jumping Frog of Calaveras County," both by Mark Twain. Some of the words you have studied in this Unit appear in* **boldface** *type. Complete each statement below the excerpt by circling the letter of the correct answer.*

1. The houseless prince, the homeless heir to the throne of England, still moved on, drifting deeper into the **maze** of squalid alleys where the swarming hives of poverty and misery were massed together. (*The Prince and the Pauper*)

Alleys that are like a **maze** are

a. intertwined **c.** dirty
b. amazing **d.** orderly

2. With **boisterous** mirth they dropped upon their knees in a body and did mock homage to their prey. The prince spurned the nearest boy with his foot, and said fiercely—

"Take thou that, till the morrow come and I build thee a gibbet!" (*The Prince and the Pauper*)

Something that is **boisterous** is NOT

a. rowdy and noisy **c.** calm and controlled
b. silly and pointless **d.** windy and wild

In one film adaptation of *The Prince and the Pauper*, twins Billy and Bobby Mauch played the roles of Tom and the Prince.

3. He was in a fine fury when he found himself described as a "sturdy **vagabond**" and sentenced to sit two hours in the stocks for bearing that character. . . . (*The Prince and the Pauper*)

A **vagabond** is someone who is a(n)

a. student **c.** witness
b. drifter **d.** official

4. In **compliance** with the request of a friend of mine, who wrote me from the East, I called on good-natured, garrulous old Simon Wheeler, and inquired after my friend's friend. . . . ("The Celebrated Jumping Frog of Calaveras County")

People who are in **compliance** are

a. curious **c.** stubborn
b. demanding **d.** accommodating

5. They used to give [the horse] two or three hundred yards start . . . but always at the [end] of the race she'd get excited and desperate-like, and come cavorting and straddling up, and scattering her legs around **limber**, sometimes in the air, and sometimes out to one side amongst the fences. . . . ("The Celebrated Jumping Frog of Calaveras County")

A **limber** horse is one that is

a. hostile **c.** stocky
b. mature **d.** nimble

Interactive Quiz

Snap the code, or go to **SadlierConnect.com**.

Vocabulary for Comprehension

Part 1

*Read "Oseola McCarty: 1908–1999," which contains words in **boldface** that appear in Units 4–6. Then answer the questions.*

Oseola McCarty: 1908–1999

Oseola McCarty left school after sixth grade to help care for an ailing relative. She was sorry not to be able to continue her education, but her family needed her. Pursuing an education was an **elusive** dream to this lifelong **inhabitant** of Mississippi. She eked out a living washing and ironing other people's clothing and lived most of her life in a small house her uncle had once owned.

For seventy-five years, Oseola McCarty served her customers. McCarty believed in hard work, and she was 86 years old before she finally retired. She boiled, hand-scrubbed, and hang-dried her customers' laundry instead of using a washing machine or a dryer. She would iron clothes until 11 o'clock at night. "Hard work gives your life meaning," she once said. McCarty also lived a frugal lifestyle and walked wherever she had to go.

McCarty earned little money yet managed to put aside a small amount almost every week. She knew it was wise to plan for the future, and she never felt right about taking money out of her bank account. The money she put into the bank was earning interest. What must have seemed like **petty** deposits of nickels and dimes eventually grew into a fortune. By the time McCarty was 87, she had nearly $300,000.

McCarty's dreams of education had never faded. She thought she was too old to attend college but felt no **remorse** about her life. Instead she thought of an **agenda** to help others attend college. She gave $150,000 of her life's savings to the University of Southern Mississippi. All she asked of the university was that it use the money for scholarships for deserving students from southern Mississippi who could not afford college. Suddenly this elderly laundry woman became a local hero.

Oseola McCarty's generosity touched people, and many were moved to make their own contributions to increase the Oseola McCarty Endowed Scholarship Fund. Since the fund was first established, the university has been able to award many scholarships in McCarty's name.

Although McCarty became a rich woman through her dutiful saving, she remained a straightforward, honest, and humble person. Her **commentaries** on life were right to the point. "If you want to feel proud of yourself," she once said, "you've got to do things you can be proud of."

McCarty also had a simple explanation for her ability to live so modestly and save so much of what she earned: "My secret was contentment. I was happy with what I had," she said. When Oseola McCarty died at the age of 91, people throughout the United States remembered her with pride and admiration.

1. Which sentence **best** states the author's purpose in "Oseola McCarty: 1908–1999"?
   A) The author tells an inspirational true story.
   B) The author tells an inspirational fictional story.
   C) The author persuades the reader of the benefits of saving money.
   D) The author explains ways to help others.

2. As used in line 6, what does the word **elusive** suggest about Oseola McCarty's dream of pursuing an education?
   A) It was easily fulfilled.
   B) It was cherished.
   C) It was difficult to achieve.
   D) It was temporary.

3. **Part A**
   Which word best describes the author's tone in paragraphs 2 and 3 (lines 12–36)?
   A) pitying
   B) disbelieving
   C) critical
   D) respectful

   Part B
   Which statement from the passage **best** supports your answer to Part A?
   A) "For seventy-five years, Oseola McCarty served her customers." (lines 12–13)
   B) "She would iron clothes until 11 o'clock at night." (lines 19–21)
   C) "The money she put into the bank was earning interest." (lines 30–31)
   D) "What must have seemed like petty deposits of nickels and dimes eventually grew into a fortune." (lines 32–34)

4. According to the passage, what are **petty** deposits (line 32)?
   A) sensible
   B) narrow-minded
   C) major
   D) insignificant

5. Based on the evidence in lines 32–36, which statement **best** describes how McCarty amassed her wealth?
   A) Here today, gone tomorrow.
   B) Live only in the here and now.
   C) Slow and steady wins the race.
   D) Out of sight, out of mind.

6. Which word means the opposite of **remorse** in line 40?
   A) confusion
   B) guiltlessness
   C) sympathy
   D) regret

7. What does the word **agenda** mean as it is used in line 41?
   A) dream
   B) way
   C) contest
   D) plan

8. Which statement **best** provides an inference that is supported by "Oseola McCarty: 1908–1999"?
   A) One person can make a big difference in the lives of others.
   B) Live as if today were your last day on earth.
   C) The most important thing in life is a college education.
   D) Without an education, a person is permanently disadvantaged.

Vocabulary for Comprehension

Part 2

*Read these passages, which contain words in **boldface** that appear in Units 4–6. Then choose the best answer to each question based on what is stated or implied in the passages. You may refer to the passages as often as necessary.*

Questions 1–8 are based on the following passages.

Passage 1

A puppet is a figure of a person or animal moved by human aid. Throughout recorded history puppets and puppet theater have been popular all over the world. Some historians claim that puppets date back into Cro-Magnon times, around 30,000 BCE. Puppets have enjoyed enduring popularity, and some puppets have become famous through movies.

Over time, many types of puppet and styles of puppet entertainment have developed. There are hand or glove puppets, rod puppets, marionettes or string puppets, and shadow figures, in which an audience views the puppet's shadows through a translucent screen.

Puppetry is diverse, and any **synopsis** of its origins will necessarily leave out some of the cultures that contributed to its development. It is fair to say, however, that two distinct traditions developed in the **maze** of this art's history. One tradition was centered in Europe, the other in Asia. The western tradition, found chiefly in Europe, performed folk plays for popular audiences. An outstanding example is the Punch and Judy show, which featured two main characters: the **headstrong** Pulcinella (Mr. Punch) and his wife Judy. Often **boisterous** and violent, this entertainment showcased farce and slapstick comedy. This type of puppet theater reached its height in England in the early 1700s.

Passage 2

The eastern tradition in puppetry is remarkably diverse. Puppet performances are popular in numerous Asian countries. One widespread type of performance is shadow puppet theater, common in India, Indonesia, Malaysia, Thailand, and Cambodia. In these performances, puppets are two-dimensional and made of buffalo hide. The puppeteer, known as the *dalang* in Indonesia, manipulates all the figures on one side of an illuminated screen. The audience watches the action from the other side. Performances include a musical ensemble of percussion instruments known as the *gamelan*. Called *wayang kulit* in Indonesia, shadow puppetry is **deemed** one of the country's most distinctive cultural traditions.

Two ancient Indian epics **generated** the storylines and most of the characters of *wayang kulit*. These epics, the *Ramayana* and the *Mahabharata*, were probably composed sometime between 400 BCE and 400 CE. In the *Ramayana*, the hero rescues his kidnapped wife. In the *Mahabharata*, five brothers must wage a **devastating** war against their cousins. Although many shadow plays exhibit great **fidelity** to the epic stories, there is **leeway** for the addition of new characters. As a night-long performance unfolds, the eerie shadows and hypnotic musical accompaniment may **induce** a state of **reverie** in the audience. Such is the magic of wayang *kulit*.

1. According to Passage 1, historians believe that puppets may
   - A) have originated in China.
   - B) be a product of medieval cultures.
   - C) be a very ancient form of art.
   - D) have become less popular over time.

2. As it is used in line 20, "synopsis" most nearly means
   - A) outline.
   - B) judgment.
   - C) interpretation.
   - D) essay.

3. From details in Passage 2, it can reasonably be inferred that the effect of shadow puppet theater is often
   - A) subversive.
   - B) hypnotic.
   - C) satirical.
   - D) explosive.

4. As it is used in line 72, "fidelity" most nearly means
   - A) transformation.
   - B) recognition.
   - C) duplication.
   - D) loyalty.

5. Passage 1 differs from Passage 2 primarily because it
   - A) acknowledges that puppets have an ancient history.
   - B) presents a broader discussion, including a definition and historical summary.
   - C) argues that the western tradition is more significant than the eastern tradition.
   - D) claims that puppetry has a narrow, specialized appeal.

6. Which choice provides the best evidence for the answer to the previous question?
   - A) Lines 1–2 ("A puppet . . . aid")
   - B) Lines 13–18 ("There are . . . screen")
   - C) Lines 19–22 ("Puppetry . . . development")
   - D) Lines 40–42 ("Puppet . . . countries")

7. Passage 1 and Passage 2 are similar in that both passages stress
   - A) the epic tales underlying puppet traditions.
   - B) the ingenious features of puppetry.
   - C) the widespread popularity of puppetry.
   - D) the contributions of slapstick comedy to puppetry.

8. As it is used in line 78, "reverie" most nearly means
   - A) boredom.
   - B) trance.
   - C) distraction.
   - D) blackout.

Denotation and Connotation

When you look up a word in a dictionary, you find its definition, or its **denotation**. A word's denotation is its literal meaning, and it conveys a neutral tone.

Many words have additional shades of meaning called connotations. **Connotations** are the emotional associations we have with words. A word might have several synonyms, or words that have related meanings, but each synonym will have a particular connotation that sets it apart from the others. Connotations can be positive, negative, or neutral.

Consider these synonyms for the neutral word *remembrance*.

memento *souvenir* *keepsake* *relic*

Memento, souvenir, and *keepsake* have positive connotations, whereas *relic* has a more negative one, suggesting something old and outdated.

> **Think:** Travelers like to collect mementos, souvenirs, and keepsakes during trips; these objects inspire happy memories. But relics are objects that are old and worthless.

Look at these examples of words that have similar denotations but very different connotations.

NEUTRAL	POSITIVE	NEGATIVE
pacify	**soothe**	**placate**
pleased	**proud**	**smug**
agenda	**proposal**	**conspiracy**

Writers know the emotional power of words. If a writer wants to elicit emotional response from readers, he or she will choose powerful words. Think about how advertisers use words. Would you rather be the *proud owner* of a new car or a *smug purchaser*?

Shades of Meaning

Write a plus sign (+) in the box if the word has a positive connotation. Write a minus sign (–) if the word has a negative connotation. Put a zero (0) if the word is neutral.

1. amiable ☐	**2.** eerie ☐	**3.** commentary ☐	**4.** plight ☐
5. duration ☐	**6.** strife ☐	**7.** ovation ☐	**8.** maze ☐
9. reimburse ☐	**10.** clarity ☐	**11.** scan ☐	**12.** bungle ☐
13. devastate ☐	**14.** gory ☐	**15.** limber ☐	**16.** inhabitants ☐

Expressing the Connotation

Read each sentence. Select the word in parentheses that better expresses the connotation (positive, negative, or neutral) given at the beginning of the sentence.

neutral **1.** Our cat is quite (**elusive, mystifying**) and seldom makes an appearance when we have company.

negative **2.** The criticism he made was (**minor, petty**), but I don't think anyone in the class took offense.

positive **3.** Ruby is a (**determined, headstrong**) child, and she prefers getting dressed on her own.

neutral **4.** You should be (**compliant, submissive**) when addressing a police officer if he stops your car.

negative **5.** The coffee shop owner does not want people to (**loiter, tarry**) in front of her place of business.

neutral **6.** Some people (**idolize, admire**) the idea of physical beauty, but I think personality is more important.

positive **7.** When they heard that their troop had sold the most cookies, the scouts responded with (**unruly, boisterous**) shouts and applause.

negative **8.** One member banged his shoe on the desk, prompting a (**fray, disagreement**) among the politicians.

Challenge: Using Connotation

Choose vocabulary words from Units 4–6 to replace the highlighted words in the sentences below. Then explain how the connotation of the replacement word changes the tone of the sentence.

conserve	**ingratitude**	**ravenous**
remorse	**gross**	**induce**

1. Even when the judge pointed out Daniel's misdeeds, Daniel felt no **guilt** ______________.

____

____

2. It is important that we **safeguard** ______________ our natural resources so that future generations can enjoy them.

____

____

3. The movie featured a **hungry** ______________ shark that attacked a large ship and its entire crew.

____

____

Idioms

In the passage "Continue Space Exploration, Now!" (see pages 60–61), the narrator says that space program funds do not "account for" all the over-spending of the federal government.

"Account for" is an idiom that means "explain" or "to be the determining factor." An **idiom** is an informal phrase or expression whose words should not be interpreted literally. We learn idioms from everyday usage, and they become so ingrained in our daily speech that we often forget we are using them.

Choosing the Right Idiom

Read each sentence. Use context clues to figure out the meaning of each idiom in ***boldface*** *print. Then write the letter of the definition for the idiom in the sentence.*

1. Jared was **up a creek** when he arrived at class without his books. ________
2. I really wish Jamie would quit **bugging me** about going to the football game. ________
3. Our class did not win first place at the tournament, but **that's the way the cookie crumbles**. ________
4. How will Tonya react when she **gets wind of** the news that Leanne can run faster than she can? ________
5. The mayor refused to **back down** on her position about the new hike and bike trail. ________
6. If you're having a party, one of the best ways to **break the ice** is to play a name game. ________
7. After a long day at school, Megan **lets off steam** by playing with her dog. ________
8. Greg, tired of doing all the work on the class project, asked his partner to **pull his own weight**. ________
9. It was difficult for the excited child to **sit tight** and wait his turn. ________
10. My brother tried to **butter me up**, hoping I would agree to wash the dishes. ________

a. retreat or give in

b. start conversations; get people to relax

c. flatter someone in order to gain something

d. in a bad situation

e. take responsibility; do one's fair share

f. that's how things turn out differently than planned

g. be patient

h. annoying or pestering

i. releases energy or stress

j. hears about

Classical Roots

re—back; again

The Latin root *re* appears in **repent** (page 54), **revocation** (page 54), **refute** (page 64), **remorse** (page 64), and **reimburse** (page 74). Some other words based on the same root are listed below.

rebuke	**refrain**	**renege**	**retract**
redeem	**relic**	**restraint**	**revive**

From the list of words above, choose the one that corresponds to each of the brief definitions below. Write the word in the blank space in the illustrative sentence below the definition. Use a dictionary if necessary.

1. to scold, express sharp disapproval; a scolding

The babysitter had to ____________________ the children for misbehaving after dinner.

2. to go back on a promise

They were surprised when the buyer suddenly decided to ____________________ on the deal.

3. to buy back; to make up for; to fulfill a pledge

Consumers who ____________________ discount coupons they clip from magazines and newspapers can lower their weekly grocery bills.

4. something that has survived the passage of time

We marveled at the delicate artistry in the Indian ____________________ we saw at the museum.

5. to take back something that has been said, offered, or published

The angry candidate demanded that the newspaper ____________________ the scandalous story.

6. to give new life to; to restore

Lively cheers from a hopeful crowd may ____________________ a team's dampened spirits.

7. a device that restricts or confines; control over the expression of one's feelings or behavior

The police officers placed ____________________ on the violent prisoner.

8. to hold oneself back; a repeated verse, chorus

On Thanksgiving, it is always hard for me to ____________________ from eating too much delicious food.

*Read the following passage, taking note of the **boldface** words and their contexts. These words are among those you will be studying in Unit 7. As you complete the exercises in this unit, it may help to refer to the way the words are used below.*

Made for the Shade

<Informational Essay>

Most people who wear sunglasses might say they wear shades to protect their eyes from the sun's harmful ultraviolet rays or to ward off glare. They aren't **prevaricating**. Those *are* the most popular reasons people wear sunglasses. But the "coolness factor" is another reason. With so many shapes, sizes, and colors to choose from, just about everyone can pick shades that look stylish. But modern sunglasses are a far cry from earlier models.

People today might not **relish** wearing the "sunglasses" of the ancient Inuit. The Inuit wore sun goggles made from bone, ivory, and wood. These were fashioned into eye coverings with slits so the wearer could see. These goggles were functional, but not exactly a fashion statement.

Roman emperors used a more glamorous way of protecting their eyes. Supposedly, the emperor Nero shielded his eyes with pieces of emerald. But lowly citizens were not **authorized** to do the same, even if they could afford the gems.

In the twelfth century, Chinese judges hid their eyes behind planes of smoky quartz crystals to appear detached or impartial. The judges could **immerse** themselves in the trial without betraying their thoughts about the alleged **culprit** or witnesses. This gesture **quashed** any suspicion that they were taking sides.

Centuries later, sunglasses similar to modern shades were developed. Around 1750, British optician, designer, and inventor James Ayscough experimented with tinted lenses. He **dissected** and remade existing spectacles to create shaded ones. He was trying to correct specific eye ailments. While he might have felt his early efforts **pathetic**, he **persevered**. Although Ayscough was not designing the glasses for sun protection, he is still known as the father of modern sunglasses.

Snow goggles helped protect the Inuit from snow blindness.

Advancements in the manufacture of sunglasses followed over the years. In 1929, entrepreneur Sam Foster started selling his own inexpensive shades in Atlantic City, New Jersey. That is when sunglasses really became both fashionable and functional. Foster founded Foster Grant—still a successful company today.

Foster could not have picked a better time to start his company. As the film industry took off in the twentieth century, sunglasses became popular among movie stars. Silent-film stars wore shades to disguise red eyes caused by lamps used while shooting films. Even after this problem was fixed, stars continued to wear shades—probably for the glamour factor. Or perhaps celebrities who want to remain incognito believe that the public is **gullible** enough not to recognize a star wearing shades.

Audrey Hepburn in *Breakfast at Tiffany's*

Although celebrities and the general public alike wear them to be fashionable, sunglasses have become a staple in various professions. In 1936, photography pioneer Edwin H. Land developed polarized sunglasses using his patented Polaroid filter. These fast became popular with fishermen. The polarized lenses reduced glare and allowed fishermen to see into the water. There are also special shades for athletes, airline pilots, and astronauts. Astronauts need sunglasses for inside the spacecraft as well as out. Sunlight is much stronger in space.

Nowadays, sunglasses are more popular than ever. It is a **testimonial** to their staying power. Some people **expend** time carefully **scouring** websites for the odd or unusual pair of shades. A person might look at vintage shades and **reminisce** about the past. But **dawdling** fondly over old memories and the "good old days" might be a case of looking at the world through rose-colored glasses. If only those who yearn for vintage shades could see the primitive methods of blocking the sun's rays, they might not see sunglasses in such a romantic light.

Astronauts require eye protection from the sun outside and inside their spacecraft.

Audio

For iWords and audio passages, snap the code, or go to **SadlierConnect.com**.

Definitions

Note the spelling, pronunciation, part(s) of speech, and definition(s) of each of the following words. Then write the word in the blank spaces in the illustrative sentence(s) following. Finally, study the lists of synonyms and antonyms.

1. authorize (ô′ thə rīz)

(*v.*) to approve or permit; to give power or authority to

I wonder if Congress will someday ____________ U.S. citizens to cast official votes over the Internet.

SYNONYMS: order, entitle, empower
ANTONYMS: forbid, ban, prohibit

2. culprit (kəl′ prit)

(*n.*) a person who has committed a crime or is guilty of some misconduct; an offender

Thanks to their efficient tracking methods, the police were able to catch the ____________ red-handed.

SYNONYMS: lawbreaker, wrongdoer

3. dawdle (dôd′ əl)

(*v.*) to waste time; to be idle; to spend more time in doing something than is necessary

It's relaxing to ____________ in the shower, but it wastes water.

SYNONYMS: delay, loiter, dillydally
ANTONYMS: hurry, hasten, speed up, bustle

4. dissect (di sekt′)

(*v.*) to cut apart in preparation for scientific study; to analyze with great care

I can't wait to ____________ a frog in biology class next week.

SYNONYM: examine
ANTONYMS: sew together, fuse, weld

5. expend (ek spend′)

(*v.*) to pay out, spend; to use up

The most experienced long-distance runners learn not to ____________ their energy too soon.

SYNONYMS: utilize, consume, disburse
ANTONYMS: save, hoard

6. fatality (fā tal′ ə tē)

(*n.*) an event resulting in death; an accidental death

The driver slammed on the brakes, but it was too late to prevent the traffic ____________.

SYNONYMS: casualty, mortality
ANTONYM: injury

7. gullible (gəl′ ə bəl)
(*adj.*) easily fooled, tricked, or cheated

Are you ____________________ enough to believe everything you hear on the radio?

SYNONYMS: trusting, naïve, credulous
ANTONYMS: suspicious, skeptical

8. illicit (i lis′ it)
(*adj.*) not permitted, unlawful, improper

Students will be suspended for one week if they bring any ____________________ materials to school.

SYNONYMS: illegal, unauthorized, forbidden
ANTONYMS: lawful, permissible, aboveboard

9. immerse (i mərs′)
(*v.*) to plunge or dip into a fluid; to involve deeply

I find it's easier to ____________________ my entire body in a swimming pool than try to get used to the water slowly.

SYNONYMS: dunk, engross
ANTONYMS: dredge up, pull out

10. inflammatory (in flam′ ə tôr ē)
(*adj.*) causing excitement or anger; leading to unrest, violence, or disorder

The candidate made an ____________________ speech that incensed all those who heard it.

SYNONYMS: provoking, incendiary, provocative
ANTONYMS: soothing, lulling, quieting

11. memorandum (mem ə ran′ dəm)
(*n.*) a note to aid one's memory; an informal note or report (*pl.*, memorandums *or* memoranda)

The principal's weekly ____________________ reminds teachers of programs, deadlines, and special events.

SYNONYM: reminder

12. pathetic (pə thet′ ik)
(*adj.*) marked by strong emotion, especially pity and sorrow; able to move people emotionally; worthy of pity; woefully inadequate or lacking

It was a ____________________ sight to see so many starving people desperately begging for food.

SYNONYMS: moving, distressing, pitiable, heartrending
ANTONYMS: funny, hilarious, frightening

13. persevere (pər sə vēr′)
(*v.*) to keep doing something in spite of difficulties; to refuse to quit even when the going is tough

The patient needs to ____________________ with the painful exercises in order to be able to walk normally again.

SYNONYMS: plug away, pursue, stick to it
ANTONYMS: give up, despair, throw in the towel, quit

14. prevaricate (pri var′ ə kāt)

(*v.*) to lie, tell an untruth; to mislead on purpose

His reputation has suffered because of his unfortunate tendency to ____________________.

SYNONYMS: stretch the truth, equivocate
ANTONYM: tell the truth

15. quash (kwäsh)

(*v.*) to crush, put down completely

Swift military action was required to ____________________ the revolt before anyone was injured.

SYNONYM: suppress
ANTONYMS: start, kindle, ignite, encourage

16. relish (rel′ ish)

(*n.*) enjoyment or satisfaction; something that adds a pleasing flavor; (*v.*) to enjoy greatly

She opened the tiny box with ____________________, knowing that it contained a piece of jewelry.

Now that I've learned about Japan in class, I ____________________ the chance to travel there.

SYNONYMS: (*n.*) pleasure, gusto; (*v.*) take delight in
ANTONYMS: (*v.*) loathe, hate, despise

17. reminisce (rem ə nis′)

(*v.*) to recall one's past thoughts, feelings, or experiences

At the family reunion, we got to hear 94-year-old Tía Luzia ____________________ about life in old Havana.

SYNONYMS: remember, recollect

18. scour (skaůr)

(*v.*) to clean or polish by hard rubbing; to examine with great care; to move about quickly in search of

The pot roast was delicious, but it won't be any fun to ____________________ the burned roasting pan.

SYNONYMS: scrub, search, comb
ANTONYMS: dirty, soil

19. testimonial (tes′ tə mō′ nē əl)

(*n.*) a statement that speaks to a person's character or to the benefits of a product; expressing the value and worth of someone or something

The famous athlete's ____________________ about the thirst-quenching drink made an impression on TV viewers.

SYNONYMS: memorial, tribute, evidence, statement

20. writhe (rīth)

(*v.*) to make twisting or turning movements in a way that suggests pain or struggle

It's so sad to see an injured bird ____________________ in pain.

SYNONYMS: twist, squirm, thrash

Choosing the Right Word

*Select the **boldface** word that better completes each sentence. You might refer to the unit selection to see how most of these words are used in context.*

1. Though he was losing his hearing, Beethoven (**authorized, immersed**) himself in his music.

2. We were impressed with Ella's (**testimonial, culprit**), as she described how a new shampoo made her hair grow faster.

3. The charges against the suspected mugger will probably not hold up in court, so the district attorney has decided to (**authorize, quash**) them.

4. Despite several rejection letters from publishers, the young writer (**prevaricated, persevered**) and continued to write stories.

5. In spite of all your talk about how hard it is to get into medical school, I intend to (**persevere, relish**) in my plans to become a doctor.

6. Is there any sight more (**pathetic, illicit**) than a kitten stranded in a tree?

Though plagued by illness, family difficulties, and the loss of his hearing, Ludwig van Beethoven created some of the world's greatest musical compositions.

7. When the class comedian imitated my way of speaking, it was all I could do not to (**writhe, reminisce**) with embarrassment.

8. What good does it do for the president of the Student Council to issue (**fatalities, memorandums**) if no one takes the trouble to read them?

9. We learned in our social studies class that the Constitution (**dissects, authorizes**) the president to arrange treaties with foreign countries.

10. She is so worried about appearing (**inflammatory, gullible**) that she sometimes refuses to believe things that are well supported by facts.

11. The more he tried to protect himself by (**scouring, prevaricating**), the more he became entrapped in his own web of lies.

12. Whenever my Aunt Joan hears a hit from the 1990s on the radio, she starts to (**reminisce, expend**) about her days in high school.

13. His sticky fingers and the crumbs around his mouth convinced us that he was the (**culprit, relish**) in the Case of the Empty Cookie Jar.

14. Although our coach can spend hours (**writhing, reminiscing**) about his victories, he doesn't have an equally good memory for his defeats.

15. She (**expends, dawdles**) so much time and energy on small matters that she can't prepare properly for the things that are really important.

16. Dictators like Hitler and Mussolini used (**pathetic, inflammatory**) language to stir up the emotions of the crowds they addressed.

17. Because my sister is so (**gullible, inflammatory**), I have to avoid reading scary stories to her before her bedtime.

18. When it became known that four explorers were lost in the jungle, special search parties were sent out to (**quash, scour**) the area for them.

19. I am afraid that our ambitious plan to modernize the gym has become a (**fatality, memorandum**) of the School Board's economy drive.

20. She was so deeply (**immersed, expended**) in the book she was reading that she did not even hear us enter the room.

21. It was plain from the way that he (**dawdled, persevered**) over breakfast that he was in no hurry to visit the dentist.

22. With the skill of a trained debater, she (**prevaricated, dissected**) her opponent's arguments one by one to reveal their basic weaknesses.

23. His scheme to make money by preparing term papers for other students is not only completely (**gullible, illicit**) but immoral as well.

24. No one (**relishes, immerses**) being reminded of his or her mistakes, but if you are wise you will try to learn from such criticism.

25. I spent three hours (**authorizing, scouring**) my room, looking for my homework.

Synonyms

*Choose the word from this Unit that is the same or most nearly the same in meaning as the **boldface** word or expression in the phrase. Write that word on the line. Use a dictionary if necessary.*

1. upsetting to learn the **heartbreaking** details ________________
2. targeted the most **innocent** people ________________
3. a monthly **notice** to all her patients ________________
4. destroying the **banned** books ________________
5. **carry on** despite many setbacks ________________
6. miracle that we suffered only one **loss of life** ________________
7. is certainly no time to **fib** ________________
8. promoting **confrontational** ideas to start a riot ________________
9. desperate to **wriggle** free from the ropes ________________
10. **submerge** the vegetables in cold water ________________

Antonyms

*Choose the word from this Unit that is most nearly opposite in meaning to the **boldface** word or expression in the phrase. Write that word on the line. Use a dictionary if necessary.*

1. a snake that **lies still** ____________________
2. suffering only a **minor wound** ____________________
3. made **calming** gestures to the group ____________________
4. sent a **long formal report** to the Board of Directors ____________________
5. participating in **legal** activities ____________________

Completing the Sentence

From the words in this Unit, choose the one that best completes each of the following sentences. Write the correct word form in the space provided.

1. You may not ____________________ being told that your carelessness was responsible for the accident, even though it happens to be true.
2. Many people were injured in the explosion, but luckily there was not a single ____________________.
3. The story of the homeless child was so ____________________ that it moved us all to tears.
4. Before you ____________________ yourself in the bath, be sure to test the temperature of the water.
5. We tried to hold Tom steady, but he ____________________ with pain as the doctor put splints on his broken leg.
6. Is it wise to ____________________ so much of your hard-earned money on things that you don't really want or need?
7. The dictator ordered his secret police to ____________________ any attempt to organize a protest rally.
8. Our supervisor prepared a(n) ____________________ that reminded the salespeople of the procedures to be followed during the holiday season.
9. "Only a bigot would dare to make such a rude and ____________________ remark, even in jest," I replied.
10. The children won't ____________________ over their homework if they know they'll be getting cheese and crackers as soon as they finish.

11. Because he was seen near the scene of the crime at the time the deed was committed, he was suspected of being the ____________________.

12. I love to listen to my grandfather ____________________ about his boyhood adventures in Coney Island.

13. The new library that will bear Ann Parker's name is a ____________________ to her commitment to teaching children how to read.

14. Do you really think that I am ____________________ enough to believe his foolish story about being a member of the Olympic team?

15. This pass ____________________ you to visit certain rooms in this museum that are not open to the general public.

16. You may be tempted to ____________________, but in the long run it will be to your advantage to own up to the truth about your unfortunate error.

17. We had to ____________________ the walls for hours to get rid of the dirt and grease with which they were encrusted.

18. Cracking down on ____________________ drug traffic is one of the biggest problems facing law-enforcement agencies in the United States.

19. No matter how talented you may be, you will never be successful unless you learn to ____________________ in what you undertake.

20. After we had ____________________ the animal, we had to point to each of its important organs and explain its main function.

Writing: Words in Action

1. Look back at "Made for the Shade" (pages 88–89). Suppose you have been put in charge of an advertising campaign for a company that manufactures sunglasses. Your job is to write a television commercial that introduces a new line of shades and persuades viewers to purchase them. Use at least two details from the passage and three Unit words to support your ad.

2. People are often very vulnerable to the claims of advertising and feel that they must have certain brand-name items: designer sunglasses, a specific manufacturer's running shoes, or an article of clothing that carries a particular logo. Write a position paper in which you state your opinion about some of the effects of advertising on people your age. What is harmful about advertising? How does it affect your daily life? What should young people know about advertising techniques? Support your opinion with your observations, specific examples, the reading (refer to pages 88–89), or your personal experience. Write at least three paragraphs, and use three or more words from this Unit.

Vocabulary in Context

Literary Text

The following excerpts are from Oliver Twist *by Charles Dickens. Some of the words you have studied in this Unit appear in* **boldface** *type. Complete each statement below the excerpt by circling the letter of the correct answer.*

1. The man shook his fist, as he uttered these words incoherently. He advanced towards Oliver, as if with the intention of aiming a blow at him, but fell violently on the ground: **writhing** and foaming, in a fit.

A person who is **writhing** is

a. talking **c.** yelling
b. praying **d.** thrashing

2. The dogs, who, in common with their masters, seemed to have no particular **relish** for the sport in which they were engaged, readily answered to the command.

People who do NOT **relish** a sport

a. enjoy it **c.** excel in it
b. dislike it **d.** fail at it

3. It was not until the two boys had **scoured**, with great rapidity, through a most intricate maze of narrow streets and courts, that they ventured to halt beneath a low and dark archway. Having remained silent here, just long enough to recover breath to speak, [Bates] uttered an exclamation of amusement and delight.

Someone who has **scoured** through a place has moved

a. joylessly **c.** intently
b. happily **d.** cautiously

Oliver Twist is about a young orphan who joins a group of boys trained to steal.

4. The snow lay on the ground, frozen into a hard thick crust, so that only the heaps that had drifted into byways and corners were affected by the sharp wind that howled abroad: which, as if **expending** increased fury on such prey as it found, caught it savagely up in clouds, and, whirling it into a thousand misty eddies, scattered it in air.

The act of **expending** involves

a. using up **c.** choosing
b. saving for **d.** approving

5. "I hope the gentleman will understand that it isn't my fault, sir?" said Mrs. Mann, whimpering **pathetically**.

A person who sobs **pathetically** does so in a(n)

a. miserable manner **c.** respectable manner
b. impartial manner **d.** playful manner

Interactive Quiz

Snap the code, or go to **SadlierConnect.com**.

*Read the following passage, taking note of the **boldface** words and their contexts. These words are among those you will be studying in Unit 8. As you complete the exercises in this unit, it may help to refer to the way the words are used below.*

From Big Dream to Big Top

<Interview>

This month, Teen Talk Magazine *interviews Mike Quintus Bessy, an aerialist with the Empire Circus. Mike tells TT about the history of the circus, his job, and circus life.*

Editor's Note: Englishman Philip Astley (1742–1814) is one of the most important figures in circus history. He was a skilled equestrian who opened a popular riding school and performing arena, and then became a circus impresario when he built Astley's Amphitheatre in London in 1770. Astley worked hard, took risks, gained money and **affluence**, and was living proof that there is no luck except when there is discipline.

TT: Mike, many circus performers are born into a family of performers, but your parents are dentists. What made you want to join the circus?

Mike Q. Bessy: When I was quite young, I read a book about Philip Astley. I was fascinated and started taking tumbling classes. Astley is known as the father of the modern circus because his circus is the **template** for the circuses we see today.

TT: How did Astley go about founding a circus?

MQB: From the **onset**, Astley had a passion for horses. He enlisted in a cavalry regiment and then took up performing. One of his specialties was to **retrieve** a handkerchief from the ground while his horse cantered. He could maintain his balance better if his horse traveled in circles, so that's why he had a ring for his circus. Back then, animals and trick riders were the stars, and Astley's circus

Philip Astley was one of the great showmen of his time.

supposedly featured a horse that could perform card tricks and a pig that could solve math problems. I would pay to see that!

TT: What was a typical show like back in Astley's time?

MQB: Astley staged massive spectacles featuring a **minimum** of 100 horses and riders. There would also be fireworks, music, magicians, tightrope walkers, clowns, performing dogs...you name it! Well, except for wild-animal acts—that **innovation** came later. There was a stage, a circular pit, and audience galleries. There was no **partition** between the stage and the arena, so the shows were held

Astley's Amphitheatre was home to the first true modern circus.

simultaneously. The amphitheatre was rebuilt a number of times after fires, and it was eventually demolished in the 1890s because bad decisions and bad luck left the owner in **arrears**. Meanwhile, Astley retired from performing when he was still in his 30s, but he was often the ringmaster, dressed in his customary military costume.

TT: The story goes that although Astley was charming, he also had a quick temper. I guess even circus folk aren't always happy-go-lucky.

MQB: It's a mistake to assume that circus performers are happy and **jovial** 100 percent of the time. We're all **crotchety** sometimes—even clowns!

TT: Besides a taste for adventure, what makes a good aerialist?

MQB: You have to have a strong, **taut** body, and you must be alert, quick, and **nimble** to fly through the air and catch your partners.

TT: Do you feel as if the circus is your home?

MQB: I do, although I know some people don't care for circuses. They think the atmosphere is a little creepy and **sinister**, or they're uncomfortable with crowds, or they harbor an image of elephants in **manacles** and chains. It makes me **cringe** to hear that animals are abused. I believe most circuses treat their animals with kindness and respect, the same way Philip Astley cared for his beloved horses.

Audio

For iWords and audio passages, snap the code, or go to **SadlierConnect.com**.

Definitions

Note the spelling, pronunciation, part(s) of speech, and definition(s) of each of the following words. Then write the word in the blank spaces in the illustrative sentence(s) following. Finally, study the lists of synonyms and antonyms.

1. affluence (af′ lü əns)
(*n.*) wealth, riches, prosperity; great abundance, plenty
Education, hard work, and a very strong desire to succeed can raise a person from poverty to ______________.
SYNONYM: opulence; ANTONYMS: poverty, want, destitution, scarcity

2. arrears (ə rērz′)
(*n., pl.*) unpaid or overdue debts; an unfinished duty
Bad spending habits and unexpected expenses left my aunt in ______________.
SYNONYMS: in default, in the red, late, overdue

3. cascade (kas kād′)
(*n.*) a steep, narrow waterfall; something falling or rushing forth in quantity; (*v.*) to flow downward (like a waterfall)
We were thrilled when we hit the jackpot, which produced a ______________ of loudly jangling coins.
I watched the clear, sparkling water ______________ down the mountainside.
SYNONYMS: (*v.*) plunge, rush, tumble
ANTONYMS: (*n.*) dribble, drop; (*v.*) trickle, ooze

4. cringe (krinj)
(*v.*) to shrink back or hide in fear or submissiveness
My father told me to be brave and not to ______________ when the doctor vaccinated me.
SYNONYMS: flinch, duck, fawn; ANTONYMS: strut, swagger

5. crotchety (kräch′ ə tē)
(*adj.*) cranky, ill-tempered; full of odd whims
It is unfortunate that the teacher asked me to work with the most ______________ partner in the class.
SYNONYMS: grumpy, grouchy, crabby, disagreeable
ANTONYMS: sociable, friendly, agreeable, amiable

6. immobile (i mō′ bəl)
(*adj.*) not movable; not moving
Models must remain ______________ for a long time in order for an artist to draw or paint them accurately.
SYNONYMS: fixed, unmoving; ANTONYMS: movable, nimble, agile

7. impassable (im pas′ ə bəl)
(*adj.*) blocked so that nothing can go through
Fallen trees formed an ______________ barrier across the highway after the storm.
SYNONYMS: closed, impenetrable; ANTONYMS: unblocked, clear

8. innovation (i nō vā′ shən)

(*n.*) something new, a change; the act of introducing a new method, idea, device, etc.

Our furnace has an energy-saving ____________ that turns the heat on and off at certain intervals.

SYNONYMS: novelty, modernization, new wrinkle

9. jovial (jō′ vē əl)

(*adj.*) good-humored, in high spirits; merry

My ____________ friend is very entertaining and is always the life of the party.

SYNONYMS: jolly, cheerful, festive
ANTONYMS: gloomy, morose, melancholy, cheerless

10. manacle (man′ ə kəl)

(*n., usually pl.*) a handcuff, anything that chains or confines; (*v.*) to chain or restrain (as with handcuffs)

The kidnappers clamped ____________ on their frightened hostages.

The guards ____________ the uncooperative prisoner to the chair.

SYNONYMS: (*v.*) put in chains, fetter
ANTONYMS: (*v.*) unchain, set free, emancipate, release

11. martial (mär′ shəl)

(*adj.*) warlike, fond of fighting; relating to war, the army, or military life

The army band plays ____________ music as the troops formally march past the visiting general.

SYNONYMS: hostile, bellicose
ANTONYMS: peace-loving, pacific, unwarlike

12. minimum (min′ ə məm)

(*n.*) the smallest possible amount; (*adj.*) the lowest permissible or possible

I need to sleep a ____________ of seven hours every night.

The ____________ age to get a driver's license in this state is sixteen.

SYNONYM: (*adj.*) least
ANTONYMS: (*n.*) maximum; (*adj.*) highest, most

13. nimble (nim′ bəl)

(*adj.*) quick and skillful in movement, agile; clever

As the ____________ climber scaled Mount Everest, it looked as if she was barely exerting any energy at all.

SYNONYMS: lively, keen, flexible
ANTONYMS: awkward, clumsy, stiff, inflexible

14. onset (än′ set)

(*n.*) the beginning, start (especially of something violent and destructive); an attack, assault

At the ____________________ of the heavy storm, frightened people ran to find shelter.

SYNONYMS: outset, commencement
ANTONYMS: conclusion, close, end

15. partition (pär tish′ ən)

(*n.*) something that divides (such as a wall); the act of dividing something into parts or sections; (*v.*) to divide or subdivide into parts or shares

A cloth ____________________ in the study gave each of us some privacy.

If you like, we can easily ____________________ the backyard into four separate play areas.

SYNONYMS: (*n.*) divider, separation
ANTONYMS: (*v.*) join, combine, consolidate, merge

16. perishable (per′ ə shə bəl)

(*adj.*) likely to spoil or decay

You must keep ____________________ foods chilled, or they will spoil.

SYNONYMS: short-lived, fleeting
ANTONYMS: long-lasting, undying, permanent

17. retrieve (ri trēv′)

(*v.*) to find and bring back, get back; to put right, make good

I don't relish having to ____________________ the tennis balls every time you hit them over the fence!

SYNONYMS: regain, fetch, remedy, rectify

18. sinister (sin′ ə stər)

(*adj.*) appearing evil or dangerous; threatening evil or harm

A ____________________ message left on our voicemail made us suspect the caller had the wrong number.

SYNONYMS: frightening, ominous
ANTONYMS: cheering, encouraging, reassuring, benign

19. taut (tôt)

(*adj.*) tightly drawn, tense; neat, in good order

A ____________________ chain kept the curious dog away from the swimming pool.

SYNONYMS: tight, strained, orderly, shipshape
ANTONYMS: loose, slack, drooping, messy, sloppy

20. template (tem′ plit)

(*n.*) a pattern, typically in the form of metal, wood, or plastic; something that is used as a model to imitate

The carpenter created a wooden ____________________ for a stair step so that he could easily construct the staircase.

SYNONYMS: mock-up, stencil, guide, shape, mold

Choosing the Right Word

*Select the **boldface** word that better completes each sentence. You might refer to the unit selection to see how most of these words are used in context.*

1. Robin Hood's faithful merry men were not only (**crotchety, jovial**) companions, but brave and clever fighters as well.

2. Some hikers are surprised when they get a poison ivy rash, as its (**cringe, onset**) can sometimes be several days after the encounter with the vine.

3. Although we all recognize that there must be changes, it is a mistake to think that every (**arrears, innovation**) is necessarily an improvement.

4. Instead of acting as though you were permanently (**manacled, retrieved**) to your small circle of friends, you should try to meet new people.

5. More than once, our skillful running backs managed to find a way through our opponents' supposedly (**impassable, affluent**) line.

Howard Pyle, an American illustrator and writer, arranged all the Robin Hood tales into a unified story.

6. Normally, I'm very even tempered, but I can become a little (**martial, crotchety**) when I'm tired or hungry.

7. We learned in our history class that the ancient Romans were very fine soldiers and excelled in all the (**martial, perishable**) arts.

8. Everyone in the auditorium (**retrieved, cringed**) when the singer hit a sour note while performing his most famous song.

9. I felt that there was something thoroughly (**sinister, immobile**) about the way he kept trying to duck questions on that subject.

10. With the (**affluence, onset**) of the heat wave, vast numbers of city dwellers began to stream toward the beaches and mountains.

11. Of all the different types of writing, humor may be the most (**perishable, jovial**), since each generation has its own idea of what is funny.

12. To keep a (**nimble, sinister**) mind, doctors advise working on crossword puzzles or learning a foreign language.

13. In the moment of danger, my nerves were so (**taut, sinister**) that I would have screamed if someone had touched me.

14. Although we are proud of our high standard of living, we should not forget that there are those who do not share in this (**affluence, minimum**).

15. Her blond hair fell upon her shoulders like a shimmering (**onset, cascade**) of gold.

16. Thanks to my brother's (**templates, innovations**) to a classic recipe, we won first prize at the fair for best hot sauce.

17. Her mind is so (**impassable, nimble**) that she always seems to be one step ahead of us in any matter under discussion.

18. The self-styled "tough guy" (**cringed, manacled**) in terror and begged the police not to shoot.

19. The first thing the bankrupt firm must do with its funds is pay the (**arrears, templates**) due on the employees' wages.

20. A high school student looking for a vacation job usually can't expect to earn more than the (**perishable, minimum**) wage.

21. Despite all his efforts, he was never able to (**retrieve, partition**) the fine reputation he had lost by that crooked deal.

22. In the eighteenth century, Russia, Prussia, and Austria made a series of deals to (**partition, cringe**) and annex Poland right out of existence.

23. The speed with which the boxer darted about the ring made his lumbering opponent seem utterly (**nimble, immobile**) by comparison.

24. Did you know that most computer software provides several different (**templates, onsets**) for letter writing?

25. This facial cream claims that it will help keep your skin (**taut, jovial**) and youthful.

Synonyms

*Choose the word from this Unit that is the same or most nearly the same in meaning as the **boldface** word or expression in the phrase. Write that word on the line. Use a dictionary if necessary.*

1. **recover** data from my computer ______________________
2. in the **clogged** section of the pipe ______________________
3. under strict **military** law ______________________
4. a **menacing** look in his eyes ______________________
5. installed to make it remain **stationary** ______________________
6. begged not to be **shackled** ______________________
7. to **cower** when the storm approaches ______________________
8. avoid eating food that **can become rotten** ______________________
9. as confetti **spilled** onto the stage ______________________
10. resisting the latest **improvement** ______________________

Antonyms

*Choose the word from this Unit that is most nearly opposite in meaning to the **boldface** word or expression in the phrase. Write that word on the line. Use a dictionary if necessary.*

1. using a **transportable** device ______________________
2. materials that are strong and **durable** ______________________
3. water **dripping** from the spout ______________________
4. living among **peaceable** people ______________________
5. looking for an **open** lane ______________________

Completing the Sentence

From the words in this Unit, choose the one that best completes each of the following sentences. Write the correct word form in the space provided.

1. The ______________________ mood of our cheerful little gathering changed abruptly to sorrow when news of the tragedy came over the radio.
2. It's a pleasure to watch the expert typist's ______________________ fingers move swiftly over the keyboard.
3. The patients will have a much better chance to recover quickly if they receive treatment at the ______________________ of the fever.
4. Sherlock Holmes detected in the wicked scheme the ______________________ hand of the evil Professor Moriarty.
5. Can you explain why there is not only a maximum speed limit but also a(n) ______________________ speed limit on many modern highways?
6. We plan to update the ______________________ of our school brochure to make it more attractive and readable.
7. I know that my payments on the car are in ______________________, but I will catch up as soon as I get my next paycheck.
8. Today ______________________ foods are transported in refrigerated trucks to prevent spoilage.
9. Unless you pull the ropes ______________________, the tennis net will sag.
10. Although we are sure that the prisoners will make no attempt to escape, the law requires us to place ______________________ on them.

11. Frank Lloyd Wright was a great American architect who was responsible for many ____________ in the design of buildings.

12. The sunlight caught the waters of the stream as they ____________ over the steep cliff and formed a brilliant rainbow.

13. I was able to ____________ my baggage promptly after leaving the plane.

14. The more we tried to humor the ____________ crossing guard, the more irritable and demanding he seemed to become.

15. His back injury was so severe that he has been placed in a cast and will have to remain ____________ for months.

16. I don't expect you to be a hero, but do you have to ____________ in that cowardly fashion whenever anyone so much as disagrees with you?

17. During the war years, the government tried all kinds of propaganda to arouse the ____________ spirit of the people.

18. All roads throughout the area became ____________ as a result of the record-breaking snowstorm.

19. The feeling of ____________ I had when I was paid lasted only until I had finished taking care of my bills.

20. We made use of a(n) ____________ to break up the floor space into a large number of small offices.

Writing: Words in Action

1. Look back at "From Big Dream to Big Top" (pages 98–99). Suppose that you are a circus performer, and you want others to consider a career with the circus. Write a letter to young people to persuade them that the circus offers challenging and interesting career paths. Use at least two details from the passage and three Unit words.

2. Some people feel that animals should not be trained to perform in circuses. Others feel that circuses are educational, allowing people to see how intelligent animals are and marvel at the amazing feats they can perform. Write a brief essay in which you state your position on this topic. Support your opinion with your observations, specific examples, the reading (refer to pages 98–99), or personal experience. Write at least three paragraphs, and use three or more words from this Unit.

Vocabulary in Context
Literary Text

The following excerpts are from The Adventures of Sherlock Holmes *by Sir Arthur Conan Doyle. Some of the words you have studied in this Unit appear in* **boldface** *type. Complete each statement below the excerpt by circling the letter of the correct answer.*

1. "Get back into your chair!" said Holmes sternly. "It is very well to **cringe** and crawl now, but you thought little enough of this poor Horner in the dock for a crime of which he knew nothing." ("The Adventure of the Blue Carbuncle")

To **cringe** is to

a. change
b. escape
c. cower
d. mumble

2. The trees and wayside hedges were just throwing out their first green shoots, and the air was full of the pleasant smell of the moist earth. To me at least there was a strange contrast between the sweet promise of the spring and this **sinister** quest upon which we were engaged. ("The Adventure of the Speckled Band")

Something that is **sinister** is definitely NOT

a. terrifying
b. comforting
c. startling
d. chilling

3. . . .I met Mr. Rucastle coming out through this door, his keys in his hand, and a look on his face which made him a very different person to the round, **jovial** man to whom I was accustomed. His cheeks were red, his brow was all crinkled with anger, and the veins stood out at his temples with passion. ("The Adventure of the Copper Beeches")

A person who is **jovial** is

a. joyful
b. thoughtful
c. crabby
d. dangerous

Basil Rathbone played Sherlock Holmes in this 1939 film adaptation of *The Adventures of Sherlock Holmes.*

4. "Yet if the lady is correct in saying that the flooring and walls are sound, and that the door, window, and chimney are **impassable**, then her sister must have been undoubtedly alone when she met her mysterious end." ("The Adventure of the Speckled Band")

If something is **impassable**, it is

a. stubborn
b. old-fashioned
c. stiff
d. blocked

5. . . .[W]ith a cry, she sprang at a small deal box which lay upon the table and tore the lid from it. Out there fell a **cascade** of children's bricks. ("The Man with the Twisted Lip")

A **cascade** is something that

a. fails
b. streams
c. crumbles
d. cries

Interactive Quiz

Snap the code, or go to **SadlierConnect.com**.

*Read the following passage, taking note of the **boldface** words and their contexts. These words are among those you will be studying in Unit 9. As you complete the exercises in this unit, it may help to refer to the way the words are used below.*

From Fire Arrows to Space Flight: A History of Rockets

<Informational Essay>

As early as 400 BCE, **logical** and observant inventors in Greece used steam to propel simple devices. A man named Archytas used steam to send a wooden pigeon gliding along high wires. These early steam-propelled devices were of little practical use. They were mainly used for entertainment. Over a thousand years later and thousands of miles away from Greece, Chinese alchemists learned to make gunpowder. By around 1100 CE, the Chinese were using gunpowder to make fireworks, which were used for celebrations. Simple grenade-like bombs were used in war. Before long, the Chinese learned to use gunpowder to propel "fire arrows" through the air. The same basic principle of propulsion was at work in Archytas's **giddy** pigeon and in Chinese fire arrows. But the special properties of gunpowder made the fire arrows useful tools of war.

In 1232, Chinese soldiers used fire arrows to defeat Mongol invaders at the Battle of Kai-Keng. This is the first known use of rockets in the history of warfare. To make these simple rockets, the Chinese filled a short bamboo tube with gunpowder. They capped one end of the tube. Then they attached it to an arrow. Then the gunpowder was ignited. It produced fire, smoke, and gas that escaped through the open end of the tube. This force propelled the rocket through the air. The arrow helped to keep the rocket steady during flight, though its course remained quite **variable**. These earliest rockets may not always have done much damage on **impact**. But a **deluge** of many fire arrows could cause **outright** fear in the enemy. Gaining something in defeat, the Mongols learned to make similar rockets. The new technology spread rapidly across Asia and Europe. But improvements in the basic design proceeded slowly at a **sluggish** pace until more modern days.

Early Chinese fire arrow rockets, c. 1000

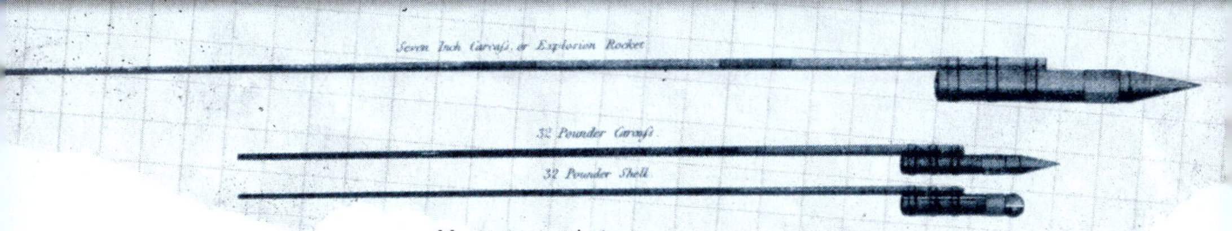

Mysorean rockets

By the **verge** of the industrial age, military rockets were becoming more effective weapons. In 1780, Hyder Ali of Mysore, a kingdom in India, used heavy, iron-cased rockets to defeat British forces. His son, Tipu Sultan, used the same rockets against the British with similar success. Mysorean rockets were not used merely to scare and **intimidate** the enemy. They were deadly weapons that cut down troops in their path. They were also used to set fire to ammunition and supplies. Determined to **avenge** themselves, British forces finally defeated Tipu Sultan's army in 1799. The Kingdom of Mysore **ceded** territory to the British Empire and became **subordinate** to its authority. The British soon developed their own weapons. The British based their rockets on the Mysorean rockets. A model described by William Congreve in 1807 set the standard for the Congreve rocket.

The British used the Congreve rocket against the United States during the War of 1812. The "rockets' red glare" remembered in the "Star-Spangled Banner" refers to the fiery **tint** of Congreve rockets in action.

By the nineteenth century, technology no longer moved at a **saunter**. The rate of change in tools of peace and war was accelerating as never before. Advances in artillery made rockets obsolete for several decades. But by the twentieth century, engineers were designing sophisticated rockets for use as spacecraft and as devastating missile systems. Rockets returned to the forefront of military technology. They also helped **liberate** humanity from Earth's gravity to explore outer space. And while rocket science has come a long way since its beginnings, it's likely to wind up light years ahead of its present state, in time.

Saturn V launch

Audio

For iWords and audio passages, snap the code, or go to **SadlierConnect.com**.

Definitions

Note the spelling, pronunciation, part(s) of speech, and definition(s) of each of the following words. Then write the word in the blank spaces in the illustrative sentence(s) following. Finally, study the lists of synonyms and antonyms.

1. avenge (ə venj′)

(*v.*) to get revenge for, get even for, settle a score; to punish someone or get satisfaction for a wrong or injury

In Shakespeare's *Hamlet*, the title character vows to ____________ his father's death.

SYNONYM: retaliate

2. cede (sēd)

(*v.*) to give up, surrender; to hand over to another

Spain ____________ territory to France.

SYNONYMS: deliver up, transfer

3. deluge (del′ yüj)

(*n.*) a great flood; a heavy fall of rain; anything that comes in a vast quantity (like a flood); (*v.*) to flood

Owners are hoping this summer will bring a ____________ of visitors to their new theme park in Minneapolis.

A torrential downpour ____________ the entire town.

SYNONYMS: (*v.*) swamp, inundate
ANTONYMS: (*n.*) trickle, dribble

4. discretion (dis kresh′ ən)

(*n.*) good judgment; care in speech and action; freedom to judge or choose

My teacher suggested I use ____________ in dealing with my difficult classmate.

SYNONYMS: prudence, tact, discrimination

5. giddy (gid′ ē)

(*adj.*) dizzy; light-headed; lacking seriousness

After the long and grueling race, the marathoner felt ____________ and exhausted.

SYNONYMS: faint, frivolous, flighty
ANTONYMS: levelheaded, serious, earnest, sober

6. impact (*n.*, im′ pakt; *v.*, im pakt′)

(*n.*) the striking of one object against another; the shock caused by a collision; (*v.*) to affect, especially forcefully

The ____________ of the car crash destroyed both vehicles, but miraculously no one was hurt.

Budget cuts will ____________ the number of hours the public library can stay open.

SYNONYMS: (*n.*) collision, blow, effect

7. intimidate
(in tim′ ə dāt)

(*v.*) to make timid or frighten by threats; to use fear to get someone to do (or not to do) something

Bullies may try to ____________________ us, but if we act brave and stand tall, we can diminish their threats.

SYNONYMS: browbeat, hector

8. liberate
(lib′ ə rāt)

(*v.*) to free from bondage or domination; to release

The police ____________________ the anxious hostages after sixteen hours of confinement.

SYNONYMS: untie, unshackle
ANTONYMS: imprison, fetter, shackle, bind

9. logical
(läj′ ə kəl)

(*adj.*) reasonable; making use of reason and good sense

Our parents are constantly encouraging us to look for ____________________ solutions to our problems.

SYNONYMS: rational, sensible
ANTONYMS: absurd, ridiculous, unsound, preposterous

10. misrepresent
(mis rep ri zent′)

(*v.*) to give a false or untrue idea

If witnesses ____________________ the facts, the defense attorney has proof to support our story.

SYNONYMS: falsify, twist, exaggerate

11. optional
(äp′ shə nəl)

(*adj.*) left to one's own choice; not required

The hotel will charge us for breakfast and dinner, but lunch is ____________________.

SYNONYMS: voluntary, discretionary
ANTONYMS: required, mandatory, compulsory

12. outright
(aůt′rīt)

(*adj.*) complete; instantaneous; without reservation, thoroughgoing; (*adv.*) completely, instantaneously

When the teacher asked her why she didn't do her homework, she told an ____________________ lie.

Even though they had already heard it several times, the hilarious joke made them laugh ____________________.

SYNONYMS: (*adj.*) total, out-and-out; (*adv.*) utterly, instantly
ANTONYMS: (*adj.*) partial, incomplete; (*adv.*) by degrees

13. rendezvous
(rän′ dā vü)

(*v.*) to meet in accordance with a plan; (*n.*) a meeting by agreement; a meeting place

Let's all agree to ____________________ by the fountain on Saturday afternoon.

They kept their ____________________ a secret.

SYNONYMS: (*n.*) date, assignation

14. rotund (rō tənd′)

(*adj.*) rounded and plump; full or rich in sound

My friends like to display the largest and most ____________ pumpkin outside their front door.

SYNONYMS: portly, sonorous; ANTONYMS: angular, lanky, gaunt

15. saunter (sôn′ tər)

(*v.*) to stroll; walk in an easy, leisurely way; (*n.*) a stroll

The star ____________ past his adoring fans.

It's such a beautiful day to take a ____________.

SYNONYMS: (*v.*) ramble, amble; (*n.*) promenade
ANTONYMS: (*v.*) speed, race, hurry, dash, scurry, rush

16. sluggish (sləg′ ish)

(*adj.*) lazy; slow-moving; not active, dull

After a big lunch, I feel ____________.

SYNONYMS: unhurried, lethargic; ANTONYMS: energetic, brisk

17. subordinate (*adj., n.,* sə bôr′ də nət; *v.,* sə bôr′ də nāt)

(*adj.*) lower in rank or position, secondary; (*n.*) one who is in a lower position or under the orders of someone else; (*v.*) to put in a lower or secondary position

A corporal is ____________ to a sergeant.

Let's ask a ____________ to help us file.

Parents often ____________ their own wishes for the sake of their children's needs.

SYNONYMS: (*n.*) assistant, helper
ANTONYMS: (*adj.*) superior, higher; (*n.*) chief, supervisor

18. tint (tint)

(*n.*) a delicate color or hue; a slight trace of something; (*v.*) to give color to something; to dye

He's painting his room a ____________ of blue.

I want to ____________ my sunglass lenses pink.

SYNONYMS: (*n.*) tone; (*v.*) color, stain; ANTONYM: (*v.*) bleach

19. variable (vâr′ ē ə bəl)

(*adj.*) likely to undergo change; changeable; (*n.*) a value or quantity that varies; a symbol for such

Spring weather can be extremely ____________.

In math, the letter *x* can stand for a ____________.

SYNONYMS: (*adj.*) fluctuating, shifting, inconstant
ANTONYMS: (*adj.*) constant, unchanging, steady

20. verge (vərj)

(*n.*) the point at which something begins or happens; a border; (*v.*) to incline, tend toward, approach; to be in the process of becoming something else

I was on the ____________ of tears today.

That chatter ____________ on baby talk.

SYNONYMS: (*n.*) threshold, edge

Choosing the Right Word

*Select the **boldface** word that better completes each sentence. You might refer to the unit selection to see how most of these words are used in context.*

1. In times of crisis, we may be called on to (**deluge, subordinate**) our personal interests to the needs of the nation as a whole.

2. I look forward to the time when my parents will agree that I have reached the "age of (**discretion, misrepresentation**)."

3. Modern household appliances have done much to (**liberate, deluge**) homemakers from tedious and time-consuming chores.

4. Many Western films include a character who is out to (**intimidate, avenge**) a wrong done to a close friend or relative.

5. Wasn't it annoying to see Michael (**verge, saunter**) into the party as though he were the coolest person ever to walk the face of the earth?

President Kennedy, in his famous Inaugural Address, said: "Ask not what your country can do for you—ask what you can do for your country."

6. He soon learned that the moods of a youngster—happy one moment, miserable the next—can be as (**variable, sluggish**) as the winds.

7. If you know that you are late for school, why do you (**saunter, rendezvous**) along as though you had all the time in the world?

8. A fastball pitcher will often try to (**liberate, intimidate**) an opposing batter by "shaving" him with an inside pitch.

9. At the State Fair, we separated to visit different exhibits, but we agreed to (**saunter, rendezvous**) at the refreshment stand at five o'clock.

10. This biased editorial has deliberately (**misrepresented, avenged**) the stand of our candidate on the important issues of the election.

11. Though once her peer, I became Caitlin's (**variable, subordinate**) when she was promoted to company president.

12. We held a meeting to discuss why the sale of tickets to the class dance has been so (**sluggish, rotund**) and what we can do about it.

13. Only the (**optional, outright**) repeal of this unfair nuisance tax will satisfy the voters.

14. I knew my dog was not feeling well when he suddenly became (**deluged, sluggish**) and refused to get up.

15. The aged millionaire, wishing to spend his last years in peace and quiet, (**ceded, impacted**) all his business interests to his sons.

16. It is good for you to "stand up for your rights," but you should not do so in a way that (**verges, subordinates**) on discourtesy.

17. It is up to the teacher's (**discretion, impact**) what topics can be chosen for our research papers.

18. It is shocking to see how, in just a few years, the lean young athlete has allowed himself to become flabby and (**giddy, rotund**).

19. Many people, unhappy with what nature has given them, seek to improve their appearance by (**tinting, ceding**) their hair.

20. There are times in life when you should be guided more by your feelings, without trying to be strictly (**outright, logical**) about everything.

21. The invitation to the party said that formal wear was (**optional, variable**).

22. Letters of protest (**deluged, tinted**) the Mayor's office when he proposed an increase in the sales tax.

23. We had regarded her as a rather (**logical, giddy**) young girl, but in this tough situation she showed that she had courage and good sense.

24. I plan to write a term paper that will discuss the different ways in which commercial television has had a major (**impact, verge**) on American life for more than sixty years.

25. The people rejoiced after being (**liberated, intimidated**) from oppression.

Synonyms

Choose the word from this Unit that is the same or most nearly the same in meaning as the ***boldface*** *word or expression in the phrase. Write that word on the line. Use a dictionary if necessary.*

1. taking an **elective** class ____________
2. an **aide** to the principal ____________
3. on the **brink** of a new beginning ____________
4. according to the judge's **ruling** ____________
5. could **bully** us into giving in ____________
6. kissed the baby's **chubby** cheek ____________
7. the jarring sound of the **crash** ____________
8. as if they made an **appointment** with danger ____________
9. had to **yield** that point in the debate ____________
10. not to **distort** the facts of the case ____________

Antonyms

*Choose the word from this Unit that is most nearly opposite in meaning to the **boldface** word or expression in the phrase. Write that word on the line. Use a dictionary if necessary.*

1. eating right in order to stay **lean** ______________________
2. your attendance is **obligatory** ______________________
3. expected to **tell the truth** ______________________
4. to **part** without saying goodbye ______________________
5. apologizing for their **tactlessness** ______________________

Completing the Sentence

From the words in this Unit, choose the one that best completes each of the following sentences. Write the correct word form in the space provided.

1. Many older residents of Paris can still recall the day in 1944 when Allied troops ______________________ the city from German occupation.

2. After the heavy meal, we felt so ______________________ that we just sat in the living room and watched whatever was on television.

3. Next year, when we have a stronger, more experienced team, we hope to ______________________ the crushing defeat we have just suffered.

4. By not ordering ______________________ features, we can hold down the cost of the new car we want to buy.

5. By late September, the leaves on the trees in the woods have begun to take on their normal autumn ______________________.

6. After being defeated in a war that lasted from 1846 to 1848, Mexico was forced to ______________________ vast territories to the United States.

7. Her argument was so ______________________ that she convinced us that her solution to the math problem was the correct one.

8. Our "truth in advertising" laws are designed to discourage manufacturers from ______________________ the virtues of their products.

9. We believe that the world is now on the ______________________ of new and exciting developments that may dramatically change the way we live.

10. Because of the lawyer's long experience in legal matters, we left it to his ______________________ how to proceed with the case.

11. When they realized that sweet talk and flattery were getting them nowhere, they tried to ______________________ me into doing what they wanted.

12. Every eye was on us as we ______________________ down Main Street in our new outfits.

13. The force of the head-on collision was so severe that the drivers of both vehicles were killed ______________________.

14. You may like to live where the sun shines all the time, but I prefer a more ______________________ climate.

15. Uncle Eddie, with his ______________________ figure, is often called on to play Santa Claus.

16. According to the eyewitness, the great ______________________ that arrived after the hurricane caused more damage than the winds.

17. Even fans sitting high in the stands could hear the ______________________ when the big fullback crashed into the line.

18. As a young and inexperienced employee, you cannot expect to hold more than a(n) ______________________ job in that big company.

19. Many people say that they become quite ______________________ when they look down from the top of a tall building.

20. The two groups of hikers, setting out from different points, have planned a(n) ______________________ at four o'clock at Eagle Rock.

Writing: Words in Action

1. Look back at "From Fire Arrows to Space Flight: A History of Rockets" (pages 108–109). Think about how Archytas's wooden pigeon led to the invention of rockets. Write a letter to Archytas in which you tell him some of the effects, or consequences, of his invention over the centuries. Incorporate at least two details from the passage and three Unit words in your writing.

2. Imagination is what motivates people to invent. Write an editorial for your local newspaper stating what you think can be done to encourage creativity and technological innovations in your own community. Support your opinion with your observations, specific examples, the reading (refer to pages 108–109), or personal experience. Write at least three paragraphs, and use three or more words from this Unit.

Vocabulary in Context

Literary Text

The following excerpts are from Anne of the Island *by L.M. Montgomery. Some of the words you have studied in this Unit appear in* ***boldface*** *type. Complete each statement below the excerpt by circling the letter of the correct answer.*

1. Gilbert and Anne, happily unconscious that their future was thus being settled by Mrs. Rachel, were **sauntering** through the shadows of the Haunted Wood.

The act of **sauntering** involves

a. hiding **c.** running
b. tumbling **d.** wandering

2. "But this morning I was quite well, so it couldn't have been the fever. I suppose if I did catch it last night it couldn't have developed so soon. I can remember that in daytime, but at three o'clock at night I never can be **logical**."

Someone who is **logical** is definitely NOT

a. confused **c.** elderly
b. lucid **d.** coherent

The 1934 film version of *Anne of Green Gables* focuses on the developing romance between Anne Shirley and Gilbert Blythe.

3. "This has been Patty's Place ever since my brother Aaron left it to me in his will, and Patty's Place it shall remain until I die and Maria dies. After that happens the next possessor can call it any fool name he likes," concluded Miss Patty, much as she might have said, "After that—the **deluge**."

A **deluge** is a(n)

a. agenda **c.** proposal
b. flood **d.** residence

4. To their right lay the harbor, taking on **tints** of rose and copper as it stretched out into the sunset. Before them the water shimmered, satin smooth and silver gray, and beyond, clean-shaven William's Island loomed out of the mist, guarding the town like a sturdy bulldog.

Tints of colors are

a. noble **c.** delicate
b. loud **d.** measurable

5. But Joseph [the cat] rashly sat up and yawned. [The other cat] Rusty, burning to **avenge** his disgrace, swooped down upon him. Joseph, pacific by nature, could fight upon occasion and fight well. The result was a series of drawn battles.

An animal who wants to **avenge** an action

a. gets even **c.** falls back
b. ignores it **d.** acts aloof

Interactive Quiz

Snap the code, or go to **SadlierConnect.com**.

Vocabulary for Comprehension

Part 1

*Read "Two Friends," which contains words in **boldface** that appear in Units 7–9. Then answer the questions.*

Two Friends

by Guy de Maupassant

Besieged Paris was in the throes of famine. Its days of **affluence** had passed, and everyone had to subsist with the **minimum** amount possible. Even the sparrows on the roofs and the rats in the sewers were growing scarce. People were eating anything they could get.

Monsieur Morissot, watchmaker by profession with a tendency to **dawdle**, was sauntering along the boulevard one bright January morning. Hands in his trousers pockets and stomach empty, he suddenly came face-to-face with an acquaintance—Monsieur Sauvage, a fishing chum.

Before the war it was Morissot's habit, every Sunday morning, of setting forth with a bamboo rod in his hand and a tin box on his back. He took the Argenteuil train, got out at Colombes, and walked thence to the Ile Marante. The moment he arrived he began fishing.

Every Sunday he met in this very spot Monsieur Sauvage, a stout, **jovial** man, a draper in the Rue Notre Dame de Lorette, and an ardent fisherman. They often spent half the day side by side, rod in hand and feet dangling over the water, and a warm friendship had sprung up between them.

Some days they did not speak. At other times they were immersed in conversation. Never an inflammatory word passed between them. They understood each other perfectly without the aid of words, having similar tastes and feelings.

In the spring, when the early sun caused a light mist to float on the water and gently warmed the backs of the two anglers, Morissot would remark:

"My, but it's pleasant here."

To which the other would reply:

"I can't imagine anything better!"

These few words sufficed to make them understand and appreciate each other.

In the **variable** autumn weather, toward day's end, the sunset shed a blood-red glow over the sky. The reflection of the crimson clouds **tinted** the river red, brought a glow to the faces of the two friends. As the sun gilded the trees, whose leaves were turning at the first touch of winter, Monsieur Sauvage would sometimes smile and say:

"What a glorious spectacle!"

And Morissot would answer, without taking his eyes from his float:

"Isn't this better than the boulevard?"

On this day, as soon as they recognized each other they shook hands cordially, affected at the thought of meeting under such changed circumstances.

Monsieur Sauvage murmured:

"These are sad times!"

Morissot shook his head mournfully.

"And such weather! This is the first fine day of the year."

The sky was of a bright, cloudless blue.

They reminisced as they walked along, side by side, reflective and sad.

"And to think of the fishing!" said Morissot. "What good times we had!"

1. What is the author's purpose in the first paragraph (lines 1–8)?
   A) to reveal the awful economic situation
   B) to show the residents' resourcefulness
   C) to describe Paris
   D) to compare past and present Paris life

2. What does the word **affluence** mean as it is used in line 2?
   A) newness
   B) dominance
   C) history
   D) wealth

3. Which word means the opposite of **minimum** as it is used in line 4?
   A) melancholy
   B) maximum
   C) pessimism
   D) realism

4. What does the word **jovial** in line 28 **most likely** suggest about Monsieur Sauvage?
   A) He is formal.
   B) He is competitive.
   C) He is young.
   D) He is merry.

5. According to the passage, what is **variable** (line 53) weather?
   A) colorful weather
   B) harsh weather
   C) changing weather
   D) mild weather

6. **Part A**
   How has the relationship between Monsieur Sauvage and Monsieur Morissot evolved over time?
   A) The war altered their friendship.
   B) The friends have become closer over the years.
   C) The friends are unable to communicate with each other.
   D) An argument destroyed their friendship.

   Part B
   Which choice provides the **best** evidence for the answer to the previous question?
   A) "he met in this very spot Monsieur Sauvage" (lines 26–27)
   B) "a warm friendship had sprung up between them" (lines 32–34)
   C) "brought a glow to the faces of the two friends" (lines 57–58)
   D) "meeting under such changed circumstances" (lines 71–72)

7. Why is the memory of the fishing experiences important to the two friends?
   A) They recall a time when they were rivals.
   B) It calls to mind a happier time before the war.
   C) They remember the day they first met.
   D) They recall their financial struggles before they became wealthy.

8. Which sentence **best** states what the passage is about?
   A) Difficult circumstances forge a stronger friendship between two men, who have much to discuss when they meet by their old fishing hole.
   B) Two friends share an unbreakable bond of friendship after the war.
   C) A man reflects on a warm friendship that existed before the war began and then unexpectedly meets the old friend.
   D) While on fishing trips, two men daydream about pre-war life in Paris.

Vocabulary for Comprehension Part 2

*Read this passage, which contains words in **boldface** that appear in Units 7–9. Then choose the best answer to each question based on what is stated or implied in the passage. You may refer to the passage as often as necessary.*

Questions 1–8 are based on the following passage.

This passage is adapted from Alice Dunbar Nelson, "The Fisherman of Pass Christian." Published in 1899.

You've never been for a hay-ride and fish-fry on the shores of the Mississippi Sound, have you? When the summer boarders and the Northern visitors undertake to give one, it is a dull affair. During those times, due regard is had for one's clothes, and there are servants to **expend** energy on the hardest work. Then it isn't enjoyable at all. But sometimes the boys and girls who live there make up their minds to have fun. Then you may depend upon its being just the best kind.

This time there were twenty boys and girls, a mamma or so, several papas, and a grizzled fisherman to quash any **inflammatory** behavior. The cart was vast and solid, and two comfortable, sleepy-looking mules to pull it. There were also tin horns, some guitars, an accordion, and a quartet of much praised voices. The hay in the bottom of the wagon was freely mixed with pine needles, whose prickiness through your hose was compensated for by its delicious fragrance.

After a triumphantly noisy passage down the beach one comes to the almost **impassable** stretch of heavy sand that lies between Pass Christian proper and Henderson's Point. This is a hard pull for the mules, and the more ambitious riders get out and walk. Then, after a final strain through the shifting sands, bravo! The shell road is reached, and one goes cheering through the pine-trees to Henderson's Point.

If ever you go to Pass Christian, you must have a fish-fry at Henderson's Point. To **dissect** the landscape is to notice the pine-thicketed, white-beached peninsula jutting out from the land. One side of the land is on the verge of the waters of the Sound and the other is purred over by the blue waves of the Bay of St. Louis. Here is the beginning of the great three-mile trestle bridge to the town of Bay St. Louis. Tonight from the beach could be seen the lights of the villas glittering across the Bay like masses of unsleeping eyes.

Here upon a firm stretch of white sand camped the **giddy** merry-makers. At the **onset** of the event, a great fire of driftwood and pine cones tossed its flames at a radiant moon in the sky, and the fishers were casting their nets in the sea. The more daring of the girls waded in the water, holding pine-torches, spearing flounders with **nimble** hands and peering for soft-shell crabs.

Annette had wandered farther in the shallow water than the rest. Suddenly she fell over a stone. The **impact** of the fall caused the torch to drop and splutter at her feet. With a little helpless cry she **scoured** the stretch of unfamiliar beach and water to find herself all alone.

1. Why does the author begin with a description of summer boarders and Northern visitors to the Mississippi Sound?
A) to detail each part of their elaborate hay-rides and fish-fries
B) to narrate the servants' experiences while working on the Mississippi Sound
C) to show the variety within the landscape of the Mississippi Sound
D) to contrast their dull entertainment with the residents' joyful entertainment

2. What is the main idea of the third paragraph (lines 29–40)?
A) Some young people prefer to walk to Henderson's Point rather than ride in the cart.
B) Getting from Pass Christian to Henderson's Point is difficult but worthwhile in the end.
C) Young people are noisy as they move from Pass Christian to Henderson's Point.
D) It takes a long time to arrive at the shell road leading to Henderson's Point.

3. As it is used in line 31, the word "impassable" means
A) blocked.
B) hilly.
C) flat.
D) vast.

4. Lines 42–55 serve to
A) compare Henderson's Point with other local beaches.
B) illustrate a fish-fry at Henderson's Point.
C) present the specific landscape of Henderson's Point.
D) illustrate a fish-fry at Henderson's Point.

5. As it is used in line 43, the word "dissect" means to
A) analyze in great detail.
B) paint a landscape.
C) discover a new idea.
D) find language for an emotion.

6. As it is used in line 57, the word "giddy" means
A) lacking energy.
B) lacking seriousness.
C) lacking personality.
D) lacking maturity.

7. It can reasonably be inferred that Annette
A) is one of the more daring girls in the group.
B) works as a servant for the boarders and visitors.
C) wants to separate herself from the merry-makers.
D) is a summer boarder at the Mississippi Sound.

8. Which choice provides the best evidence for the answer to the previous question?
A) Lines 3–6 ("When the . . . dull affair")
B) Lines 6–9 ("During . . . hardest work")
C) Lines 56–58 ("Here . . . merry-makers")
D) Lines 62–66 ("The more . . . crabs")

Denotation and Connotation

The literal meaning of a word, which you can find in a dictionary, is its **denotation**. The emotional association connected to a word is its **connotation**. The connotation can be either positive or negative.

A connotation is an implied, or suggested, meaning. Several words may share the same basic denotation, but that doesn't mean the words are interchangeable. You can end up conveying an unintended meaning if you don't carefully consider the implied meanings of the words you use. Consider these synonyms for the neutral word *walk*.

saunter *stroll* *trudge* *plod*

Saunter and *stroll* have positive connotations, suggesting leisure and ease, whereas *trudge* and *plod* have negative connotations, suggesting effort and exertion.

Think: If you saunter or stroll, you're walking easily and with little effort. If you trudge or plod, your walk is a struggle!

Look at these examples of words that have similar denotations. Notice how the connotation of each word varies.

NEUTRAL	POSITIVE	NEGATIVE
cancel	**overturn**	**quash**
continue	**persevere**	**persist**
tint	**highlight**	**stain**

Writers choose their words carefully, knowing that readers are aware of connotations and draw on those emotional associations as they read. For example, a writer knows that describing the star of an action movie as "burly" will have a very different effect from describing him as "hefty." Good writers keep in mind how a word's connotation might affect their audience.

Shades of Meaning

Write a plus sign (+) in the box if the word has a positive connotation.
Write a minus sign (–) if the word has a negative connotation.
Put a zero (0) if the word is neutral.

1. fatality ☐ **2.** onset ☐ **3.** sluggish ☐ **4.** pathetic ☐

5. affluence ☐ **6.** partition ☐ **7.** template ☐ **8.** innovation ☐

9. illicit ☐ **10.** nimble ☐ **11.** jovial ☐ **12.** testimonial ☐

13. cringe ☐ **14.** dawdle ☐ **15.** optional ☐ **16.** crotchety ☐

Expressing the Connotation

Read each sentence. Select the word in parentheses that expresses the connotation (positive, negative, or neutral) given at the beginning of the sentence.

positive	**1.**	The day was so enjoyable that we wanted to (**dawdle, linger**) on the beach for a few more hours.
negative	**2.**	The (**gullible, trusting**) man entrusted his entire life savings to a swindler.
neutral	**3.**	Melinda is the only employee at the bank who can (**sanction, authorize**) a cashier's check.
negative	**4.**	The gang members hung out on the street corner, hoping to (**deter, intimidate**) passers-by.
positive	**5.**	I spent hours (**polishing, scouring**) the silverware for the New Year's Eve party.
positive	**6.**	It was fun to (**reminisce, chat**) about our previous summers at the camp.
negative	**7.**	No one was laughing when Henry accidentally (**immersed, dunked**) his motorcycle in the lake.
neutral	**8.**	Years of irresponsibility with money left my cousin in (**debt, arrears**).

Challenge: Using Connotation

Choose vocabulary words from Units 7–9 to replace the highlighted words in the sentences below. Then explain how the connotation of the replacement word changes the tone of the sentence.

rendezvous	**giddy**	**retrieve**
sinister	**logical**	**culprit**

1. Not used to staying up late, Chuck began acting **odd** ____________ in the hours after midnight.

____

____

2. My brother tried to drag me to that **spooky** ____________ haunted house, but I told him I wouldn't go within a mile of the place.

____

____

3. The police chief was pleased to announce that his officers had caught the **wrongdoer** ____________ after a lengthy sting operation.

____

____

Adages

In the passage "Made for the Shade" (see pages 88–89), the writer remarks that people seeking out vintage sunglasses might be "looking at the world through rose-colored glasses." What the writer means is that these consumers are optimistic or overly cheerful.

"Looking at the world through rose-colored glasses" is an adage. **Adages** are wise and clever traditional or "folksy" sayings that have been passed down from generation to generation. Adages can be serious or humorous, but they are always colorful. It is easy to see why they are often sprinkled throughout daily speech and informal writing.

Choosing the Right Adage

*Read each sentence. Use context clues to figure out the meaning of each adage in **boldface** print. Then write the letter of the definition for the adage in the sentence.*

1. Instead of trying to find a new partner for your group, **dance with the one that brought you**. _______
2. You should think twice about hanging out with those troublemakers; **people are known by the company they keep**. _______
3. Don't worry about how you'll juggle coursework, team sports, and a job when you're in college; **cross that bridge when you come to it.**_______
4. Our neighbor never says hello to us, which is rather sad, since **courtesy costs nothing**. _______
5. Yes, I guess it was dangerous to try and break up the fight, but **fools rush in where angels fear to tread**. _______
6. It's not surprising that the organist's daughter is also a musician. After all, **the apple doesn't fall far from the tree**. _______
7. Our cat has gained so much weight that we've stopped giving him the snacks he likes. Sometimes **you have to be cruel to be kind**. _______
8. You shouldn't take Ryan's tough-guy talk very seriously, because **barking dogs seldom bite**. _______
9. If you want to be on the team, you need to build some muscle, because **a chain is only as strong as its weakest link**. _______
10. Every time I enjoy a walk or observe nature, I realize that **the best things in life are free**. _______

a. People who do a lot of tough talking seldom act on their words.

b. It's always a good idea to be polite.

c. Deal with problems when you have to; don't worry about them in advance.

d. Children often take after their parents.

e. Team members need to pull their own weight.

f. True happiness comes not from money but from simple things.

g. The people you associate with will affect your reputation.

h. Inexperienced people often don't know where danger lurks.

i. You sometimes have to be strict in order to help another.

j. Stay loyal to those who look after you.

Classical Roots

log, logue—speech, word, discourse

The Greek root *log* appears in **logical** (page 111). The word means "capable of reasoning," and reasoning is expressed through speech and discourse. Some other words about speech or speaking are based on the same root. They are listed below.

apology	**dialogue**	**eulogy**	**neologism**
decalogue	**epilogue**	**monologue**	**prologue**

From the list of words above, choose the one that corresponds to each of the brief definitions below. Write the word in the blank space in the illustrative sentence below the definition. Use a dictionary if necessary.

1. an introductory statement, act, or event; a preface; opening remarks

   The novel's ____________________ offers background on the main character.

2. words of regret to express remorse and ask pardon for an accident, fault, failure, or offense; an explanation, defense, or excuse

   "If you'd like me to accept your ____________________," he explained, "I need to believe that you know what you did wrong and that you will strive to do better."

3. a concluding section at the end of a play or literary work, intended to provide further comment, interpretation, or information; an afterword

   After the curtain fell, a narrator gave a brief ____________________ to tie up loose ends.

4. a speech or written tribute composed to honor someone who has died

   Lincoln's Gettysburg Address was delivered on November 19, 1863, as a(n) ____________________ to those who died at the Battle of Gettysburg.

5. a conversation between two or more people or characters; the lines in a script that are to be spoken; an airing of ideas or views

   Abbott and Costello's wacky routine, "Who's on First?," is one of the funniest baseball ____________________ in American comedy.

6. a newly invented word, expression, or usage; new meaning for an old word

   Evolving technology has led to many ____________________, such as *smartphone* and *blog*, that have become part of our everyday language.

7. a set of ten authoritative rules or laws; (*usu. cap.*) the Ten Commandments (*in the Bible*)

   The stained-glass window shows Moses holding the ____________________.

8. a long speech made by one person; a speech that monopolizes conversation; a series of jokes or comedic stories delivered by one comedian

   The opening ____________________ given by talk-show hosts, consisting of light banter and political humor, has become a staple of late-night television.

*Read the following passage, taking note of the **boldface** words and their contexts. These words are among those you will be studying in Unit 10. As you complete the exercises in this unit, it may help to refer to the way the words are used below.*

Farewell, Blue Yodeler

<Obituary>

June 1, 1933
Asheville Evening Post
by Floyd O. Merryll

With the passing last week of Jimmie Rodgers, the country lost a great performer. But it's a testament to the kind of man he was that many of his fans will take the loss personally, as if that Blue Yodeler, as we like to call him and will remember him, was a friend of ours. Thankfully, we've got his records to keep with us as **mementos**.

James Charles Rodgers was born in Meridian, Mississippi, in 1897. His mama died when he was just a kid, and Jimmie was raised by relatives in Mississippi and Alabama. When he was a little older, he returned to Meridian to live with his father, Aaron, who was a maintenance foreman on the Mobile and Ohio Railroad.

Jimmie had no **rigorous** musical training, but he learned to sing and play guitar. Still a boy, Jimmie proved to be a **nonconformist**. He secretly organized a traveling show. When Aaron Rodgers found out, he had the good sense to **foil** his son's plans—he tracked Jimmie down, and dragged him home. But the stunt was more than the **bumbling** behavior of an unruly kid. Jimmie showed the same **initiative** again, **formulating** a second plan to get out on the road and sing. He charged a pricey canvas tent in his father's name and hit the road to make music. His father might have understood Jimmie's love of music, but he probably didn't want the boy to **delude** himself about a musician's life. He set out again to **pry** his son from the road. Soon Aaron got Jimmie a job as a waterboy with the railroad. Within a few years, Jimmie was a brakeman on the New Orleans and Northeastern Railroad. Now Jimmie was a steady working man. But he never lost his love of music.

Jimmie came down with the deadly respiratory disease called tuberculosis in 1924, when he was 27 years old. As a **consequence** of that **abominable** disease, he had to quit his railroad job. Ever **resourceful**, Jimmie organized a traveling show and played across the Southeast. He worked as a brakeman again and later as a switchman but couldn't keep those jobs because of his tuberculosis. But his travels gave him a look at the whole **panorama** of Southern music. In 1927, Jimmie went to Asheville, North Carolina, where the city's first radio station had just hit the airwaves, and he played on the radio and earned himself a weekly slot. The exposure served him well in **subsequent** months. He recorded songs for a record company. One of them, "Blue Yodel," sold like hotcakes and made Jimmie Rodgers a star.

Propelled by fame, the Blue Yodeler traveled the country for the next few years. It was hard times for the nation. But while so many people were on the **dole** and looking for work, Jimmie was living his dream. He was making music, touring, and starring in a movie short called "The Singing Brakeman." Eventually, his illness caught up with him. During a recording session in New York City last week, he couldn't get through all of his songs. He took the day off to recover, but Jimmie was in a race against time. So before he'd sung his last song, Jimmie Rodgers was gone. But in a few years as a recording artist and a few more as a performer who rambled around the country, he made such a mark for **posterity** that we'll never forget him. Jimmie leaves behind his wife, Carrie, and daughter, Carrie Anita, and a legion of fans and recordings.

Farewell, Blue Yodeler.

Audio

For iWords and audio passages, snap the code, or go to **SadlierConnect.com**.

Left: Promotional photo for "The Singing Brakeman"

Inset: Jimmie posing with his sweet Model A Ford, in 1930

Definitions

Note the spelling, pronunciation, part(s) of speech, and definition(s) of each of the following words. Then write the word in the blank spaces in the illustrative sentence(s) following. Finally, study the lists of synonyms and antonyms.

1. abominable (ə bäm′ ə nə bəl)

(*adj.*) arousing hatred; disgusting, detestable

Unfortunately, there are many ________________ ideas circulating on the Internet.

SYNONYMS: hateful, despicable, loathsome
ANTONYMS: praiseworthy, delightful, charming

2. bumbling (bəm′ bliŋ)

(*adj.*) blundering and awkward; (*n.*) clumsiness

The ________________ burglars were so inept that they actually left some of their own money at the home they were planning to rob!

The old cartoon character Mr. Magoo was well known for his ________________.

SYNONYMS: (*adj.*) clumsy, stumbling
ANTONYMS: (*adj.*) forceful, effective, skillful, adroit

3. consequence (kän′ sə kwens)

(*n.*) a result, effect; importance

Does he truly comprehend the ________________ of his actions?

SYNONYMS: outcome, significance
ANTONYMS: cause, source

4. delude (di lüd′)

(*v.*) to fool, deceive; to mislead utterly

Don't ________________ yourself into thinking that you will become a famous concert pianist just because you played one song at the school's talent show.

SYNONYMS: trick, hoodwink

5. dole (dōl)

(*v.*) to give out in small amounts; (*n.*) money, food, or other necessities given as charity; a small portion

Let's ________________ out scraps of food to the hungry dogs.

The people at the homeless shelter lined up to receive their weekly ________________.

SYNONYMS: (*v.*) ration, allot, distribute; (*n.*) handout

6. engulf (en gəlf′)

(*v.*) to swallow up, overwhelm, consume

The truck was ________________ in flames after its fuel tank exploded.

SYNONYMS: encompass, immerse

7. foil (foil)

(*v.*) to defeat; to keep from gaining some end; (*n.*) a thin sheet of metal; a light fencing sword; a person or thing serving as a contrast to another

The police will ____________________ the criminals' plot.

Glum characters make a good ____________________ for the upbeat star of that new comedy.

SYNONYMS: (*v.*) frustrate, thwart, counter; (*n.*) rapier
ANTONYMS: (*v.*) aid, abet, assist, advance, promote

8. formulate (fôr′ myə lāt)

(*v.*) to express definitely or systematically; to devise, invent; to state as a formula

The town board will ____________________ a tax policy.

SYNONYMS: define, articulate, frame, specify

9. initiative (i nish′ ə tiv)

(*n.*) the taking of the first step or move; the ability to act without being directed or urged from the outside

Dad is proud of my ____________________ with chores.

SYNONYMS: leadership, enterprise
ANTONYMS: laziness, sloth, shiftlessness

10. memento (mə men′ tō)

(*n.*) something that serves as a reminder

This cap is a ____________________ of our recent trip.

SYNONYMS: remembrance, souvenir, token

11. nonconformist (nän kən fôr′ mist)

(*n.*) a person who refuses to follow established ideas or ways of doing things; (*adj.*) of or relating to the unconventional

Jake, a ____________________, is not swayed by opinion.

Her ____________________ poetry appears in several small literary magazines.

SYNONYMS: (*n.*) maverick, individualist, bohemian
ANTONYMS: (*n.*, *adj.*) traditionalist, conventionalist; (*adj.*) traditional, conventional, conservative

12. null and void (nəl and void)

(*adj.*) without legal force or effect; no longer binding

This contract becomes ____________________ at noon.

SYNONYMS: canceled, repealed, abolished
ANTONYMS: in effect, binding

13. panorama (pan ə ram′ ə)

(*n.*) a wide, unobstructed view of an area; a complete survey of a subject; a continuously passing or changing scene; a range or spectrum

Displays of old picture postcards present an entertaining ____________________ of twentieth-century life.

SYNONYM: overview

14. posterity (pä ster′ ət ē)

(*n.*) all of a person's offspring, descendants; all future generations

Let's keep the photo album for ____________________.

ANTONYMS: ancestry, ancestors, forebears, the past

15. pry (prī)

(*v.*) to pull loose by force; to look at closely or inquisitively; to be nosy about something

We can use this tool to ____________________ the lid off a can of paint.

SYNONYMS: snoop, meddle

16. refurbish (ri fər′ bish)

(*v.*) to brighten, freshen, or polish; to restore or improve

Every five years, the hotel ____________________ the décor of its elegant lobby.

SYNONYMS: remodel, renew
ANTONYMS: dilapidate, run down

17. resourceful (ri sôrs′ fəl)

(*adj.*) able to deal promptly and effectively with all sorts of problems; clever in finding ways and means of getting along

A ____________________ guide will know how to handle any questions or surprises that come up on the tour.

SYNONYMS: inventive, ingenious, skillful
ANTONYMS: uninventive, incompetent

18. rigorous (rig′ ər əs)

(*adj.*) severe, harsh, strict; thoroughly logical

"Boot camp" is the nickname for the place where new soldiers receive ____________________ basic training.

SYNONYMS: tough, trying, challenging, rousing
ANTONYMS: easy, lax, indulgent, tiresome

19. subsequent (səb′ sə kwent)

(*adj.*) coming after; following in time, place, or order

The country enjoyed peace and prosperity in the years ____________________ to the war.

SYNONYMS: later, following, ensuing
ANTONYMS: previous, prior, preceding

20. unerring (ən er′ iŋ)

(*adj.*) making no mistakes, faultless, completely accurate

Even a pilot with ____________________ judgment can be surprised by sudden changes in the weather.

SYNONYMS: sure, certain, unfailing
ANTONYMS: faulty, fallible, unreliable

Choosing the Right Word

*Select the **boldface** word that better completes each sentence. You might refer to the unit selection to see how most of these words are used in context.*

1. In devising the Constitution, the Founding Fathers sought to "secure the blessings of liberty to ourselves and our (**posterity, foils**)."

2. Our foreign policy embraces a vast (**consequence, panorama**) of aims and objectives, problems and concerns.

3. Here I am on my first vacation in years, and I have to put up with this (**abominable, bumbling**) weather day after day!

4. All these things in the attic may seem like a lot of junk to you, but to me they are priceless (**mementos, nonconformists**) of childhood.

Among the fifty-five framers of the U.S. Constitution were George Washington and Benjamin Franklin.

5. Sasha was pleasantly surprised with all the perks, such as free tickets, that the producers (**doled, foiled**) out to the actors.

6. She hopes to win the election by convincing voters that the city's troubles result from the (**unerring, bumbling**) policies of the present mayor.

7. With his serious face and his dignified way of speaking, he is an excellent (**foil, memento**) for the clownish comedian.

8. It is too late to attempt to (**formulate, refurbish**) the old city charter; we must have a completely new plan for our city government.

9. Since you have failed to carry out your promises, I must tell you that the agreement between us is now (**resourceful, null and void**).

10. By coaxing and questioning hour after hour, Tom finally managed to (**pry, delude**) the big secret from his sister.

11. When we reached the top of the volcano, the (**panoramic, resourceful**) view was well worth the five-hour hike.

12. The war that began with Germany's invasion of Poland in 1939 spread until it had (**refurbished, engulfed**) almost the entire world.

13. Brad is the kind of (**rigorous, resourceful**) quarterback who can always come up with something new when it is a matter of victory or defeat.

14. My father, an electrical engineer, is an expert at computing (**rigorous, abominable**) math problems.

15. We worked several hours shoveling dirt and removing roots, hoping to (**engulf, pry**) the tree stump loose from the ground.

16. Why is it that such hardworking, self-reliant people now have to depend on a (**posterity, dole**) of food and other necessities from charitable agencies?

17. We all know that it is a long time since the speeding laws in our community have been (**rigorously, subsequently**) enforced.

18. Do you think the United States should take the (**initiative, dole**) in trying to bring about a compromise in the region?

19. I thought the first chapter was dull, but (**null and void, subsequent**) chapters were fascinating.

20. If you think that you can get away with selling overpriced products to the people of this town, you are (**deluding, refurbishing**) yourself.

21. He may look like an ordinary man, but he is in fact a figure of real (**panorama, consequence**) in the state government.

22. One of the signs of a truly democratic nation is that it gives protection and freedom to (**initiatives, nonconformists**) who espouse unpopular views.

23. "We must (**formulate, engulf**) a plan to deal with this new situation and carry it out as quickly as possible," the president said.

24. Perhaps he doesn't seem to be very bright, but he has an (**abominable, unerring**) instinct for anything that might make money for him.

25. Many comics get laughs for their (**unerring, bumbling**) antics on the stage.

Synonyms

*Choose the word from this Unit that is the same or most nearly the same in meaning as the **boldface** word or expression in the phrase. Write that word on the line. Use a dictionary if necessary.*

1. a contract that is considered **invalid** ____________________
2. to discuss it at our **next** meeting ____________________
3. **creative** use of recycled materials ____________________
4. must pass a **demanding** exam ____________________
5. **prepare** an answer for the defense ____________________
6. a dramatic **vista** of red rock formations ____________________
7. devised a **perfect** plan ____________________
8. a precious **keepsake** of Sally's childhood ____________________
9. if we decide to **spruce up** the kitchen ____________________
10. huge waves that **envelop** the tiny beach ____________________

Antonyms

*Choose the word from this Unit that is most nearly opposite in meaning to the **boldface** word or expression in the phrase. Write that word on the line. Use a dictionary if necessary.*

1. declared **valid** by the courts ____________________
2. to **demolish** the old building ____________________
3. due to my **flawed** sense of direction ____________________
4. **lovely** behavior for a twelve-year-old ____________________
5. waves that **retreat from** the dunes ____________________

Completing the Sentence

From the words in this Unit, choose the one that best completes each of the following sentences. Write the correct word form in the space provided.

1. A truly ____________________ administrator always seems to be able to find an effective way of dealing with any problem that may come up.

2. Like so many other young people, he has been ____________________ into the false belief that there is an easy way to success.

3. Professional baseball players get themselves into shape for the upcoming season by undergoing a ____________________ training period each spring.

4. The first meeting will be in the school auditorium, but all ____________________ meetings will be held in the homes of our members.

5. You may think that the crude way he has behaved is slightly amusing, but I think it is ____________________ and inexcusable.

6. Huge clouds of smoke and ash from the active volcano ____________________ the sleepy little villages that nestled on its flanks.

7. From the observation deck of the skyscraper one may enjoy a sweeping ____________________ of the city.

8. What a disappointment to hear that dull and ____________________ speech when we were expecting a clear, forceful, and interesting statement!

9. Many an artist whose work has been overlooked in his or her own lifetime has had to trust to ____________________ for appreciation.

10. All that you will need to ____________________ that dilapidated old house is lots of time, lots of skill, lots of enthusiasm, and lots of money.

11. As a tennis player, Sue doesn't have much speed or power, but she hits the ball with ____________________ accuracy.

12. Since I was able to prove in court that the salesperson had lied to me, the contract I had signed was declared ____________________.

13. These old photographs may not look like much, but I treasure them as a(n) ____________________ of the last summer my entire family spent together.

14. During World War II, food became so scarce in Great Britain that the government ____________________ it out to consumers in very small amounts.

15. Anyone who ____________________ into someone else's business runs the risk of opening a can of worms.

16. The alert employee ____________________ an attempted robbery by setting off the alarm promptly.

17. At the time it occurred, that mistake didn't seem to be too important, but it had ____________________ that still hurt me today.

18. We must ____________________ a detailed response that leaves no doubt about our position on this important issue.

19. Rather than sit back and wait for the enemy to attack him, the general took the ____________________ and delivered the first blow.

20. The term "____________________" was first applied in the 1660s to English Protestants who dissented from the Church of England.

Writing: Words in Action

1. Look back at "Farewell, Blue Yodeler" (pages 126–127). Suppose that you are a musician who traveled with Jimmie when he was a boy. You want to persuade his father, Aaron Rodgers, that Jimmie should continue to travel with the show and hone his skills as a musician. Write a letter to Aaron Rodgers supporting your position. Use at least two details from the passage and three Unit words.

2. *"Music has charms to soothe a savage breast."—William Congreve*

   It is a common sentiment that music soothes the soul. Do you agree with this statement? Should music always "soothe" the soul, or does it have other purposes? What roles does music play in contemporary life? In a brief essay, support your opinion with specific examples from your observations, studies, the reading (refer to pages 126–127), or personal experience. Write at least three paragraphs, and use three or more words from this Unit.

Vocabulary in Context

Literary Text

The following excerpts are from The Works of Edgar Allan Poe, Volume I *by Edgar Allan Poe. Some of the words you have studied in this Unit appear in* **boldface** *type. Complete each statement below the excerpt by circling the letter of the correct answer.*

1. . . . upon the **subsequent** disposal of the trinkets and jewels . . . it was found that we had greatly undervalued the treasure. ("The Gold-Bug")

A discovery made **subsequent** to an action occurs

a. after **c.** suddenly
b. previously **d.** gradually

2. . . . and I fell down in the bottom of the car, trembling with unmitigated terror. Indeed, I now perceived that I had entirely overdone the business, and that the main **consequences** of the shock were yet to be experienced. ("The Unparalleled Adventure of One Hans Pfaall")

Consequences are

a. fears **c.** results
b. reminders **d.** memories

3. . . . I should have been unable to accomplish even as much as I had now accomplished, and the wonderful adventures of Hans Pfaall would have been utterly lost to **posterity**, I had therefore every reason to be grateful . . . ("The Unparalleled Adventure of One Hans Pfaall")

Posterity refers to things in the

a. future **c.** basement
b. news **d.** present

4. . . . [L]ooking dizzily around, [I] was . . . struck with the idea of our being among breakers; so terrific, beyond the wildest imagination, was the whirlpool of mountainous and foaming ocean within which we were **engulfed**. ("Ms. Found in a Bottle")

Someone **engulfed** by the ocean is

a. fishing in it **c.** floating on it
b. thrilled by it **d.** immersed in it

5. . . . [T]here still remained in his possession a small remnant of his patrimony; and, upon the income arising from this, he managed, by means of a **rigorous** economy, to procure the necessaries of life. ("The Murders in the Rue Morgue")

A **rigorous** economy is definitely NOT

a. energizing **c.** stimulating
b. lenient **d.** invigorating

Bela Lugosi played the role of the mad scientist in the 1932 film *Murders in the Rue Morgue*, based on Poe's short story.

Interactive Quiz

Snap the code, or go to **SadlierConnect.com**.

*Read the following passage, taking note of the **boldface** words and their contexts. These words are among those you will be studying in Unit 11. As you complete the exercises in this unit, it may help to refer to the way the words are used below.*

Here I Am: Galápagos Log

<Log>

Written by Samantha Z. Rosenstern, marine biologist with the Center for Island Research

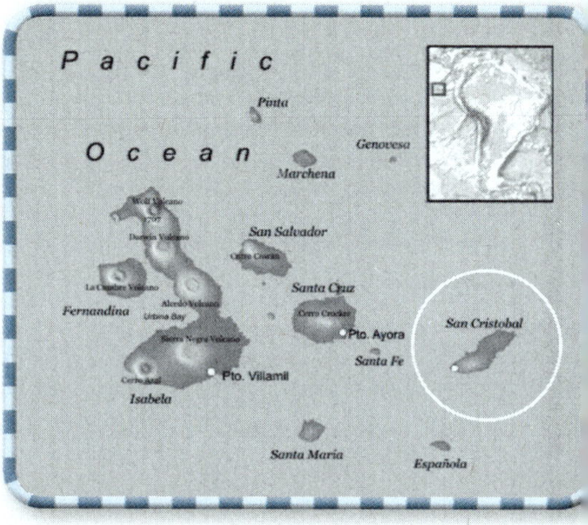

Wed., Apr. 12 After a delay at the airport, our research team arrived at the Galápagos. I often think that a good **alias** for these islands would be "reptile heaven." No land bridge ever linked the Galápagos with the coast of South America, over 600 miles away. As an unavoidable and **inevitable** consequence, reptiles **prevailed** over mammals in these spots of land straddling the equator. Only reptiles such as the giant tortoise and the land iguana possess the endurance to make long ocean crossings with no fresh water. The **dogged** persistence of these creatures made it possible for them to establish themselves here.

The name Galápagos refers to the islands' most prominent creatures. In old Spanish, *galápago* means "tortoise." Different giant tortoises have different shells. Some are dome-shaped, while others have an arched shell that looks like a saddle.

Sat., Apr. 15 My third day of field work on San Cristóbal Island at the eastern edge of the Galápagos archipelago. In mid afternoon, I **amble** down the beach. My leisurely pace would leave most of the Galápagos giant tortoises **dumbfounded**. I calculated that the **burly** giants move at about 0.2 miles per hour. That's barely ten percent of the rate of a human walker!

It really is true that human nature is the same the world over. This morning, I saw tour groups representing seven different nationalities. All were equally in awe of the animals of the Galápagos.

Thurs., Apr. 20 The population of saddlebacks on San Cristóbal has been estimated at 1,800. Long ago, there were tortoises at the southern end of the island. That population is now **extinct**. The **relic** of a specimen of this race poses a new question: Were these tortoises the same as

today's animals, named *Geochelone chathamensis*, or were they a different subspecies of giant tortoise?

One of my goals is to measure the impact of predators on tortoise hatchlings. The first newborns emerged this week after six months of incubation. I cannot help admiring their determination and **grit**. Feral dogs and goats, as well as hawks, are their chief enemies. If youngsters survive, however, they will enjoy a life on an epic scale. When fully grown, the males will weigh up to 800 pounds and measure over six feet from end to end. Amazingly, the tortoises have the longest life span of any creature on Earth—an estimated 150 years. No wonder there are so many gaps in the scientific literature about these animals. It is understandable that scientists' reports might be **distorted**. No one scientist could ever observe the tortoises' entire natural lifespan.

Wed., Apr. 26 Another goal of mine is to document dominance contests among adult saddlebacks. Last night I **rummaged** through my field notes from the last few weeks. Many of the dominance contests take place in plain view. As yet, I have witnessed only a few.

Fri., Apr. 28 Whatever the causes for their **ingrained** hostility, it is clear that superior height gives the winning tortoise its key advantage, as in the sparring contest I witnessed this morning. Saddlebacks can be especially aggressive toward one another. Is this because they have to **skimp** on sparse resources within their habitat, such as food, plants, water, and shade? Some more **sleuthing** during my next month here should answer these questions, as well as a few I haven't yet asked!

Audio

For iWords and audio passages, snap the code, or go to **SadlierConnect.com**.

Definitions

Note the spelling, pronunciation, part(s) of speech, and definition(s) of each of the following words. Then write the word in the blank spaces in the illustrative sentence(s) following. Finally, study the lists of synonyms and antonyms.

1. alias (ā′ lē əs)

(*n.*) an assumed name, especially as used to hide one's identity; (*adv.*) otherwise called

"Mr. Plante" was just one ________________ used by the elusive spy.

Superman, ________________ Clark Kent, began as a comic book character created in 1938.

SYNONYM: (*n.*) pseudonym
ANTONYMS: (*n.*) real name, given name, legal name

2. amble (am′ bəl)

(*v.*) to walk slowly, stroll; (*n.*) an easy pace; a leisurely walk

It's a lovely day to ________________ to work and enjoy the many sights and sounds along the way.

When we woke to see the sun shining, we planned a long ________________ in the park.

SYNONYMS: (*v.*) saunter; (*n.*) ramble
ANTONYMS: (*v., n.*) gallop, dash, sprint, run, race, rush

3. burly (bər′ lē)

(*adj.*) big and strong; muscular

That guy is as ________________ as a lumberjack, so he would be the perfect one to help me move my furniture.

SYNONYMS: strapping, hefty, beefy
ANTONYMS: weak, puny, delicate, frail

4. distort (dis tôrt′)

(*v.*) to give a false or misleading account of; to twist out of shape

A magazine known to ________________ the facts would be an unreliable source of information.

SYNONYMS: disfigure, misshape, falsify

5. dogged (dôg′ əd)

(*adj.*) persistent, stubbornly determined, refusing to give up

The troops fought with ________________ determination and courage.

SYNONYM: untiring
ANTONYMS: wishy-washy, faltering, irresolute

6. dumbfounded (dəm′ faůnd əd)

(*adj.*) so amazed that one is unable to speak, bewildered

When the shocking news finally reached us, we were completely ________________.

SYNONYMS: speechless, stunned, flabbergasted
ANTONYMS: unsurprised, expectant

7. extinct
(ek stiŋkt′)

(*adj.*) no longer in existence; no longer active; gone out of use

The ____________ volcano is no longer a threat.

SYNONYMS: died out, vanished
ANTONYMS: still alive, surviving, extant

8. grit
(grit)

(*n.*) very fine sand or gravel; courage in the face of hardship or danger; (*v.*) to grind; to make a grating sound

Cars stall if ____________ clogs a fuel line.

It upsets me to see Dad get angry and ____________ his teeth.

SYNONYMS: (*n.*) dirt, mettle
ANTONYMS: (*n.*) timidity, cowardice, faintheartedness

9. inevitable
(in ev′ ə tə bəl)

(*adj.*) sure to happen, unavoidable

Is it ____________ that all comedies have happy endings?

SYNONYMS: inescapable, fated
ANTONYMS: avoidable, escapable, preventable

10. ingrained
(in grānd′)

(*adj.*) fixed deeply and firmly; working into the grain or fiber; forming a part of the inmost being

Biting my lower lip is an ____________ habit.

SYNONYMS: deep-seated, entrenched, indelible
ANTONYMS: superficial, shallow, skin-deep

11. meteoric
(mē tē ôr′ ik)

(*adj.*) resembling a meteor in speed; having sudden and temporary brilliance similar to a meteor's

The young actor's ____________ rise to fame became legendary.

SYNONYMS: brilliant, blazing; ANTONYMS: slow, sluggish, gradual

12. parody
(par′ ə dē)

(*n.*) a humorous or ridiculous imitation; (*v.*) to make fun of something by imitating it

The audience roared with laughter at the comedy troupe's hilarious ____________.

The new film successfully ____________ political life in England.

SYNONYMS: (*n.*) satire, travesty; (*v.*) lampoon, burlesque

13. prevail
(pri vāl′)

(*v.*) to triumph over; to succeed; to exist widely, be in general use; to get someone to do something by urging

We hope to ____________ over all obstacles we may encounter on this project.

SYNONYMS: win, rule, overcome, conquer
ANTONYMS: be defeated, go under, succumb

14. relic (rel′ ik)

(*n.*) an object from the past with historical value or interest; a trace of an outdated custom; remaining fragments, ruins

The old Model T in my grandfather's barn is a ____________________ of the first American touring cars.

SYNONYMS: (*n.*) artifact, historical object

15. rend (rend)

(*v.*) to tear to pieces; split violently apart (*past tense,* rent)

The abominable tactics of this trial could ____________________ public confidence in the legal system.

SYNONYMS: cleave, splinter, tear asunder

16. replenish (ri plen′ ish)

(*v.*) to fill again, make good, replace

Airport crews work quickly to ____________________ a plane's supply of food, water, and safety supplies.

SYNONYMS: restock, refresh, restore
ANTONYMS: empty, drain, sap

17. rummage (rəm′ əj)

(*v.*) to search through, investigate the contents of; (*n.*) an active search; a collection of odd items

It can be an adventure to ____________________ around our garage for remnants of our childhood.

She found an old saddle in the ____________________.

SYNONYMS: (*v.*) delve into, sift through, poke around

18. skimp (skimp)

(*v.*) to save, be thrifty; to be extremely sparing with; to give little attention or effort to

If you ____________________ on regular meals, you may be tempted to snack on too much junk food.

SYNONYMS: be stingy, scrimp, cut corners
ANTONYMS: be extravagant, splurge, lavish

19. sleuth (slüth)

(*n.*) a detective

A skilled ____________________ can find hidden clues in unusual places.

SYNONYMS: investigator, gumshoe

20. vandalism (van′ dəl iz əm)

(*n.*) deliberate and pointless destruction of public or private property

The city realizes that it needs to create tougher laws to discourage ____________________.

SYNONYM: willful destruction

Choosing the Right Word

*Select the **boldface** word that better completes each sentence. You might refer to the unit selection to see how most of these words are used in context.*

1. The defenders of the Alamo put up a (**burly, dogged**) resistance against the enemy.

2. All I need is a meal, a hot shower, and a good night's sleep to (**replenish, rend**) my energies.

3. Isn't it foolish to think that just because of his (**meteoric, burly**) physique he has no interest in art or music?

4. No, I wasn't (**ingrained, dumbfounded**) to be chosen the most popular member of the class, but maybe I was just a little surprised!

5. Suddenly, the stillness of the early morning hours was (**rent, rummaged**) by a single shot!

Though from Tennessee, Davy Crockett helped to defend the Alamo.

6. To avoid a lot of unwanted attention, the famous rock star registered in the hotel under a(n) (**rummage, alias**).

7. There are several organizations whose goal is to protect endangered species, such as the giant panda, to keep them from becoming (**relics, extinct**).

8. The aging actor trying to play the part of a young man seemed no more than a (**sleuth, parody**) of the great performer he once was.

9. With all of his absences and goofing off in class, it was (**inevitable, meteoric**) that he would not pass the test.

10. Is there anything more romantic than a nighttime (**amble, vandalism**) upon the moonlit decks of a mighty ocean liner?

11. "I'll have two hot dogs with all the fixings," I said to the vendor, "and don't (**prevail, skimp**) on the mustard!"

12. Nikki (**distorted, rummaged**) the truth about her whereabouts in order to conceal her alliance with the defendant.

13. The prejudices of a bigot are sometimes so (**ingrained, burly**) that it is very difficult to get rid of them.

14. When I discovered the abandoned cave that was used for an enemy hideout during WWII, I was amazed with how many war (**aliases, relics**) still remained.

15. I hope to pick up some real bargains at the (**rummage, grit**) sale being held in our civic center.

16. I know that you don't like the idea of painting the house, but you'll just have to (**replenish, grit**) your teeth and do it.

17. Whether the window was broken accidentally or as an act of (**parody, vandalism**), the fact remains that it is broken and must be paid for.

18. After months of looking for employment, my sister, known for her (**skimpy, dogged**) persistence, finally obtained her dream job as a video game reviewer.

19. An art historian who is trying to verify the authenticity of a painting acts more like a (**sleuth, relic**) than a critic.

20. Although it is sometimes hard, we must have faith that in the long run justice and decency will (**skimp, prevail**).

21. It may be, as you say, that this volcano has been (**extinct, dumbfounded**) for many years, but isn't there some danger that it may come to life again?

22. Since it is possible for nations to settle their disagreements in a reasonable way, we refuse to believe that war is (**inevitable, meteoric**).

23. We scorn all those who would deliberately bend the truth and (**distort, amble**) history in order to suit the political needs of their day.

24. His (**dogged, meteoric**) success at such an early age left him unprepared to handle the disappointments and failures that came to him later in life.

25. Don't you find those TV shows that (**parody, skimp**) famous people hilarious?

Synonyms

*Choose the word from this Unit that is the same or most nearly the same in meaning as the **boldface** word or expression in the phrase. Write that word on the line. Use a dictionary if necessary.*

1. **deep-rooted** sense of right and wrong ____________________
2. ways to **misrepresent** the truth ____________________
3. tried to **ridicule** the governor ____________________
4. memoirs of her **dazzling** career ____________________
5. where science **reigns** over superstition ____________________
6. greedily **dismember** its prey ____________________
7. protected by a **brawny** bodyguard ____________________
8. **refill** the empty bird feeder ____________________
9. admiring the **determination** of hardy pioneers ____________________
10. ruined by **malicious defacement** ____________________

Antonyms

*Choose the word from this Unit that is most nearly opposite in meaning to the **boldface** word or expression in the phrase. Write that word on the line. Use a dictionary if necessary.*

1. hoping you will **glorify** our leader ____________
2. after **depleting** the ice ____________
3. **restoration** of an historic statue ____________
4. reviewing a **lackluster** career ____________
5. hoping to **unite** the quarrelsome couple ____________

Completing the Sentence

From the words in this Unit, choose the one that best completes each of the following sentences. Write the correct word form in the space provided.

1. We saw a bolt of lightning ____________ a huge limb from the mighty oak tree.
2. After our furious gallop across the countryside, we allowed our tired horses to ____________ back to the stable.
3. The grime on the mechanic's hands was so deeply ____________ even a thorough scrubbing couldn't entirely remove it.
4. The old custom of celebrating the Fourth of July with a fireworks display still ____________ in many American towns.
5. Isn't it a shame that our school board must spend thousands of dollars every year just to repair the damage caused by ____________?
6. The cruise ship stopped at the port both to give the passengers a chance to go ashore and to ____________ the water supply.
7. Isn't it fun on a rainy day to ____________ about in the attic and look for interesting odds and ends?
8. In the late 19th century, Sir Arthur Conan Doyle created one of the most famous ____________ in literature, Sherlock Holmes.
9. There is an old saying that nothing is really ____________ except death and taxes.
10. Whenever our team needs a few yards to make a first down, we call on our big, ____________ fullback to crash through the line.

11. We were nothing less than ____________________ when we saw the immense damage that the hurricane had done in so brief a time.

12. Even though so many people were criticizing and ridiculing him, he had the ____________________ to continue doing what he felt was right.

13. We greatly admired the ____________________ determination and patience that the disabled veteran showed in learning to master a wheelchair.

14. Her ability to ____________________ the words and gestures of prominent Americans makes her an excellent comic impressionist.

15. The old con artist had used so many ____________________ over the course of his criminal career that he sometimes forgot his real name!

16. If you truly want to improve your math grades, you should not continue to ____________________ so often on your homework.

17. The rock singer enjoyed a sudden ____________________ rise in popularity, but his career faded just as quickly as it had blossomed.

18. As the buffalo began to decrease sharply in numbers, conservationists feared that the species might become totally ____________________.

19. There are archeological sites in Greece that contain sacred ____________________ that the ancients believed held supernatural powers.

20. Her face was so ____________________ with pain and suffering that at first I did not recognize her.

Writing: Words in Action

1. Look back at "Here I Am: Galápagos Log" (pages 136–137). Suppose that Samantha Rosenstern decides to choose one student to join her in the study of saddlebacks. You are on the short list of candidates. Write a letter to Ms. Rosenstern, convincing her that you are the best person to join her in San Cristóbal. Use at least two details from the passage and three Unit words.

2. If you could choose a place anywhere in the world to visit for scientific research, where would it be? Why? What discovery would you hope to make? In a brief essay, identify your choice and support it with specific examples, details from the reading (refer to pages 136–137), or personal experience. Write at least three paragraphs, and use three or more words from this Unit.

Vocabulary in Context

Literary Text

The following excerpts are from White Fang *by Jack London. Some of the words you have studied in this Unit appear in* ***boldface*** *type. Complete each statement below the excerpt by circling the letter of the correct answer.*

1. And here, in the Klondike, the leader was indeed the leader. The wisest as well as strongest dog was the leader, and the team obeyed him and feared him. That White Fang should quickly gain this post was **inevitable**.

Something that is **inevitable** is NOT

a. avoidable
b. predictable
c. understandable
d. sensible

2. So near did the wolves approach, that the dogs became frantic with terror, and it was necessary to **replenish** the fire from time to time in order to keep the adventurous marauders at safer distance.

To **replenish** a fire means to

a. stay near it
b. avoid it
c. let it die out
d. build it up

3. The she-wolf stood over against her cub, facing the men, with bristling hair, a snarl rumbling deep in her throat. Her face was **distorted** and malignant with menace, even the bridge of the nose wrinkling from tip to eyes, so prodigious was her snarl.

Something that is **distorted** is

a. shaped
b. encouraged
c. twisted
d. confirmed

White Fang, part wolf and part dog, goes from a wild existence to gradual domestication.

4. Kiche licked White Fang soothingly with her tongue, and tried to **prevail** upon him to remain with her. But his curiosity was rampant, and several minutes later he was venturing forth on a new quest.

To **prevail** is to

a. prepare
b. urge
c. calm
d. force

5. Public-spirited citizens took down their rifles and went out after him. A pack of bloodhounds followed the way of his bleeding feet. And the **sleuth**-hounds of the law, the paid fighting animals of society, with telephone, and telegraph, and special train, clung to his trail night and day.

A hound that is characterized as a **sleuth** is a(n)

a. tracker
b. consumer
c. fighter
d. idler

Interactive Quiz

Snap the code, or go to **SadlierConnect.com**.

*Read the following passage, taking note of the **boldface** words and their contexts. These words are among those you will be studying in Unit 12. As you complete the exercises in this unit, it may help to refer to the way the words are used below.*

Vampires We Have Known

<Humorous Essay>

To the extent that vampires make appearances in television dramas nowadays, and in movies and novels, too, we can say that we're all quite familiar with these creatures. That's an **indisputable** fact, is it not? And there's nothing **ambiguous** about the claim that there have been reports of vampires for hundreds of years already. The traditional legends of these ominous creatures seem to have **thrived** originally in eastern Europe. One early case stretches back to the year 1672 in old Croatia. There, a legend sprang up around a man named Jure Grando. He had died and been buried and some twenty years later was reportedly back on his feet. It is not precisely clear by what **incalculable** logic the locals derived this knowledge. But it is rather clear that they were convinced that Jure Grando had emerged from the ground as something called a vampire. By secret, **stealthy** tactics and **maneuvers**, the now vampiric Grando was determined to drink the blood of good civilians. He especially liked to trouble his former wife, the poor living widow, Mrs. Grando.

Do you **balk** at believing these strange tales from another age? How can we **confer** now and discuss the case of Jure Grando? Most of the evidence, if there was any, is lost to history. The **scant** traces that remain of any Grando, or of any facts, or of any vampires, show us next to nothing.

Equally well-founded reports of vampires spread through Europe in the century after this episode. By what **earmarks** does one know a vampire?

6. earmark (ir′ mark)

(*v.*) to set aside for a special purpose; to mark an animal's ear for identification; (*n.*) an identifying mark or feature

Let's ____________________ the money we received for the new building fund.

SYNONYMS: (*v.*) reserve; (*n.*) trait, attribute

7. frigid (frij′ id)

(*adj.*) extremely cold; lacking in warmth or feeling

Antarctica has a very ____________________ climate.

SYNONYMS: freezing, unresponsive
ANTONYMS: hot, balmy, torrid, warm, friendly

8. implement (im′ plə mənt)

(*n.*) an instrument, tool; (*v.*) to put into effect

The harrow is a farm ____________________ that is used to pulverize and smooth soil.

The highway patrol will ____________________ the new speed limit as of July 1 of this year.

SYNONYMS: (*n.*) device, utensil; (*v.*) fulfill, accomplish, achieve, apply, carry out

9. incalculable (in kal′ kyə lə bəl)

(*adj.*) too great to be counted; unpredictable, uncertain

Concerned scientists worry that global warming may cause ____________________ damage to our environment.

SYNONYMS: countless, measureless
ANTONYMS: measurable, countable, predictable

10. indisputable (in dis pyüt′ ə bəl)

(*adj.*) beyond question or argument, definitely true

With such ____________________ evidence, Judge Lee must rule to drop all charges against my client.

SYNONYMS: irrefutable, undeniable, incontestable
ANTONYMS: questionable, debatable, arguable

11. intensive (in ten′ siv)

(*adj.*) thorough, deep; showing great effort; concentrated

It took ____________________ physical therapy for the injured athlete to regain her strength and speed.

SYNONYMS: thoroughgoing, heightened, exhaustive
ANTONYMS: relaxed, easygoing, laid-back

12. maneuver (mə nü′ vər)

(*n.*) a planned movement; a skillful plan; a scheme; (*v.*) to perform or carry out such a planned movement

The troops carried out a night ____________________ as part of the training mission.

It takes a steady hand to ____________________ the high-speed power drill.

SYNONYMS: (*n.*) move, tactic; (*v.*) guide, manipulate

13. sabotage (sab′ ə täzh)

(*n.*) an action taken to destroy something or to prevent it from working properly; (*v.*) to take such destructive action

Foreign embassies worry about ____________________.

Protesters decided to ____________________ the factory.

SYNONYMS: (*v.*) vandalize, cripple, subvert, destroy

14. scant (skant)

(*adj.*) not enough; barely enough; marked by a small or insufficient amount

Somehow, we made the ____________________ supply of food stretch for nearly a week.

SYNONYMS: inadequate, meager, skimpy, bare
ANTONYMS: abundant, plentiful, profuse, excessive

15. stealthy (stel′ thē)

(*adj.*) done in a way so as not to be seen or observed; sneaky, underhanded

The nervous robber took ____________________ glances at the cash register.

SYNONYMS: sly, furtive; ANTONYMS: open, direct, aboveboard

16. strapping (strap′ iŋ)

(*adj.*) tall, strong, and healthy

That ____________________ young man is a good wrestler.

SYNONYMS: sturdy, husky, brawny, athletic, hefty
ANTONYMS: weak, frail, fragile, puny

17. strident (strīd′ ənt)

(*adj.*) harsh, shrill; unpleasant sounding

Her ____________________ laughter showed harsh ridicule.

SYNONYMS: piercing, grating
ANTONYMS: mellow, soothing, musical, honeyed

18. thrive (thrīv)

(*v.*) to grow vigorously; to grow in wealth and possessions

Angie hopes that her business will ____________________ in today's Internet culture.

SYNONYMS: flourish, blossom, prosper; ANTONYMS: wither, fail

19. titanic (tī tan′ ik)

(*adj.*) of enormous size, strength, power, or scope

The movie plot explores the ____________________ struggle between the forces of good and evil.

SYNONYMS: gigantic, huge; ANTONYMS: tiny, miniature, diminutive

20. valiant (val′ yənt)

(*adj.*) possessing or acting with bravery or boldness

Sir Galahad was a ____________________ knight of King Arthur's Round Table.

SYNONYMS: brave, bold, gallant, heroic
ANTONYMS: timid, cowardly, fainthearted, "chicken"

Choosing the Right Word

*Select the **boldface** word that better completes each sentence. You might refer to the unit selection to see how most of these words are used in context.*

1. Of all the evergreens that tower in America's forests, none can surpass the height and girth of the (**titanic, indisputable**) California redwoods.

2. Truthfulness and sincerity are the (**earmarks, compacts**) of an honest person.

3. The brave defenders of the fort waged a (**scant, valiant**) battle against the enemy's troops.

4. Why is that big, (**strapping, incalculable**) fellow in the advertisement always kicking sand into the face of the 98-pound weakling?

5. When he says that his analysis of the problem is (**valiant, indisputable**), all he means is that he's not willing to listen to anyone else's ideas.

6. The first Pilgrim settlers signed an agreement called the "Mayflower (**Compact, Maneuver**)."

National Park Service Director Stephen T. Mather, left, urged the U.S. Congress to preserve the redwood forests.

7. What do you think the United States should do when its representatives are (**sabotaged, abducted**) and held for ransom?

8. "It's an (**indisputable, ambiguous**) fact that the finest guitar players in rock music were from the 1970s," Brandon said.

9. Creeping (**stealthily, ambiguously**) through the underbrush, the enemy came within a few yards of the stockade before the guards saw them.

10. Although our club is run more or less democratically, we don't have the time to (**confer, abduct**) about every minor detail.

11. As election day gets closer, the tone of the candidates' political oratory becomes more and more (**titanic, strident**).

12. Aunt Lorna (**conferred, balked**) when the waiter at the seafood restaurant told her that the dinner special—the "catch of the day"—was $41.00.

13. When we made our appeal for funds, their response was so (**incalculable, frigid**) that we realized we would have to find other ways of raising money.

14. The future is indeed (**incalculable, strapping**), but we must face it with faith and confidence.

15. We have worked out a good plan on paper; now we must decide how we are going to (**implement, balk**) it.

16. Whenever I go out to eat, I (**thrive, sabotage**) my diet by ordering dessert.

17. Because her condition was so poor after the operation, she was placed in the hospital's (**stealthy, intensive**) care unit.

18. The Labrador retriever received a medal from the fire department for its (**valiant, compact**) act of saving a drowning man.

19. After straining and sweating in the hot sun for an hour, we realized that we had pushed the stalled car only a(n) (**scant, intensive**) quarter mile.

20. Since *presently* means both "right now" and "in the future," any statement containing it must be considered (**strident, ambiguous**).

21. I don't think democracy can (**balk, thrive**) in an atmosphere of racial and religious hatred.

22. In her floor exercise, the champion gymnast performed some of the most amazing (**earmarks, maneuvers**) I have ever seen.

23. When their pitcher committed the (**balk, earmark**), the umpire advanced our runner from first to second base.

24. When a conquering army overruns a country, the only way the people may have to strike back is by acts of (**ambiguity, sabotage**).

25. The extra money being raised by the band booster club has been (**earmarked, maneuvered**) to fund future band trips.

Synonyms

*Choose the word from this Unit that is the same or most nearly the same in meaning as the **boldface** word or expression in the phrase. Write that word on the line. Use a dictionary if necessary.*

1. may use that **gadget** to move the baggage ____________________
2. **resist** because of fear ____________________
3. lending us **limitless** support ____________________
4. its **pocket-size** motor ____________________
5. the **inarguable** star of the team ____________________
6. a most **standoffish** welcome ____________________
7. the king who has been **taken hostage** ____________________
8. to interpret that **vague** remark ____________________
9. as they put forth an **immense** effort ____________________
10. a **hearty** young athlete ____________________

Antonyms

*Choose the word from this Unit that is most nearly opposite in meaning to the **boldface** word or expression in the phrase. Write that word on the line. Use a dictionary if necessary.*

1. drives an **oversized** car ____________________
2. worries about **minor** details ____________________
3. met the **delicate** daughter of the earl ____________________
4. decided to **abandon** the plan ____________________
5. expected to **release** the hostages ____________________

Completing the Sentence

From the words in this Unit, choose the one that best completes each of the following sentences. Write the correct word form in the space provided.

1. The millionaire has hired special guards to make sure that his valuable, prize-winning show dog, Lucy, will not be ____________________.

2. Even mighty warships were endangered by the ____________________ waves that loomed like mountains above them.

3. In Shakespeare's words, "Cowards die many times before their deaths; the ____________________ never taste of death but once."

4. At first the zebras did not notice the ____________________ movements of the lions inching their way closer to the herd.

5. The new recruits were rudely awakened from their peaceful sleep by the ____________________ voice of the sergeant barking commands.

6. I was amazed to see how skillfully Felicia ____________________ that huge car through the heavy downtown traffic.

7. No doubt our antipollution program will be expensive, but the cost of doing nothing would be simply ____________________.

8. When the winds begin to turn ____________________ in November, our thoughts turn to our warm and sunny island off the coast of Florida.

9. Because I'm afraid of heights, I usually ____________________ at the idea of sitting in the first row of the topmost balcony in a theater.

10. Since the time we have to prepare for the final exams is exceedingly ____________________, we had better make the best of every hour.

11. Each year a portion of the school budget is ____________________ for the purchase of new books for the library.

12. As the day of the big game approached, our practice sessions became more and more ____________________.

13. I prefer the ____________________ edition of the dictionary because it is so much lighter and less bulky than the unabridged version.

14. In your training to become a dental assistant, you will become familiar with many of the ____________________ that dentists use.

15. The breakdown of all these machines at the same time cannot simply be a coincidence; we suspect deliberate ____________________.

16. Why must you always be so ____________________ when I want you to give me a straight yes-or-no answer?

17. The president will ____________________ well-deserved honors on the retiring ambassador.

18. When our team saw their ____________________ 200-pound defensive linemen, we realized that we would have a hard time running against them.

19. For a person who loves to argue as much as Gene does, there is nothing that is really ____________________.

20. The cactus is an example of a plant having natural adaptations that enable it to ____________________ even in a very dry climate.

Writing: Words in Action

1. Look back at "Vampires We Have Known" (pages 146–147). Imagine you are a reporter. Rumors are spreading about a vampire-like creature attacking animals in your community. Alleviate your community's fears by writing an article that summarizes the history of vampires. Convince readers that there are no vampires. Use at least two details from the passage and three Unit words.

2. What is your opinion about the existence of monsters? Why do you think some people create stories about them? Why do some others believe in them? Write a brief essay, supporting your views with specific examples, observations, the reading (refer to pages 146–147), or personal experience. Write at least three paragraphs, and use three or more words from this Unit.

Vocabulary in Context
Literary Text

The following excerpts are from Tales of Terror and Mystery *by Sir Arthur Conan Doyle. Some of the words you have studied in this Unit appear in* **boldface** *type. Complete each statement below the excerpt by circling the letter of the correct answer.*

1. The eyes glimmered like two disks of phosphorus in the darkness. They appalled and yet fascinated me. I could not take my own eyes from them. Nature plays strange tricks with us at such moments of **intensity**, and those glimmering lights waxed and waned with a steady rise and fall. ("The Brazilian Cat")

Intensity refers to

a. meekness
b. ignorance
c. fear
d. concentration

2. Nothing could be more hearty than his manner, and he set me at my ease in an instant. But it needed all his cordiality to atone for the **frigidity** and even rudeness of his wife, a tall, haggard woman, who came forward at his summons. ("The Brazilian Cat")

People who convey **frigidity** are

a. aloof
b. keen
c. dull
d. shy

3. The court next morning was crammed to overflowing, and a murmur of excitement passed over it when Mr. Humphrey was observed to enter in a state of emotion, which even his trained nerves could not conceal, and to **confer** with the opposing counsel. ("The Black Doctor")

To **confer** with someone is to

a. babble
b. discuss
c. lie
d. inspire

Sir Arthur Conan Doyle's *Tales of Terror and Mystery* is a compilation of six horror stories and seven mysteries.

4. In the silence of the night I could distinctly hear that someone was coming down the corridor. It was a **stealthy** step, faint and intermittent, as of a man who paused cautiously after every stride. ("The Beetle-Hunter")

Someone trying to be **stealthy** is NOT

a. prepared
b. crafty
c. obvious
d. secretive

5. At the time when I was able to fulfill my **compact** I was living in a cottage at Fontainebleau, and as the evening trains were inconvenient, he asked me to spend the night in his house. ("The Leather Funnel")

A person fulfilling a **compact** is honoring a(n)

a. colleague
b. host
c. country
d. agreement

Interactive Quiz

Snap the code, or go to **SadlierConnect.com**.

Vocabulary for Comprehension

Part 1

*Read "An International Science Lab," which contains words in **boldface** that appear in Units 10–12. Then answer the questions.*

An International Science Lab

"Science lab" usually means a clean, bright room in which researchers work with high-tech equipment. Antarctica, the fifth largest of Earth's seven continents, is itself an enormous, ice-cold science lab. It has no native population. Few living things can survive in its brutal climate. But scientists are attracted to the rare features of this desolate continent.

Antarctica is more than 95 percent ice-covered all year long. It has had the lowest air temperature ever measured, as well as some of the highest winds. Because it has no industrial pollution, its ice and snow are pure. All that ice makes it doubtful that any settlement or economic development will ever take place in Antarctica, but many tiny outposts have sprung up since the 1950s.

In that decade, twelve nations set up research stations all over Antarctica. Representatives of those nations got together to draft a **compact** devoting the continent to peaceful study. This pact went into effect in 1961. It forbids military action and nuclear weapons. It promotes a free exchange of ideas.

Antarctic scientists devise and carry out a wide range of tests. They study glaciers, weather patterns and conditions, icebergs, magnetism, volcanoes, the movement of rock plates, and animal and plant biology. They openly share their findings with the global scientific community.

Life in such a difficult place demands planning, special gear, and **grit**. Scientists must figure out how to do their research safely and effectively. They must guard their health and well-being. Internet and satellite technologies surely help. Researchers so far from home can **confer** with the family, friends, and co-workers they left behind. They can stay up-to-date on world events. But they cannot easily come and go. Scientists often arrive before the Antarctic winter, when near-total darkness **engulfs** the area. They typically stay for six to ten long, cold, lonely months.

Dressing for the job of an Antarctic scientist is a unique challenge. An optimal number of layers in the right fabrics is needed to protect the body against wind, cold, and moisture during long, **rigorous** workdays outdoors. The scientific research stations themselves are challenging to build. The buildings must be designed to consider snow patterns, the effects of melting ice, and insulation against the **frigid** climate and fierce winds. Antarctica has no trees or other naturally found resources for construction, so materials are usually brought by ship and assembled on site. But they must be assembled quickly so that supply ships can leave before they are frozen in!

Despite the difficulties they encounter, researchers in Antarctica have made many important scientific achievements. These include the detection of massive under-ice lakes and canyons, the discovery of previously unknown species of animals, and the identification of ways Earth is changing both naturally and because of human activity.

1. What is the central idea of "An International Science Lab"?
  A) Antarctica is almost totally covered with ice all year.
  B) Important international scientific research is conducted in Antarctica.
  C) Antarctica, the fifth-largest continent, has no native population.
  D) It is easy to do scientific research in Antarctica.

2. What is the main purpose of the second paragraph (lines 11–21)?
  A) to describe the rare features mentioned in the previous paragraph
  B) to inform readers on how to survive like the researchers in Antarctica
  C) to describe life inside the science lab
  D) to convince the reader of the importance of peaceful study

3. What does the word **compact** mean as it is used in line 26?
  A) small car
  B) speech
  C) agreement
  D) dense

4. What is the meaning of **grit** as it is used in line 41?
  A) grind
  B) persistence
  C) gravel
  D) courage

5. According to line 47, what does **confer** mean?
  A) consult
  B) argue
  C) play
  D) study

6. **Part A**
What does the word **rigorous** most likely mean as it is used in line 61?
  A) easy
  B) foolish
  C) full of life
  D) challenging

Part B
Which text evidence provides the best clue to the meaning of **rigorous**?
  A) "twelve nations set up research stations all over Antarctica." (lines 22–24)
  B) "forbids military action and nuclear weapons." (lines 28–29)
  C) "study glaciers, weather patterns and conditions, icebergs, magnetism, volcanoes, the movement of rock plates, and animal and plant biology." (lines 33–36)
  D) "stay up-to-date on world events." (line 49)

7. Which word means the opposite of **frigid** in line 67?
  A) relaxed
  B) balmy
  C) icy
  D) freezing

8. Why does the author **most likely** describe what Antarctic scientists wear and how scientific research stations are built?
  A) to reveal how a supply ship was frozen in
  B) to share the most important scientific discoveries
  C) to emphasize the difficulties of working in Antarctica
  D) to weigh the pros and cons of research

Vocabulary for Comprehension
Part 2

*Read these passages, which contain words in **boldface** that appear in Units 10–12. Then choose the best answer to each question based on what is stated or implied in the passages. You may refer to the passages as often as necessary.*

Questions 1–8 are based on the following passages.

Passage 1

Nearly 40,000 people died on our roads in 2015—and almost all road accidents are caused by human error. If American drivers were as reliable as the cars they drive, our roads would be much less dangerous than they are. Modern automobiles must conform to **intensive** codes of safety, but they can only ever be as safe as their drivers—and even the best drivers make mistakes.

Self-driving cars will manage the **titanic** task of eliminating human error by taking over the driving responsibilities. They avoid the kinds of risks that human drivers often take without thinking. Their computerized guidance systems can calculate braking distances, relative speeds, **maneuverability**, and other important data more rapidly and accurately than any human driver. They base their decisions and predictions on accurate information rather than intuition and guesswork. They do not pick up lazy habits, or neglect necessary safety procedures—they refuse to move until their passengers are safely buckled up.

Self-driving cars are law-abiding. They never exceed the speed limit, and they are strictly teetotal. They not get angry, either with their passengers or with other road users, and they are never distracted. Experts have noted a recent **meteoric** rise in the number of deaths on our roads, and attribute it to the **abominable** use of smartphones. Self-driving cars will never endanger the lives of their passengers by texting their friends.

Passage 2

Self-driving cars promise safety. **Strident** supporters of the self-driving car movement proclaim that they will eliminate the 94 percent of road accidents that the Department of Transport identifies as the **consequence** of human error. We are told the world should get ready for the **valiant** new technology of self-driving cars—but are self-driving cars ready for the world?

When there is no longer a human driver processing the data and making the decisions, the car has to be infallible. Recently, a self-driving car was in a fatal collision with a tractor-trailer rig on a Florida highway. The car was apparently unable to detect the white truck against the bright sky. The passenger in the self-driving car seems to have been watching a movie—by encouraging human drivers to pay **scant** attention to the road, self-driving cars may be creating new hazards. The manufacturer has since advised human drivers to keep at least one hand on the steering wheel, and to be ready to take over driving duties at any time. This precaution may be sensible, but aren't self-driving cars supposed to take over the driving duties from us?

Consumers are told that self-driving trucks will make heavy transport safer and more efficient by forming long convoys, called "platoons." These platoons would resemble freight trains riding along railroad tracks. Freight trains will always be safer and faster—and they already exist.

1. Passage 1 claims that human error
   A) cannot be eliminated.
   B) is caused by guesswork and intuition.
   C) caused 40,000 road deaths in 2015.
   D) causes the majority of road deaths.

2. As it is used in line 8, "intensive" most nearly means
   A) exhausting.
   B) thorough.
   C) incomprehensible.
   D) long-lasting.

3. As it is used in line 43, "strident" most nearly means
   A) obstinate.
   B) loud.
   C) feverish.
   D) passionate.

4. As it is used in line 64, "scant" most nearly means
   A) less.
   B) excessive.
   C) meager.
   D) casual.

5. Which of these words in Passage 2 conveys a sense of irony about the claims made in Passage 1?
   A) strident (line 43)
   B) valiant (line 50)
   C) infallible (line 56)
   D) sensible (line 71)

6. Which choice provides the best evidence for the answer to the previous question?
   A) Lines 48–52 ("We . . . world")
   B) Lines 53–56 ("When . . . infallible")
   C) Lines 61–66 ("The passenger . . . hazards")
   D) Lines 66–71 ("The manufacturer . . . time")

7. In Passage 1, the author states that self-driving cars will eliminate human error. In Passage 2, the author demonstrates that self-driving cars are
   A) not ready to take over driving.
   B) capable of human error.
   C) inattentive to road conditions.
   D) more dangerous than human drivers.

8. Which statement best describes the overall relationship between Passage 1 and Passage 2?
   A) Passage 1 shows how self-driving cars will reduce the number of road accidents, and Passage 2 shows how self-driving cars will make the roads more dangerous.
   B) Passage 1 is forward-thinking and ready to accept new technology, while Passage 2 rejects progress and clings to old technology, such as freight trains.
   C) The author of Passage 1 believes that self-driving cars are ready to make a contribution to road safety, and the author of Passage 2 believes they will never help to prevent road accidents.
   D) Passage 1 demonstrates a belief in the immediate effectiveness of self-driving car technology, and Passage 2 demonstrates that self-driving cars are not yet ready for the world.

Denotation and Connotation

A word's dictionary definition is its **denotation**. A denotation is the word's literal meaning, and it conveys a neutral tone.

Words also have connotations. **Connotations** are the emotional associations that people make to certain words. These associations can be either positive or negative.

Consider these synonyms for the neutral word *individualist*:

nonconformist *maverick* *eccentric* *oddball*

Nonconformist and *maverick* have positive connotations, whereas *eccentric* and *oddball* are negative.

Think: People often admire nonconformists and mavericks, because they are usually confident, independent thinkers. People may be wary of eccentrics or oddballs, however, because their ideas may seem too way out or unusual.

Look at these examples of words. Notice how the connotation of each word varies.

NEUTRAL	POSITIVE	NEGATIVE
restore	**refurbish**	**overhaul**
satire	**parody**	**lampoon**
cold	**bracing**	**frigid**

Words can evoke powerful associations in readers. For example, the word *forest* might make some readers think of a beautiful woodland perfect for camping. Others might think of the dark, mysterious forests in fairy tales. Writers must be aware of connotations and choose words carefully so that they can convey the right mood and message.

Shades of Meaning

Write a plus sign (+) in the box if the word has a positive connotation. Write a minus sign (–) if the word has a negative connotation. Put a zero (0) if the word is neutral.

1. compact ☐ **2.** thrive ☐ **3.** dumbfounded ☐ **4.** maneuver ☐

5. bumbling ☐ **6.** vandalism ☐ **7.** confer ☐ **8.** scant ☐

9. subsequent ☐ **10.** abduct ☐ **11.** pry ☐ **12.** resourceful ☐

13. delude ☐ **14.** valiant ☐ **15.** prevail ☐ **16.** distort ☐

Expressing the Connotation

Read each sentence. Select the word in parentheses that better expresses the connotation (positive, negative, or neutral) given at the beginning of the sentence.

negative	**1.**	It was quite common for outlaws of the Wild West to have several (**names, aliases**).
neutral	**2.**	The gymnast achieved (**meteoric, rapid**) fame after her Olympic debut.
negative	**3.**	Our cat (**balked, hesitated**) when I opened the door to let him outside, and he saw that it was raining.
positive	**4.**	We ate our lunch on the veranda and watched the tourists (**amble, trudge**) along the beach.
neutral	**5.**	The movers had a difficult time trying to get the (**titanic, large**) piano into the small loft.
negative	**6.**	The (**strident, loud**) screams from the fans made the security staff a little nervous.
positive	**7.**	After spending the entire summer working out, Ted became a (**beefy, burly**) athlete.
positive	**8.**	Randy saved the program from the ceremony as a (**keepsake, relic**) of the happy event.

Challenge: Using Connotation

Choose vocabulary words from Units 10–12 to replace the ***boldface*** *words in the sentences below. Then explain how the connotation of the replacement word changes the tone of the sentence.*

unerring	**replenished**	**sabotaged**
foiled	**stealthy**	**engulfed**

1. Once again the police were victorious when they **interrupted** ____________ the heist of the notorious diamond burglar.

____

____

2. The unexpected snowstorm **undermined** ____________ our winter getaway, causing all flights to warmer climates to be cancelled.

____

____

3. Now that the serious drought has been broken, it will not take long before the lakes will be **refilled** ____________.

____

____

Idioms

In the passage "Farewell, Blue Yodeler" (see pages 126–127), the writer describes Jimmie Rodgers's last days and states that he was "in a race against time." The writer means that Jimmie did not have much time to complete his recordings, as he was about to die.

"Race against time" is an **idiom**. Idioms are words, phrases, or expressions based on colorful comparisons. Their meanings should not be taken literally. People usually learn idioms by hearing and using them in everyday speech. Idioms are unique to every language. When you learn a new idiom and its meaning, you are also learning how different cultures, communities, and generations see the world.

Choosing the Right Idiom

Read each sentence. Use context clues to figure out the meaning of each idiom in ***boldface*** *print. Then write the letter of the definition for the idiom in the sentence.*

1. I know I was angry at James for a while, but that is all **water under the bridge** now. ______
2. "No matter how much money I save from what I earn babysitting," Alison complained, "it just seems to be **a drop in the bucket**." ______
3. "I can't worry about the game tonight," Sam said. "I've got **bigger fish to fry**." ______
4. Tim tried to explain his tardiness to the teacher, but she did not fall for his **old song and dance**. ______
5. Marie is very health conscious; **once in a blue moon**, though, she'll eat something sugary. ______
6. We just got a new boss, so this is not the time to **make any waves**. ______
7. Garret is still **finding his feet** in his new job as a grocery store cashier. ______
8. I couldn't **believe my ears** when I heard you were moving. ______
9. **A little bird told me** that Gwen was getting braces next week. ______
10. I don't mean to **rain on your parade**, but I heard the concert was cancelled. ______

a. excuses or lies

b. getting comfortable in

c. a very small amount

d. very infrequently

e. cause trouble; draw attention to yourself

f. believe what I'm hearing

g. a past event that is no longer important

h. spoil your fun

i. A secret source I can't reveal gave me the information.

j. more important business to attend to

Classical Roots

co, col, com, con, cor—with, together

A form of this Latin prefix appears in **consequence** (page 128), **compact** (page 148), and **confer** (page 148). Some other words in which this prefix appears are listed below.

coincidence	**colleague**	**compute**	**confide**
collaborate	**composure**	**concurrent**	**correspond**

From the list of words above, choose the one that corresponds to each of the brief definitions below. Write the word in the blank space in the illustrative sentence below the definition. Use a dictionary if necessary.

1. to work with others; to aid or assist an enemy of one's country

They agreed to ____________________ on the science project so they could pool their resources and ideas.

2. to exchange letters; to be in agreement

My cousin and I decided to ____________________ by e-mail after he moved to Montana.

3. occurring at the same time; agreeing

The convicted felon was sentenced to ____________________ prison terms.

4. the chance occurrence of two things at the same time or place

"What a ____________________ to bump into you here at the passport office!" she exclaimed.

5. a fellow worker, associate

The proud retiree was honored by her longtime ____________________ at the library.

6. to tell something as a secret; to entrust a secret

I would never ____________________ such details to anyone but a close friend.

7. to determine by arithmetic; to calculate

The mechanic used a calculator to ____________________ the total repair bill.

8. calmness of mind, bearing, or appearance; self-control

Even the car alarms wailing outside the auditorium did not ruffle the speaker's ____________________.

*Read the following passage, taking note of the **boldface** words and their contexts. These words are among those you will be studying in Unit 13. As you complete the exercises in this unit, it may help to refer to the way the words are used below.*

Polar Opposites

<Compare and Contrast Essay>

Although they may seem similar, the polar regions of planet Earth are really very different. They **affirm** the old adage that there are two sides to the same coin.

The astonishing climate **traits** of both the Arctic and Antarctica are **stupefying**. Temperatures of –60°F are not unusual. If the harsh winds and vast ice sheets do not **deter** visitors, these strangers will find the elements **disquieting** at the very least. During polar winters, the sun never rises, while during the summers, it never sets. For centuries, explorers had to give careful thought to how to **cope** with these forces of nature. It was essential to **adhere** closely to a more rigorous program of safety precautions than explorers used in more temperate lands.

The Arctic is a region of immense diversity. Although the terrain seems forbidding, many animals **prowl** the land, including polar bears, caribou, wolves, foxes, hares, and weasels. Migrant birds visit from as far away as Central and South America. Possibly the most famous of these birds is the arctic tern. This summer visitor traverses thousands of miles every year, from Antarctica to the Arctic! The ocean **surges** with abundant marine life, especially when warm currents move around some of the Arctic coasts. Surprisingly, vegetation is widespread. Algae, lichens, and dwarf shrubs persist, even in areas of permanent ice.

The Arctic is also home to a broad range of native peoples. For example, the Inuit and Aleuts reside in northern North America and Greenland. The Eurasian Arctic is home to the Sami, sometimes

The arctic fox has a thick coat and furred paws to allow for survival in an extremely cold climate.

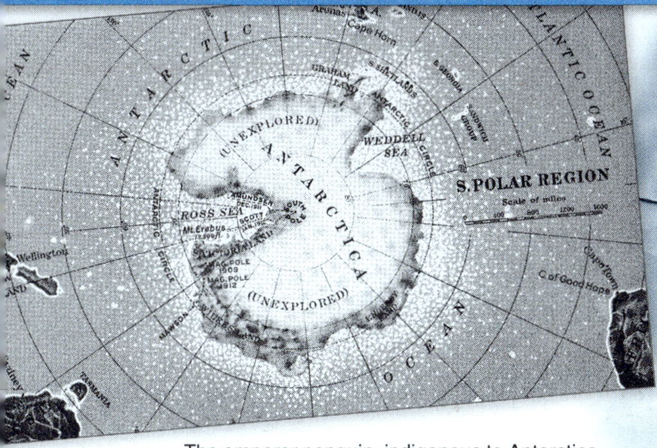

The emperor penguin, indigenous to Antarctica, is the largest species of penguins.

called the Lapps, as well as to the Nenets (Samoyed) and the Evenks (Tungus). To suppose that these peoples view their environment as hostile would be a **misapprehension**. According to anthropologists, many Arctic residents are **optimists**. They perceive their surroundings as benevolent and **empowering**, offering an abundant livelihood.

By contrast with the Arctic, which is made up of portions of several continents, Antarctica is a true continent, the fifth largest on Earth. Its landmass covers 5.5 million square miles and lies almost wholly beneath a vast ice sheet. The ice measures 7 million cubic miles—that's about 90 percent of all the ice on Earth. In 1983, the lowest recorded temperature on Earth was measured at an Antarctic research center, Vostok Station: –128.6°F.

Unlike the Arctic, the interior of Antarctica may boast only of invertebrate microfauna, such as nematodes and ciliate protozoans. Seals and birds live on the edges of the land. Probably the most spectacular resident of Antarctica is the emperor penguin, a flightless bird standing between three and four feet tall.

Antarctica is the only continent on Earth without a native human population. Although the North and South Poles were first reached at roughly the same time in the early 1900s, the Arctic and Antarctic regions have had different exploration histories. Study of Antarctica **lagged** for some time, largely because trade routes from North America and Europe to the East seemed much more appealing in the far north.

The 1950s, however, witnessed two important events for Antarctica. First was the development of the tourist industry. Second was the Antarctic Treaty, a breakthrough in international diplomacy. This treaty preserved Antarctica from corrupt or **unscrupulous** exploitation that would **mangle** the environment. The agreement set aside the continent as a scientific preserve.

Despite differences between these two polar regions, both have been an equal source of fascination and inspiration for people throughout the centuries.

Audio

For iWords and audio passages, snap the code, or go to **SadlierConnect.com**.

Definitions

Note the spelling, pronunciation, part(s) of speech, and definition(s) of each of the following words. Then write the word in the blank spaces in the illustrative sentence(s) following. Finally, study the lists of synonyms and antonyms.

1. adhere (ad hēr′)

(*v.*) to stick to, remain attached; to be devoted or loyal as a follower or supporter

Things will work out better if we ____________________ to our original plan.

SYNONYMS: cling, hold fast
ANTONYMS: unfasten, unglue, abandon, betray

2. affirm (ə fərm′)

(*v.*) to declare to be true, state positively; to confirm

Unexpected kindness from a stranger during a time of need can ____________________ one's faith in human nature.

SYNONYMS: assert, ratify
ANTONYMS: deny, disavow, reject, veto, disallow

3. atrocity (ə träs′ ət ē)

(*n.*) an extremely wicked, brutal, or cruel act; something very bad or unpleasant

The Nazis took great pains to keep detailed records of each kind of ____________________ they committed.

SYNONYMS: enormity, monstrosity
ANTONYMS: good deed, kindness

4. cope (kōp)

(*v.*) to struggle successfully against; to prove to be a match for, deal with satisfactorily; (*n.*) a long religious cloak; a canopy

Education and experience provide us with the skills we need to ____________________ with difficult situations.

We exchanged wedding vows under a blue ____________________.

SYNONYMS: (*v.*) make do, get along, handle

5. deter (di tər′)

(*v.*) to discourage, scare off, or prevent through fear or doubt

Traffic jams won't ____________________ us from coming to your birthday party.

ANTONYMS: encourage, urge on

6. disquieting (dis kwī′ ət iŋ)

(*adj.*) causing uneasiness or worry

A ____________________ incident at school put all the teachers and students on edge.

SYNONYMS: disturbing, alarming
ANTONYMS: calming, reassuring, soothing, comforting

7. empower (em pau̇′ ər)

(*v.*) to give power or authority to; to enable; to permit

Signing this legal paper will ________________ me to set up my own bank account.

SYNONYMS: authorize, license
ANTONYMS: forbid, prohibit, ban, disqualify

8. fluent (flü′ ənt)

(*adj.*) speaking or writing easily and smoothly, flowing gracefully

Susannah can speak ________________ Japanese, French, and Russian.

SYNONYMS: eloquent, articulate, glib
ANTONYMS: tongue-tied, choppy

9. lag (lag)

(*v.*) to move slowly or fall behind; to bring up the rear; (*n.*) a falling behind; the amount by which someone or something is behind; an interval

Please try not to ________________ behind the others.

There is a three-hour ________________ from the time I send you an e-mail until you receive it.

SYNONYMS: (*v.*) trail, straggle; (*v., n.*) delay
ANTONYMS: (*v.*) keep up, outstrip, outdo

10. mangle (maŋ′ gəl)

(*v.*) to injure very seriously by cutting, tearing, crushing, etc.; to bring to ruin

Workers could ________________ their hands in this equipment if they don't pay attention to what they're doing.

SYNONYMS: mutilate, butcher, disfigure, rend

11. misapprehension (mis ap ri hen′ shən)

(*n.*) a wrong idea, misunderstanding

A lingering ________________ may cause ill will between friends.

SYNONYM: misconception

12. optimist (äp′ tə mist)

(*n.*) one who expects things to turn out for the best; someone who looks on the bright side of things

An ________________ holds a rosy view of life.

ANTONYMS: pessimist, prophet of doom

13. prowl (prau̇l)

(*v.*) to roam about stealthily in search of something

A panther can ________________ freely at night because its dark fur prevents it from being seen.

SYNONYMS: rove, skulk, slink, lurk

14. recitation (res′ ə tā′ shən)

(*n.*) a reading in public of something that is memorized; a memorized poem or piece of prose that is read aloud

Kent was not nervous at all when he gave his Walt Whitman ____________________ at the school assembly.

SYNONYMS: (*n.*) recital, performance, presentation

15. stupefy (stü′ pə fī)

(*v.*) to make dull or groggy; to surprise or astonish

The vet used a powerful tranquilizer to ____________________ the animal.

SYNONYMS: stun, daze, shock, amaze, astound
ANTONYMS: awaken, arouse, stimulate, enliven

16. sulky (səl′ kē)

(*adj.*) in a bad or nasty mood, resentful; gloomy

A ____________________ child does not make a very good playmate.

SYNONYMS: sullen, petulant; ANTONYMS: cheerful, amiable

17. supplement (səp′ lə ment)

(*n.*) something added to complete a thing or make up for a lack; a section added to a book or document; (*v.*) to provide such an addition or completion

The sports ____________________ is my favorite part of this magazine.

Many people ____________________ their regular diet by taking daily vitamins.

SYNONYMS: (*n.*) addition, extension; (*v.*) add to

18. surge (sərj)

(*v.*) to have a heavy, violent, swelling motion (like waves); (*n.*) a powerful forward rush

Runners who train hard and who have good stamina often ____________________ ahead of the pack.

A sudden ____________________ of electrical current could make a computer crash.

SYNONYMS: (*v.*) flood, rush, burst, gush; (*n.*) wave
ANTONYMS: (*v.*) recede, ebb; (*n.*) recession, slowdown

19. trait (trāt)

(*n.*) a quality or characteristic (especially of personality); a distinguishing feature

Your most appealing ____________________ is your unfailing sense of humor.

20. unscrupulous (ən skrü′ pyə ləs)

(*adj.*) dishonest; not guided or controlled by moral principles

Avoid dealing with ____________________ merchants whenever possible.

SYNONYMS: crooked, corrupt, shady
ANTONYMS: fair, honest, trustworthy, aboveboard

Choosing the Right Word

*Select the **boldface** word that better completes each sentence. You might refer to the unit selection to see how most of these words are used in context.*

Theodore Roosevelt, the twenty-sixth president of the United States, won the Nobel Prize for Peace in 1906.

1. Everything that I have learned about Theodore Roosevelt from history books (**stupefies, affirms**) my reverence for this great president.

2. Who (**prowled, empowered**) you to speak for everyone in our class?

3. A loud groan went through the class when we got the (**unscrupulous, disquieting**) news that there would be a full-period test later in the week.

4. I would love to be half as (**fluent, sulky**) in Spanish as José is in English.

5. All those smooth words and vague promises are not going to (**adhere, deter**) us from doing what we know is needed to improve conditions.

6. There is no one (**trait, optimist**) that makes him so likable; it is the overall effect of his personality.

7. When everything went wrong for Stan, and he saw no way out of his troubles, he muttered to himself, "I just can't (**mangle, cope**)!"

8. Come what may, I will (**adhere, affirm**) to the great ideas and ideals for which our ancestors suffered so much.

9. Jonathan was furious when his (**optimistic, unscrupulous**) boss stole his ideas for an advertising campaign.

10. My yoga class helped improve my breathing and (**supplemented, affirmed**) my training for running the marathon.

11. My definition of a(n) (**optimist, misapprehension**) is someone who looks at an almost empty bottle of juice and says, "This bottle is one-quarter full."

12. The City Council has approved funds for a new playground, but we expect a (**lag, surge**) of several months before construction begins.

13. When I saw the (**disquieting, mangled**) vehicle, I thought for sure that the driver had to be seriously injured; amazingly, though, he walked away from the wreck.

14. Even though some animals are ferocious and attack livestock, we should not be (**mangled, deterred**) from protecting their dwindling populations.

15. It is far better to know you are ignorant of something than to act on the basis of wrong information and (**misapprehensions, recitations**).

16. Shortly after World War II, Japan began the great economic (**surge, trait**) that put it among the world's top industrial nations.

17. My friend took one look at the statue I fashioned from stray pieces of junk and exclaimed, "That's not a sculpture; it's a(n) (**lag, atrocity**)!"

18. The worst way to deal with disappointments is to become (**fluent, sulky**); the best way is to smile and make up your mind to try again.

19. Ms. Edwards is having us listen to professional speakers to help prepare us for our poetry (**recitations, supplements**).

20. Jackals and other scavengers now (**prowl, deter**) through the ruins of what was once a great city.

21. Have all these years of peace and good living (**disquieted, stupefied**) us to such an extent that we are not even prepared to defend ourselves?

22. I agree fully with what the previous speaker has said, but I should like to (**cope, supplement**) his ideas with a few remarks of my own.

23. The play went along smoothly until it came to Mark Antony's funeral oration, which Fred (**empowered, mangled**) beyond all recognition.

24. A true friend would not have been so (**sulky, unscrupulous**) as to take unfair advantage of your trust and confidence.

25. Which stylistic (**traits, surges**) of Van Gogh's paintings do you find most enthralling?

Synonyms

*Choose the word from this Unit that is the same or most nearly the same in meaning as the **boldface** word or expression in the phrase. Write that word on the line. Use a dictionary if necessary.*

1. **damaged** the bicycle's lock while stealing it ______________
2. did not welcome her **grouchy** attitude ______________
3. **outrage** that stunned the world ______________
4. the most unique **attribute** of the breed ______________
5. hikers who **drop back** to the rear of the group ______________
6. drafting a **smooth and effortless** speech ______________
7. a special **addendum** to the book ______________
8. a letter containing some **troubling** news ______________
9. his dramatic **delivery** of the poem ______________
10. unsure how to **manage** without her help ______________

Antonyms

*Choose the word from this Unit that is most nearly opposite in meaning to the **boldface** word or expression in the phrase. Write that word on the line. Use a dictionary if necessary.*

1. comments that **detract from** your main point ____________________
2. witnessed the **spontaneous outburst** on the stage ____________________
3. known for her **sunny** disposition ____________________
4. **halting** public-speaking skills ____________________
5. practicing **caring acts** everyday ____________________

Completing the Sentence

From the words in this Unit, choose the one that best completes each of the following sentences. Write the correct word form in the space provided.

1. In spite of our best efforts, collections for the Community Fund this year have ____________________ far behind last year's figures.

2. Since she has a large family, she finds it necessary to ____________________ her income by working at a second job at night and on weekends.

3. Do you think that it is possible to become ____________________ in a foreign language without actually living in a country where it is spoken?

4. If you think that I would go to a party without being invited, you are under a complete ____________________.

5. As the young girl began her ____________________, her mouth became dry and her voice began to crack.

6. In World War I, soldiers in the trenches endured one ____________________ after another, such as contaminated food and water, diseases, and gangrene.

7. He is so careless in handling his textbooks that by the end of the term he has practically ____________________ all of them.

8. Naturally we were upset when we received the ____________________ news that our uncle had been taken to the hospital.

9. The unfavorable weather reports did not ____________________ us from holding the picnic that we had planned for so long.

0. In spite of all his talents, he will never gain high public office because so many voters feel that he is ____________________ and cannot be trusted.

11. We were so ____________________ by the bad news that for a few moments we just sat there without moving or speaking.

12. When he gets in one of those ____________________ moods, he is as unreasonable and unpleasant as a cranky child.

13. The Constitution ____________________ the president to name the people who will fill many of the most important positions in the government.

14. As soon as the doors were opened, the shoppers, eager for the advertised bargains, ____________________ into the store in great waves.

15. Throughout her long and noble career, her outstanding ____________________ has been her deep love for her fellow human beings.

16. If you are having so much trouble with a program of four major courses, how do you expect to ____________________ with a fifth course?

17. It is hard to be a(n) ____________________ when nothing works out for you.

18. As the robber ____________________ the streets looking for victims, he was unaware that undercover police officers were watching his every move.

19. Now that the job has been completed, I have finally become skillful in hanging the paper so that it ____________________ firmly to the wall.

20. The witness solemnly ____________________ that the evidence she was about to give was true.

Writing: Words in Action

1. Look back at "Polar Opposites" (pages 164–165). Using details from the passage, compare and contrast the Arctic and Antarctica. In your conclusion, state which polar region you would rather visit and explain why. Include at least two details from the passage and three Unit words.

2. The author of "Polar Opposites" states that Arctic residents "perceive their surroundings as benevolent and empowering." How do the weather and the environment affect a person's outlook? Write a brief essay, supporting your views with specific examples, observations, the reading (refer to pages 164–165), or personal experience. Write at least three paragraphs, and use three or more words from this Unit.

Vocabulary in Context

Literary Text

The following excerpts are from Anne of Green Gables *by L.M. Montgomery. Some of the words you have studied in this Unit appear in* ***boldface*** *type. Complete each statement below the excerpt by circling the letter of the correct answer.*

1. Every other Friday afternoon she has **recitations** and everybody has to say a piece or take part in a dialogue. Oh, it's just glorious to think of it.

Recitations are

a. parties
b. readings
c. experiments
d. picnics

2. She said she hadn't time to get sick, watching to see that I didn't fall overboard. She said she never saw the beat of me for **prowling** about. But if it kept her from being seasick it's a mercy I did prowl, isn't it?

The act of **prowling** involves

a. eating
b. swimming
c. sneaking
d. running

3. Marilla felt hot anger **surge** up into her heart again. This child had taken and lost her treasured amethyst brooch and now sat there calmly reciting the details thereof without the least apparent compunction or repentance.

Feelings that **surge**

a. diminish
b. cheapen
c. end abruptly
d. swell rapidly

Megan Follows portrays the resourceful orphan Anne Shirley in this 1985 TV adaptation of *Anne of Green Gables*.

4. . . . Matthew, noting Anne's paleness and indifference and the **lagging** steps that bore her home from the post office every afternoon, began seriously to wonder if he hadn't better vote Grit at the next election.

Someone taking **lagging** steps is

a. lingering
b. forceful
c. hasty
d. skipping

5. "We had a quarrel. I wouldn't forgive him when he asked me to. I meant to, after awhile—but I was **sulky** and angry and I wanted to punish him first. He never came back . . . . But I always felt—rather sorry. I've always kind of wished I'd forgiven him when I had the chance."

A person who is **sulky** is NOT

a. peevish
b. confident
c. friendly
d. energetic

Interactive Quiz

Snap the code, or go to **SadlierConnect.com**.

Read the following passage, taking note of the ***boldface*** *words and their contexts. These words are among those you will be studying in Unit 14. As you complete the exercises in this unit, it may help to refer to the way the words are used below.*

Madam C.J. Walker and Her Wonderful Remedy

<Biographical Sketch>

Pioneering entrepreneur Madam C.J. Walker was likely both the first woman and first African American self-made millionaire. She achieved her fortune by creating, marketing, and selling a hair tonic for African American women. She **transformed** her life and reached her **exalted** status through hard work, determination, and courage. As she liked to say, "I got my start by giving myself a start."

Madam Walker's real name was Sarah Breedlove. She was born in 1867 into a **glum** world of poverty and hardship. Her parents were newly freed slaves who worked the cotton fields on a Louisiana plantation. They left her an orphan at age seven.

Sarah Breedlove's early life was full of sadness, trouble, change, and **upheaval**. Seeking **sanctuary** from an abusive brother-in-law, she married as a 14-year-old and became a mother as a 17-year-old. She went from picking cotton to washing clothes for $1.50 a day. Despite her lack of formal education and money, she was not content to remain an obedient and **submissive** wife or employee to a tough **taskmaster**. She had other ideas.

To treat her hair loss and a scalp problem caused by poor nutrition, she began mixing homemade hair-care recipes. She hit upon a scalp conditioner and healing formula and dubbed it Madam C.J. Walker's Wonderful Hair Grower. (She used her third husband's name, C.J. Walker, **appending** "Madam" as well for sparkle.) She turned her remedy into a booming business.

Knowing that he who hesitates is lost, Madam Walker quickly took her product on the road. She traveled for years, selling her hair and beauty products successfully door-to-door to a **responsive** and eager audience. Hotels refused to **accommodate** African Americans, so she often stayed instead with local African American parishioners.

After years of struggle, business was so good she was able to hire and train sales agents. They were all African American women seeking a better life. In 1910, Madam Walker moved to Indianapolis and **amalgamated** her different business ventures into The Madam C.J. Walker Manufacturing Company. The Walker compound consisted of a factory, beauty school and salon, and training center for her growing sales force.

A **tally** of Madam C.J. Walker's many accomplishments shows she was not just a successful businesswoman. She was also a philanthropist and arts patron. She used her influence and fortune to help others. She gave large sums to charities and orphanages.

Madam Walker was vocal about social injustice. She spoke out against racist attitudes at a time when it was risky to do so. She petitioned Congress and the President to support federal anti-lynching laws. And she showed her **allegiance** to the National Association for the Advancement of Colored People (NAACP), pledging $5,000 to its anti-lynching campaign. It was the largest single donation the civil rights organization had ever received.

In 1998, the United States Postal Service issued a stamp **commemorating** Madam Walker and her extraordinary accomplishments. Her New York mansion is a National Historic Landmark, as is the former Walker Company building in Indianapolis, which now houses the Madame Walker Theatre Center. There is a street in Manhattan honoring Madam Walker and her daughter, A'Lelia, who was a famous Manhattan society figure.

Harvard Business School recognized Madam Walker as one of the great American business leaders of the twentieth century. It would not be unrealistic or **far-fetched** to say the rags-to-riches story of the little girl who dreamed big has inspired generations.

Audio

For Words and audio passages, snap the code, or go to **SadlierConnect.com**.

Beauty mogul Madam C.J. Walker at the wheel of her Model T Ford

Madam C.J. Walker's Wonderful Hair Grower sparked a beauty empire.

Definitions

Note the spelling, pronunciation, part(s) of speech, and definition(s) of each of the following words. Then write the word in the blank spaces in the illustrative sentence(s) following. Finally, study the lists of synonyms and antonyms.

1. abstain (ab stān′)

(*v.*) to stay away from doing something by one's own choice

I find it hard to ____________ from these tempting and delicious desserts.

SYNONYMS: avoid, decline, resist
ANTONYMS: yield to, give in to, indulge in

2. accommodate (ə käm′ ə dāt)

(*v.*) to do a favor or service for, help out; to provide for, supply with; to have space for; to make fit or suitable

That van is the ideal vehicle for carpooling because it can ____________ nine passengers.

SYNONYMS: oblige, lodge, adapt
ANTONYMS: disoblige, inconvenience, trouble

3. allegiance (ə lēj′ əns)

(*n.*) the loyalty or obligation owed to a government, nation, or cause

At a festive yet solemn ceremony, fifty new citizens swore ____________ to their adopted nation.

SYNONYMS: obedience, fidelity

4. amalgamate (ə mal′ gə māt)

(*v.*) to unite; to combine elements into a unified whole

Two small companies will ____________ into one large corporation on June 1.

SYNONYMS: merge, consolidate
ANTONYMS: divide, separate, carve up, break up

5. append (ə pend′)

(*v.*) to attach, add, or tack on as a supplement or extra item

We were dismayed when our teacher decided to ____________ an additional assignment to our already huge load of homework.

ANTONYMS: detach from, disconnect

6. commemorate (kə mem′ ə rāt)

(*v.*) to preserve, honor, or celebrate the memory of

Each May we ____________ Grandpa's life by lighting a special candle for him that burns for 24 hours.

SYNONYM: memorialize
ANTONYMS: dishonor, forget, overlook

7. enumerate (i nü′ mə rāt)

(*v.*) to count; to name one by one, list

These booklets ____________ and compare all the high-tech features that new televisions can offer.

SYNONYMS: check off, spell out, specify

8. exalt (eg zôlt′)

(*v.*) to make high in rank, power, character, or quality; to fill with pride, joy, or noble feeling; to praise, honor

Let us now ____________ the heroes for their courage and character in the face of all this adversity.

SYNONYMS: elevate, raise, uplift

ANTONYMS: lower, cast down, humble, degrade, demote, depose

9. extort (ek stôrt′)

(*v.*) to obtain by violence, misuse of authority, or threats

The kidnappers tried to ____________ a huge sum of money in return for releasing their prisoners unharmed.

SYNONYMS: blackmail, coerce, bilk, "shake down"

10. far-fetched (fär fecht′)

(*adj.*) strained or improbable (in the sense of not being logical or believable), going far afield from a topic

No one will believe the ____________ excuse you just gave!

SYNONYMS: unlikely, hard to swallow

ANTONYMS: likely, probable, plausible, credible

11. glum (gləm)

(*adj.*) depressed, gloomy

The losing team wore ____________ expressions on their faces as the final buzzer sounded.

SYNONYMS: dejected, morose, melancholy

ANTONYMS: cheerful, merry, rosy, sunny

12. replica (rep′ lə kə)

(*n.*) a copy, close reproduction

We visited a life-size ____________ of the *Mayflower*, the Pilgrim ship docked near Plymouth, Massachusetts.

SYNONYMS: duplicate, imitation

ANTONYMS: original, prototype

13. responsive (ri spän′ siv)

(*adj.*) answering or replying; reacting readily to requests, suggestions, etc.; showing interest and understanding

The host of the charming inn was ____________ to our every wish.

SYNONYMS: sympathetic, open, receptive

ANTONYMS: insensitive, unsympathetic

14. sanctuary (saŋk′ chə wer ē)

(*n.*) a sacred or holy place; refuge or protection from capture or punishment; a place of refuge or protection

The exhausted refugees found ________________ in a local church.

SYNONYMS: shrine, haven

15. self-seeking (self sēk′ iŋ)

(*adj.*) selfishly ambitious

That ________________ politician will promise just about anything to win a few more votes.

SYNONYMS: selfish, opportunistic, gold-digging
ANTONYMS: unselfish, selfless, altruistic

16. submissive (səb mis′ iv)

(*adj.*) humbly obedient; tending to give in to authority, obeying without protest

In some cultures, boys and men still expect girls and women to behave in a totally ________________ manner.

SYNONYMS: meek, compliant, servile, subservient
ANTONYMS: rebellious, defiant, insubordinate

17. tally (tal′ ē)

(*v.*) to count up; to keep score; to make entries for reckoning; to correspond or agree; (*n.*) a total or score

They will ________________ the votes after 9:00 P.M.

Our teacher keeps an accurate ________________ of all of our absences.

SYNONYMS: (*v., n.*) total, record

18. taskmaster (task′ mas tər)

(*n.*) one whose job it is to assign work to others; one who uses his or her power to make people work very hard

The crusty old boss was a harsh ________________ but also an efficient manager.

SYNONYMS: supervisor, overseer

19. transform (trans fôrm′)

(*v.*) to change completely in appearance or form; to make into something else

A heavy rain could ________________ the parched yellow fields into a lush green landscape again.

SYNONYMS: alter, convert
ANTONYMS: maintain, preserve

20. upheaval (əp hēv′ əl)

(*n.*) a sudden, violent upward movement; great disorder or radical change

The sudden change in leadership caused dramatic social and economic ________________.

SYNONYMS: confusion, disruption, chaos
ANTONYMS: tranquility, peace and quiet

Choosing the Right Word

*Select the **boldface** word that better completes each sentence. You might refer to the unit selection to see how most of these words are used in context.*

1. In Robert Louis Stevenson's classic story, a chemical potion (**tallies, transforms**) the good Dr. Jekyll into the evil Mr. Hyde.

Scottish writer Robert Louis Stevenson was especially known for his adventure novels *Treasure Island* and *Kidnapped*.

2. He enjoys (**abstaining, enumerating**) all the factors that enabled him to rise from poverty to great wealth, but he always omits the important element of luck.

3. I didn't have time to write a letter to Lucy, but I (**appended, enumerated**) a few sentences to my sister's letter, expressing my congratulations.

4. My trainer wants me to (**abstain, enumerate**) from eating highly processed foods, especially those made with sugar and wheat.

5. We cannot have a peaceful and just society so long as any one group is required to be (**responsive, submissive**) to another.

6. When he felt low, he found that singing (**exalted, amalgamated**) his spirits.

7. Each member of the basketball team was awarded a trophy to (**transform, commemorate**) the championship season.

8. On the weekends, my parents are (**taskmasters, upheavals**), handing out lists of chores for all the children to do.

9. Financiers are planning to (**accommodate, amalgamate**) various businesses in the United States and England into one huge multinational corporation.

10. Ms. Wilentz is the kind of manager who does not try to (**extort, exalt**) cooperation from the people under her, but earns it by being a real leader.

11. Isn't it a little (**far-fetched, self-seeking**) to suggest that the pollution of our environment is mainly caused by creatures from outer space?

12. Nina is not very (**submissive, responsive**) to the idea of hiking up Mt. Kilimanjaro for her honeymoon.

13. Experience has taught me that people who constantly boast about their unselfishness are often secretly quite (**submissive, self-seeking**).

14. After a complete makeover, the scruffy young man was (**exalted, transformed**) into a distinguished-looking gentleman.

15. The detective's suspicion was aroused when the suspect's story failed to (**tally, commemorate**) with the known facts of the case.

16. The mayor had to choose between (**allegiance, tally**) to his political party and his judgment of what was best for the city.

17. The United States has a long history of providing (**upheaval, sanctuary**) to those fleeing persecution abroad.

18. If you look so (**far-fetched, glum**) just because you can't go to the party, how are you going to react when something really bad happens?

19. Unless the poor people of the country see some hope of improving their lives, there will probably soon be a great social (**sanctuary, upheaval**).

20. The new hotel is spacious enough to (**accommodate, extort**) large groups of people attending conventions and banquets.

21. Only seven members of the Security Council voted on the resolution; the others (**abstained, tallied**).

22. Instead of working so hard to prepare (**replicas, allegiances**) of famous works of art, why don't you try to create something original?

23. Because she sets extremely high standards for herself and is always pushing herself to do better, she is her own most severe (**taskmaster, replica**).

24. It remains to be seen how (**glum, responsive**) the students will be to the new method of teaching mathematics.

25. To (**tally, commemorate**) Paul Bunyan's birthday, my uncle made flapjacks.

Synonyms

*Choose the word from this Unit that is the same or most nearly the same in meaning as the **boldface** word or expression in the phrase. Write that word on the line. Use a dictionary if necessary.*

1. **acclaimed** as a standard of beauty ______________
2. as **itemized** on the packing slip ______________
3. a **model** of the space shuttle ______________
4. an arrogant and **egotistical** person ______________
5. lit candles in the quiet **place of worship** ______________
6. fear of displeasing the **overseer** ______________
7. has clearly proven his **devotion** ______________
8. chose to **refrain** from voting ______________
9. to **house** an exchange student from Senegal ______________
10. how to **threaten** innocent victims ______________

Antonyms

*Choose the word from this Unit that is most nearly opposite in meaning to the **boldface** word or expression in the phrase. Write that word on the line. Use a dictionary if necessary.*

1. submitting a **novel idea** ______________________
2. **treat yourself to** a banana split ______________________
3. meant to **randomize** the instructions ______________________
4. never question a **noble** gesture ______________________
5. reputation for **donating** money ______________________

Completing the Sentence

From the words in this Unit, choose the one that best completes each of the following sentences. Write the correct word form in the space provided.

1. I love basketball games, but I have decided to ______________________ from attending them until I can get my grades up to where they should be.

2. Imagine how ______________________ we felt when a sudden wave of warm weather melted all the snow and ruined our plans for a winter carnival!

3. Is there anything more despicable than trying to ______________________ money from innocent people by threatening them with bodily harm?

4. Remember that the Pledge of ______________________ is not a formula to be repeated mechanically but a summary of our sacred duty to our country.

5. On Memorial Day, Americans gather in ceremonies across the country to ______________________ the nation's war dead.

6. Every entertainer likes a(n) ______________________ audience that shows it appreciates and enjoys a performance.

7. I know that Mother has given you all kinds of instructions before you leave for camp, but let me ______________________ some extra advice of my own.

8. Anne usually seems to be quiet and ______________________, but she has a way of flaring up when she feels that anyone is being unfair to her.

9. Can you see why it was logical for various labor unions in the clothing and textile industries to ______________________ into a single organization?

10. Under the U.S. Constitution, officials are never ______________________ to a point where they are more important or more powerful than the law.

11. Good employees don't need a(n) ________________ to keep them working.

12. In just a few years, she was ________________ from an awkward tomboy into a charming young woman.

13. The driving instructor ________________ carefully the bad habits and practices that are likely to lead to accidents.

14. We learned in our science class how ________________ of Earth's crust has resulted in the formation of mountains.

15. Though an injured hand kept Larry from actually bowling, he took part in the tournament by keeping a careful ________________ of the scores.

16. I enjoyed the first part of the detective story, but the surprise ending was so ________________ that I couldn't accept it.

17. When we visited New York City, we bought a small ________________ of the Statue of Liberty as a memento of our trip.

18. I would like to ________________ you, but I don't think it is right to allow you to copy my homework.

19. A portion of the forest has been set aside as a bird ________________ for the protection of endangered species in the area.

20. When Ben Franklin said, "God helps those who help themselves," he did not mean that the most important thing in life is to be ________________.

Writing: Words in Action

1. Look back at "Madam C.J. Walker and Her Wonderful Remedy" (pages 174–175). Suppose you are a sales representative. You want to persuade your company to sell Walker's beauty products. Write a persuasive proposal stating why the products would enhance company sales. Use at least two details from the passage and three Unit words.

2. Madam Walker received many honors for her extraordinary accomplishments. How would you honor a deserving citizen? In a letter to a local commemoration committee, nominate a person. Explain why this person deserves to be recognized and explain how you would like to honor him or her. Highlight the individual's accomplishments and contributions to the community. Support your letter with specific examples from your observations, personal experience, and the reading (refer to pages 174–175). Write at least three paragraphs, and use three or more words from this Unit.

Vocabulary in Context

Literary Text

The following excerpts are from The Life and Adventures of Nicholas Nickleby *by Charles Dickens. Some of the words you have studied in this Unit appear in* ***boldface*** *type. Complete each statement below the excerpt by circling the letter of the correct answer.*

1. At length, the two money-lenders obtained shelter in a house next door, and, being **accommodated** with a ladder, clambered over the wall of the back-yard—which was not a high one—and descended in safety on the other side.

If a person is **accommodated**, he or she is

a. hidden **c.** shaken down
b. disrespected **d.** helped out

2. "To put him," said Madame Mantalini, looking at Ralph, and prudently **abstaining** from the slightest glance at her husband, lest his many graces should induce her to falter in her resolution, "to put him upon a fixed allowance . . ."

The act of **abstaining** involves

a. escaping **c.** encouraging
b. avoiding **d.** glaring

3. "John, why don't you say something?"

"Say summat?" repeated the Yorkshireman.

"Ay, and not sit there so silent and **glum**."

People who are **glum** are NOT

a. cheery **c.** proud
b. sullen **d.** polite

A scene from a 6.5-hour-long stage version of *The Life and Adventures of Nicholas Nickleby* at the Gielgud Theatre in London, 2010.

4. With such expressions of sorrow, Miss Petowker went on to **enumerate** the dear friends of her youthful days one by one, and to call upon such of them as were present to come and embrace her.

To **enumerate** one's friends, one

a. avoids them **c.** calls on them
b. praises them **d.** counts them

5. "The ties of nature are strong. The weak husband and the father—the father that is yet to be relents. I apologize."

"Humbly and **submissively**?" said Nicholas.

"Humbly and submissively," returned the tragedian, scowling upwards.

An apology made **submissively** is made

a. curtly **c.** obediently
b. enthusiastically **d.** boldly

Interactive Quiz

Snap the code, or go to **SadlierConnect.com**.

*Read the following passage, taking note of the **boldface** words and their contexts. These words are among those you will be studying in Unit 15. As you complete the exercises in this unit, it may help to refer to the way the words are used below.*

Running With the Big Dogs

<Magazine Article>

Throughout history, humans have depended on working guard dogs to protect and herd their animal flocks. For centuries, these dogs have served as **beacons** of protection. A well-trained guard dog is probably the most sensible **precaution** a shepherd or rancher can take to protect his herds against dangerous **encounters** with wolves or bears. The size, strength, and speed of three breeds shed some light on their ability to **retaliate** fiercely against attackers.

First is the Great Pyrenees. This truly massive breed takes its name from the Pyrenees—mountains located between France and Spain. Comparative **data** show that this is one of the largest of the flock guardians. A Great Pyrenees may stand as high as 32 inches and weigh up to 130 pounds. The medium-long, snow-white coat is sometimes shaded with gray or tan. The Great Pyrenees's coat blends in with a flock of sheep or goats and functions as a **sham**. Would-be attackers often do not suspect that the large white shape among the herd animals is really a protector of **epic** courage and strength. A Pyrenees will stop at nothing to **chasten**, or even kill, any invader threatening his flock.

It does not **detract** from the Pyrenees's awesome reputation to note that it is easily trained and especially patient with children. This makes the Pyrenees a **wholesome** household pet. The breed combines safety, affection, and beauty.

Great Pyrenees guard sheep and goats.

Like the Great Pyrenees, the Komondor sheepdog of Hungary enjoys the benefit of camouflage. A Komondor's white coat is doubly protective because it is corded from head to tail. The breed's tangled and woolly coat perfectly enables it to **prosecute** its mission of guarding a flock. Potential predators do not suspect the strength that lurks beneath those ropy cords. In addition, the Komondor's seemingly **uncouth** jacket guards it against the fangs and claws of **berserk** enemies. Finally, a Komondor's coat superbly insulates it against harsh weather.

A Komondor is only slightly smaller than a Great Pyrenees. Males stand up to 28 inches high and may weigh 100 pounds or more. With a large head and a long, agile stride, the Komondor is truly a majestic animal.

The Komondor dog and a Leicester sheep

Farther east in Europe, the Turkish Kangal Dog offers a third canine example of outstanding strength and courage. Largely unknown outside Turkey, the Kangal is prized in its homeland as a national treasure. The photograph below **underscores** several typical characteristics of the breed. Like a Pyrenees and a Komondor, a Kangal blends in with the herd. This dog is short-coated and almost always exhibits a black mask and ears. The legs are large-boned and well-muscled, and the tail is curled. The breed's homeland is the rugged steppe, or prairie, of east-central Turkey. Unlike the Great Pyrenees and the Komondor, coated in **celestial** white, the Kangal usually sports a gray or tan-colored coat. The very appearance of a Kangal projects authority. Any illusions that attackers of the herd may harbor will surely be **punctured** if a Kangal is on duty.

Readers can find out more about each of these breeds. Nationally recognized breed associations are located throughout the country.

Inez P. Farquar is a regular contributor to Dog Days *magazine. When she's not playing fetch with her two terriers, Ms. Farquar volunteers at her local animal shelter.*

Audio

For Words and audio passages, snap the code, or go to **SadlierConnect.com**.

The Turkish Kangal Dog guarding goats

Definitions

Note the spelling, pronunciation, part(s) of speech, and definition(s) of each of the following words. Then write the word in the blank spaces in the illustrative sentence(s) following. Finally, study the lists of synonyms and antonyms.

1. beacon (bē′ kən)

(*n.*) a light or other signal that warns and guides; a lighthouse; anything that guides or inspires

Sailors returning to port on a dark night search for the glow of a familiar ______________.

SYNONYMS: beam, flare

2. berserk (bər sərk′)

(*adj., adv.*) violently and destructively enraged

A ______________ man terrified the crowd of subway riders.

The wounded lion went ______________ in his cage.

SYNONYMS: (*adj.*) mad, deranged
ANTONYMS: (*adj.*) sane, rational

3. celestial (sə les′ chəl)

(*adj.*) having to do with the sky or heavens; heavenly; yielding great bliss or happiness

The sun is the brightest ______________ body in our solar system.

SYNONYMS: ethereal, stellar, blissful
ANTONYMS: earthly, terrestrial, infernal

4. chasten (chā′ sən)

(*v.*) to punish (in order to bring about improvement in behavior, attitude, etc.); to restrain, moderate

Dad knows how to ______________ the stubborn child with a firm but soothing voice.

SYNONYMS: discipline, temper
ANTONYMS: praise, commend, reward

5. confiscate (kän′ fə skāt)

(*v.*) to seize by authority; to take and keep

The police will ______________ that car.

SYNONYMS: commandeer, expropriate
ANTONYMS: return, reinstate

6. data (dā′ tə)

(*pl. n.*) information; facts, figures, statistics

For math class, we collected ______________ on the Internet sites students visited during the past week.

7. detract (di trakt′)

(*v.*) to take away from; reduce in value or reputation

Nothing can ______________ from your beauty!

SYNONYMS: subtract from, lower
ANTONYMS: increase, heighten, enhance

8. encounter (en kaủn′ tər)

(*n.*) a meeting (especially one that is unplanned); a meeting of enemies, battle; (*v.*) to meet or come upon

Remember our ________________ with that skunk?

We might ________________ other curious animals.

SYNONYMS: (*n.*) confrontation; (*v.*) happen upon
ANTONYMS: (*v.*) avoid, sidestep

9. epic (ep′ ik)

(*n.*) a long narrative poem (or other literary composition) about the deeds of heroes; an event or movement of great sweep; (*adj.*) on a grand scale, vast, titanic

Beowulf, the English ________________, was written around the year 700.

It describes ________________ struggles between the forces of good and evil.

SYNONYMS: (*n.*) saga, chronicle

10. pantomime (pan′ tə mīm)

(*n.*) a play or story performed without words by actors using only gestures; (*v.*) to express in this way

The performer included a short ________________.

We ________________ when we're unable to speak.

SYNONYMS: (*n.*) mime show, dumb show

11. pessimist (pes′ ə mist)

(*n.*) one who believes or expects the worst; prophet of doom

A ________________ sees a glass as half empty.

SYNONYM: killjoy; ANTONYMS: optimist, Pollyanna

12. precaution (pri kô′ shən)

(*n.*) care taken beforehand; a step or action taken to prevent something from happening

I advise you to take every ________________ necessary to prevent a household fire.

SYNONYMS: foresight, prudence, safeguard
ANTONYMS: recklessness, heedlessness

13. prosecute (präs′ ə kyüt)

(*v.*) to bring before a court of law for trial; to carry out

She was told she would not be ________________ if she restored the money.

SYNONYMS: put on trial, pursue; ANTONYMS: defend, abandon

14. puncture (pəŋk′ chər)

(*n.*) a small hole made by a sharp object; (*v.*) to make such a hole, pierce

The ________________ caused the balloon to explode.

I tried not to wince as the hypodermic needle ________________ my skin.

SYNONYM: (*n.*) perforation

15. retaliate (ri tal′ ē āt)

(*v.*) to get revenge; to strike back for an injury

I would ____________________ for that cheap insult, but I fear it may only make matters worse.

SYNONYMS: pay back, get even with
ANTONYMS: pardon, forgive, turn the other cheek

16. sham (sham)

(*adj.*) fake, not genuine; (*n.*) something false pretending to be genuine; a pretender; a decorated pillow covering; (*v.*) to pretend

The play includes a ____________________ fight scene.

Her claim that she's a princess is a ____________________.

Don't ____________________ an illness in order to miss a day of school.

SYNONYMS: (*adj.*) phony, counterfeit; (*n.*) fraud
ANTONYMS: (*adj.*) authentic, bona fide

17. uncouth (ən küth′)

(*adj.*) unrefined, crude; awkward or clumsy

Although the quality of his work was good, his ____________________ attitude cost him the job.

SYNONYMS: boorish, graceless
ANTONYMS: refined, polished, graceful, genteel

18. underscore (ən′ dər skôr)

(*v.*) to draw a line under; to put special emphasis on; (*n.*) a line drawn under something

The dire situation in the hospital's emergency room ____________________ the importance of having enough doctors and nurses available.

The word with the ____________________ is in Spanish.

SYNONYMS: (*v.*) underline, stress, accent
ANTONYMS: (*v.*) downplay, de-emphasize, soft-pedal

19. wholesome (hōl′ səm)

(*adj.*) healthy; morally and socially sound and good; helping to bring about or preserve good health

He always eats ____________________ foods.

SYNONYMS: nourishing, beneficial
ANTONYMS: harmful, unhealthy, baneful

20. wistful (wist′ fəl)

(*adj.*) full of melancholy yearning or longing, sad, pensive

Her ____________________ look made me sad.

ANTONYMS: happy, contented, satisfied

Choosing the Right Word

*Select the **boldface** word that better completes each sentence. You might refer to the unit selection to see how most of these words are used in context.*

1. Laura Ingalls Wilder wrote a series of children's books that describe the (**celestial, epic**) story of Western migration.

2. Is it right to (**retaliate, confiscate**) against an evil act by performing evil acts of one's own?

3. The youth center was a (**precaution, beacon**) to young people seeking help and guidance.

4. My first (**encounter, data**) with the new neighbors was amicable, and I believed we were all going to become good friends.

5. As I watched through the soundproof hospital window, the skaters on the pond seemed to be carrying out a colorful (**pantomime, epic**).

6. The news that I had been dropped from the football squad (**detracted, punctured**) my dream of becoming a great gridiron hero.

7. Parents who fail to (**chasten, detract**) their children for rude, impolite behavior may regret their lenient attitude later.

Laura Ingalls Wilder's "Little House" books are beloved by several generations of readers.

8. My grandmother becomes (**wistful, detracted**) when she recalls her childhood in the Swiss Alps.

9. Marie is not really pretty, but her sparkling personality and (**berserk, wholesome**) charm make her very attractive.

10. She had such a (**celestial, sham**) expression on her face that I thought she'd seen a vision of heaven.

11. I, for one, was extremely offended by the teen's (**underscored, uncouth**) behavior and foul language.

12. Many a perfectly healthy employee has been known to (**retaliate, sham**) illness to avoid going to work.

13. It does not (**prosecute, detract**) in the least from his reputation as a great player to say that all the team members deserve equal credit.

14. For some strange reason, the photocopier suddenly went (**berserk, wistful**) and started spewing vast quantities of paper all over the floor.

15. Although I do not get seasick, I am going to take some anti-motion sickness medication just as a (**precaution, puncture**).

16. The report that he sent to the president of the company (**underscored, retaliated**) the need for better planning and more careful use of funds.

17. I knew that it would be difficult to raise funds for the recycling program, but I never expected to (**chasten, encounter**) so many tough problems.

18. During the long years of defeat, Lincoln searched for a general who would (**prosecute, underscore**) the war fearlessly until the Union was saved.

19. The trouble with being a(n) (**underscore, pessimist**) is that you are so taken up with what is going wrong that you are unaware of what is going right.

20. Before we can plan properly for the upcoming school year, we must have accurate (**beacons, data**) on the results of last year's programs.

21. If you try to smuggle goods into this country without paying the customs duties, the inspectors may (**puncture, confiscate**) the goods and fine you.

22. Our driving instructor has emphasized that the use of seat belts is not a "silly" (**encounter, precaution**) but a surefire way of saving lives.

23. The child gazed (**wistfully, wholesomely**) at the shiny toys in the store window.

24. Her writing style is a little (**pessimistic, uncouth**), but what it lacks in polish and refinement is more than made up for by its wonderful humor.

25. When I want a(n) (**epic, wholesome**) snack, I eat a handful of almonds.

Synonyms

*Choose the word from this Unit that is the same or most nearly the same in meaning as the **boldface** word or expression in the phrase. Write that word on the line. Use a dictionary if necessary.*

1. such a **naysayer** ________________
2. a crowd that is **out of control** ________________
3. should **emphasize** its safety features ________________
4. crowds enjoying the **charade** ________________
5. sure to certify the **numbers** ________________
6. a convincing, yet **made-up** excuse ________________
7. a small **pinprick** in the leather ________________
8. with a strong desire to **avenge** ________________
9. staring with such **heartbreaking** eyes ________________
10. might **impound** our property ________________

Antonyms

*Choose the word from this Unit that is most nearly opposite in meaning to the **boldface** word or expression in the phrase. Write that word on the line. Use a dictionary if necessary.*

1. anticipated your **sensible** behavior ______________________
2. to convey ideas through **talking** ______________________
3. the greeter's **cheerful** demeanor ______________________
4. **idealists** who always share their views ______________________
5. forced to **restore** the leather case ______________________

Completing the Sentence

From the words in this Unit, choose the one that best completes each of the following sentences. Write the correct word form in the space provided.

1. Little did I realize when I ______________________ that old man on a lonely beach that this chance meeting would change my life.
2. In the old days, whippings and other forms of physical punishment were used to ______________________ student misbehavior, even in college.
3. In polite society, it is considered ______________________ to balance peas on your knife at the dinner table.
4. Before we use the blowtorch in our industrial arts class, we are required to take the ______________________ of wearing goggles.
5. The workbook directions instruct the user to ______________________ the subject of each sentence in red and the predicate in blue.
6. My definition of a(n) ______________________ is someone who worries about the hole in the doughnut and forgets about the cake surrounding it.
7. Over the years, a great many ships have been saved from destruction by that tall ______________________ standing on the rocky coast.
8. Though many people doubted that the new program would do any real good, I thought it was a very ______________________ development.
9. Now that we have gathered a vast number of ______________________, it is up to us to draw some useful conclusions from all this information.
10. When she said she would "turn the other cheek," she simply meant that she would not ______________________ for the injury done to her.

11. So there I was with a(n) ____________________ in one of my rear tires, on a lonely road, on a dark night, and during a violent rainstorm!

12. The police have done their job in arresting the suspect; now it is up to the district attorney to ____________________ him and prove his guilt.

13. Late that afternoon, one of the inmates went ____________________ and totally wrecked the infirmary.

14. With a(n) ____________________ expression on his face, the prisoner looked through his cell window at the patch of sky that meant freedom to him.

15. Although he could speak no English, he made us understand by the use of ____________________ that he was extremely thirsty.

16. Isn't it remarkable that a(n) ____________________ poem such as *The Iliad*, written almost 3,000 years ago, still has interest for readers today?

17. Nothing can ____________________ from the fact that he stood by us in our hour of greatest need.

18. After the war, all the property that had been ____________________ by the government was turned back to its former owners.

19. In ancient times, people gazed at the sky and studied the planets and other ____________________ bodies to predict the future.

20. Freedom of speech is a(n) ____________________ and a mockery if it does not apply to people whose opinions are very unpopular.

Writing: Words in Action

1. Look back at "Running with the Big Dogs" (pages 184–185). Suppose that you are a herder who must choose one of the three dog breeds discussed in the essay—Great Pyrenees, the Komondor, or the Kangal—to protect your herd. You must convince your family that your choice is correct. Write a letter to your family in which you support your choice of herding dog using at least two details from the passage and three Unit words.

2. Dogs have held important jobs over the years. They herd and protect farm animals; they help guide the blind; they serve in the military and assist fire fighters and police officers; and they rescue people after disasters. Write a brief essay about how dogs help humans. Include specific examples, observations, studies, the reading (refer to pages 184–185), or personal experience. Write at least three paragraphs, and use three or more words from this Unit.

Vocabulary in Context

Literary Text

*The following excerpts are from "The Legend of Sleepy Hollow" by Washington Irving. Some of the words you have studied in this Unit appear in **boldface** type. Complete each statement below the excerpt by circling the letter of the correct answer.*

1. Such was one of the favorite haunts of the Headless Horseman, and the place where he was most frequently **encountered**.

   Whenever someone is **encountered**, he or she is

   a. surprised **c.** come upon
   b. inspired **d.** taken down

2. What fearful shapes and shadows beset his path, amidst the dim and ghastly glare of a snowy night! With what **wistful** look did he eye every trembling ray of light streaming across the waste fields from some distant window!

   A **wistful** look is one that is

   a. satisfied **c.** ashamed
   b. brooding **d.** mischievous

3. How often did he shrink with curdling awe at the sound of his own steps on the frosty crust beneath his feet; and dread to look over his shoulder, lest he should behold some **uncouth** being tramping close behind him!

   Something that is **uncouth** is NOT

   a. coarse **c.** courageous
   b. clumsy **d.** cultured

Schoolteacher Ichabod Crane being pursued by the Headless Horseman in an illustration by Frances Brundage.

4. All this he called "doing his duty by their parents"; and he never inflicted a **chastisement** without following it by the assurance, so consolatory to the smarting urchin, that "he would remember it and thank him for it the longest day he had to live."

   A **chastisement** is a(n)

   a. suspicion **c.** affection
   b. punishment **d.** weakness

5. Could that girl have been playing off any of her coquettish tricks? Was her encouragement of the poor pedagogue all a mere **sham** to secure her conquest of his rival?

   A **sham** is a

   a. deception **c.** lesson
   b. collection **d.** fashion

Interactive Quiz

Snap the code, or go to **SadlierConnect.com**.

Vocabulary for Comprehension

Part 1

Read "Goya: A Victim of His Art?," which contains words in ***boldface*** *that appear in Units 13–15. Then answer the questions.*

Goya: A Victim of His Art?

The masterful Spanish painter Francisco de Goya (1746–1828) **coped** with strange bouts of illness at various times in his life. Might his illness have explained the dramatic changes in his work? His early paintings were gentle and bright. His graceful portraits were lovely. But over time, his work grew dark, **wistful**, and moody. He began to paint angry, pessimistic scenes in thick, dark colors. Art historians have long debated the reasons for this shift in Goya's style. Could it have been his health?

Modern science has evidence to suggest that Goya may have had a severe case of lead poisoning. High levels of lead in the bloodstream can cause muscle and joint pains, headaches, hearing loss, dizziness, mental distress, nausea, deranged conduct, personality changes, and finally, death. This list **tallies** with the list of symptoms that Goya suffered.

Goya's **disquieting** symptoms forced him to take breaks from painting. When he felt well enough to return to painting, he would rush back to his studio. There he would grind pigments again and paint enthusiastically to make up for the **lag** in his output.

Like most artists of the past, Goya made his paints himself. Grinding the pigments put him at risk of inhaling lead dust and getting it in his eyes, mouth, and ears, and on his skin. Goya also sometimes applied lead-based pigments to his canvas using only his fingers, so he could have absorbed the lead through his skin, as well.

Goya was known to use an unusual amount of a pigment called *lead white*. This pigment commonly consisted of two forms of lead combined simply with vinegar. Many of the great masters used lead white because it was durable, dried quickly, and maintained a fresh appearance. Although other artists risked lead poisoning, few used as much lead white as Goya did. Lead white gave Goya's works their characteristic pearly glow. But it also made him sick.

Lead poisoning is not unheard of among the great artists of the past. In fact, lead poisoning is a suspected cause of the illness of famous artist Vincent Van Gogh (1853–1890). Another highly regarded painter, Candido Portinari (1903–1962), was diagnosed with lead poisoning seven years before his death. Unfortunately for Goya, modern medical understanding of the toxic effects of lead did not emerge until the late 1800s.

It no longer seems **far-fetched** to think that Goya's physical condition changed his artistic vision. One can only wonder how modern medical knowledge might have prevented his illness and allowed him to express his later genius.

1. What does the word **coped** mean as it is used in line 3?
   A) discovered
   B) suffered from
   C) dealt with
   D) avoided

2. Why does the author **most likely** include the two rhetorical questions in lines 4–6 and lines 14–15?
   A) to challenge the reader
   B) to later refute these questions with the facts
   C) to explain the structure of the passage
   D) to set the focus for the entire passage

3. **Part A**
   What is the meaning of **tallies** as it appears in line 24?
   A) totals
   B) agrees
   C) degrades
   D) merges

   Part B
   Which sentence from "Goya: A Victim of His Art?" provides the **best** clue to the meaning of the word **tallies**?
   A) "early paintings were gentle" (lines 6–7)
   B) "graceful portraits were lovely" (line 8)
   C) "reasons for this shift in Goya's style" (lines 13–14)
   D) "evidence to suggest" (lines 16–17)

4. As used in line 26, what does the word **disquieting** suggest about Goya's symptoms?
   A) They were disturbing.
   B) They were hard to describe.
   C) They were surprising.
   D) They were unusual.

5. What is the author's **most likely** reason for including lines 44–56?
   A) to praise other great artists who used lead-based pigments
   B) to list symptoms of lead poisoning
   C) to strengthen the argument that Goya's symptoms were those of severe lead poisoning
   D) to describe lead-based pigments in detail

6. Which word means the opposite of **far-fetched** as used in line 70?
   A) plausible
   B) shocking
   C) sympathetic
   D) improbable

7. Which of the following **best** outlines the structure of this passage?
   A) Goya's later work, lead poisoning, Goya's symptoms
   B) changes in Goya's work, symptoms, lead-based pigments, lead poisoning
   C) Goya's biography, lead poisoning
   D) lead-based pigments, lead poisoning

8. Which statement about the author's point of view is **best** supported by "Goya: A Victim of His Art"?
   A) The author believes that Goya is Spain's greatest genius.
   B) The author is horrified by Goya's many physical symptoms.
   C) The author thinks that Goya's later paintings are superior to his early work.
   D) The author suspects that severe lead poisoning caused great changes in Goya's work.

Vocabulary for Comprehension

Part 2

*Read this passage, which contains words in **boldface** that appear in Units 13–15. Then choose the best answer to each question based on what is stated or implied in the passage. You may refer to the passage as often as necessary.*

Questions 1–8 are based on the following passage.

Although some people believe that the term "modern" in modern architecture relates to a contemporary period of design, that is a **misapprehension**. Modern refers to a specific **trait** of architecture that was dominant from the mid-nineteenth century to the 1970s. Modern architecture emphasizes shape, form, light, and transparency rather than ornate embellishments. Industrial metals like steel, concrete, and glass give modern architecture its distinctive look. The style is defined by clean lines and minimalist interiors. Modern architects let the design speak for itself. Therefore, they do not add **supplements** to enhance the design. Many modern designs have angular roof lines and vaulted ceilings and their blueprints have fewer walls and create open living spaces. Modern architecture also asserts that design should be **submissive** to nature rather than dominating it.

The architect most commonly associated with modernism is Frank Lloyd Wright. Early in his career, Wright worked with Louis Sullivan. Sullivan was an American architect known as "the father of skyscrapers." Sullivan dreamed of identifying a uniquely American style of architecture. Through his **encounters** with Sullivan, Wright was later able to **transform** this dream into reality. In 1893, Wright designed the Winslow House in River Forest, Illinois. The house had expansive, open interior spaces, and it represented Wright's style, which would later be known as "organic architecture."

In 1915, the Japanese emperor commissioned Wright to design the Imperial Hotel in Tokyo. Wright created a modernist masterpiece while taking several **precautions** to ensure that the building was earthquake proof. After the Great Kanto earthquake of 1923 decimated the city, Wright's Imperial Hotel was the only large building to survive the earthquake. In the mid-1930s, Wright was commissioned to build a house for a family in Pennsylvania. This home, called Fallingwater, is distinguished by its several balconies and terraces built on top of a waterfall. This home is one of Wright's most notable works, and it remains a national landmark.

In 1934, Wright began the project that would consume the next 16 years of his life: designing the Guggenheim Museum in New York City. After 700 sketches and 6 working drawings for the building, Wright achieved his goal. Visitors to this building are **stupefied** by its white cylindrical exterior and all of the other geometric shapes that comprise the internal structure. There was some artistic **upheaval** after the building was designed. These artists believed that the exterior of the building should not overpower the art inside it. Nonetheless, the Guggenheim Museum still stands, decades after Wright's death, as a modernist marvel and an architectural **beacon** for all who see it.

1. As it is used in line 5, "misapprehension" most nearly means
   A) misunderstanding.
   B) miscalculation.
   C) misgiving.
   D) misfortune.

2. The author includes lines 8–25 to
   A) name some of the significant buildings that use modern architecture.
   B) distinguish modern architecture from previous forms of architecture.
   C) reveal the philosophy that guides modern architecture.
   D) describe some of the important features of modern architecture.

3. As it is used in line 24, "submissive" most nearly means
   A) subversive.
   B) subservient.
   C) subterranean.
   D) substitute.

4. Why does a passage about modernism have information about Frank Lloyd Wright?
   A) Wright worked with "the father of skyscrapers."
   B) Wright's style was "organic architecture."
   C) Wright identified a uniquely American style of architecture.
   D) Wright is a famous modernist architect.

5. Which choice provides the best evidence for the answer to the previous question?
   A) Lines 26–28 ("The architect ... Wright")
   B) Lines 30–31 ("Sullivan ... skyscrapers'")
   C) Lines 32–34 ("Sullivan ... architecture")
   D) Lines 38–42 ("The ... architecture'")

6. What is the meaning of the word "encounters" as it is used in line 34?
   A) auditions
   B) sidesteps
   C) meetings
   D) fights

7. The author implies that it took Wright 16 years to design the Guggenheim Museum because
   A) designing a cylindrical exterior had never been accomplished previously.
   B) it was a complex project that involved 700 sketches and 6 working drawings.
   C) he was concerned about the artistic upheaval that his designs received.
   D) he was ambivalent about the geometrical interior of the building.

8. What is the main idea of the passage?
   A) Wright designed several buildings, including the Imperial Hotel, Fallingwater, and the Guggenheim.
   B) Designing the Guggenheim Museum was Wright's highest achievement.
   C) Modernism's influence on Wright was evident in his designs.
   D) Wright transformed modernism into an architectural movement.

Denotation and Connotation

Words have two kinds of meanings. **Denotation** refers to the word's literal meaning, which you'll find in a dictionary entry. The denotation conveys a neutral tone.

Connotations are the emotional and cultural associations that people make to words. These associations are the "shades of meaning" we perceive in words that have similar, but not identical, denotations. A connotation can have a positive or negative tone.

Consider these synonyms for the word *copy:*

replica *facsimile* *sham* *fraud*

Replica and *facsimile* have neutral connotations, while *sham* and *fraud* have deeply negative connotations.

Think: A museum might display a replica or a facsimile of a famous artwork or document, but it would never exhibit a work considered to be a sham or fraud.

Look at these examples of words that are similar in denotation but have different connotations.

NEUTRAL	POSITIVE	NEGATIVE
pronounce	**affirm**	**dictate**
satisfied	**proud**	**self-seeking**
meet	**encounter**	**confront**

Remember that writers choose their words deliberately. They understand that people associate feelings with words. Writers know how to influence their audiences, and thus readers should be mindful of the specific connotations carried by certain words.

Shades of Meaning

Write a plus sign (+) in the box if the word has a positive connotation.
Write a minus sign (–) if the word has a negative connotation.
Put a zero (0) if the word is neutral.

1. mangle ☐ **2.** pantomime ☐ **3.** submissive ☐ **4.** optimist ☐

5. empower ☐ **6.** glum ☐ **7.** data ☐ **8.** beacon ☐

9. commemorate ☐ **10.** recitation ☐ **11.** berserk ☐ **12.** atrocity ☐

13. fluent ☐ **14.** unscrupulous ☐ **15.** celestial ☐ **16.** uncouth ☐

Expressing the Connotation

Read each sentence. Select the word in parentheses that better expresses the connotation (positive, negative, or neutral) given at the beginning of the sentence.

positive **1.** The office manager kept (**promoting, exalting**) her resourceful young assistant, hoping to procure a large raise for her in the next fiscal year.

neutral **2.** Rhonda wants to become a (**taskmaster, manager**) at the hotel when she graduates from school.

positive **3.** I'd like to (**commemorate, remember**) my father with a special gathering on the anniversary of his death.

positive **4.** The professor shared all of her knowledge with her graduate students, hoping to (**empower, help**) them in their future careers.

neutral **5.** In order to (**inflate, supplement**) his income, my uncle took a second job that he could do from home.

negative **6.** Brandi was amused when her host (**mangled, stumbled over**) the pronunciation of her last name.

negative **7.** Several homeowners were suspicious of the man (**wandering, prowling**) around their neighborhood.

negative **8.** Don't let the price (**frighten, deter**) you; this house is really a very good deal, and you won't regret buying it.

Challenge: Using Connotation

*Choose vocabulary words from Units 13–15 to replace the **boldface** words in the sentences below. Then explain how the connotation of the replacement word changes the tone of the sentence.*

sulky	**uncouth**	**abstain**
exalt	**lag**	**responsive**

1. During Lent, many Catholics **withdraw** ______________ from eating meat on Fridays.

____

____

2. Those young actors are very **sensitive** ______________ when the director offers suggestions on how they can improve their performances.

____

____

3. Although Bernie thought that eating with his mouth open was funny, family members found his behavior to be **ill-mannered** ______________.

____

____

Proverbs

The author in the passage about Madam C.J. Walker (see pages 174–175), describing Walker's incentive to sell hair products, uses the old saying "he who hesitates is lost." This proverb means that if someone spends too much time thinking about what action to take, the opportunity will vanish.

A **proverb** is a short saying that conveys a simple truth about life. Proverbs offer wise, everyday advice, and they can be used in many contexts. Many proverbs originate from the Bible, Shakespeare's plays, and other classic literature.

Choosing the Right Proverb

*Read each sentence. Use context clues to figure out the meaning of each proverb in **boldface** print. Then write the letter of the definition for the proverb in the sentence.*

1. **Lightning never strikes twice**, so stop worrying that you're going to fall down on stage again! ________
2. **It's often said that when the cat's away, the mice will play**, but our class always stays on task when our teacher has to leave the room. ________
3. "**Don't change horses in the middle of the stream**, Marie," I said. "Stick to your original topic and finish the report you started writing." ________
4. Joyce lost the debate, but **there's no point in crying over spilt milk**. ________
5. They **never do things by halves** in my uncle's auto repair shop. ________
6. I know you want to blame Eric, but **it takes two to make a quarrel**. ________
7. John should reconsider giving Monique a loan; **lend your money and lose your friend**. ________
8. I'm not upset that Katie's business card looks just like mine; **imitation is the sincerest form of flattery**. ________
9. Knowing that **he who pays the piper calls the tune**, Claude ordered for everyone at the table. ________
10. You should **learn to walk before you run** and stop expecting to paint a masterpiece in your first art class. ________

a. Undertake tasks wholeheartedly.

b. In an argument, both sides share blame.

c. The person who pays the bill decides how to spend the money.

d. Master a skill patiently, step by step.

e. The same misfortune is unlikely to occur twice to the same person.

f. Don't fret over something that has already happened.

g. Avoid making a change after an activity has begun.

h. Lending money to friends can ruin the relationship.

i. Copying someone is an unintended compliment.

j. People take advantage of a situation when there's no supervision.

Classical Roots

pre—before

This Latin prefix appears in **precaution** (page 187). Some other words in which this prefix appears are listed below.

prearrange	**prefer**	**preliminary**	**preoccupy**
precise	**prehistoric**	**premature**	**preside**

From the list of words above, choose the one that corresponds to each of the brief definitions below. Write the word in the blank space in the illustrative sentence below the definition. Use a dictionary if necessary.

1. coming before the main business or action; introductory; something that comes before the main event, a curtain-raiser

Although the young boxer lost the ______________ bout, knowledgeable fans could readily see that he had promise.

2. to like better, choose over something else; to put forward, press

Although many customers ______________ to order healthy appetizers and main courses, restaurant owners report an increased interest in rich desserts.

3. unexpectedly early in development; coming too soon

The expectant mother was alerted to the possibility of a ______________ birth, so she took extra good care of herself.

4. to absorb one's attention completely or at the expense of other things

She was so ______________ with the novel that she forgot to return my phone call.

5. very definite or clear, exact; very careful; strict

The doctor left ______________ instructions on how to clean the wound.

6. to arrange ahead of time

One important task of a travel agent is to ______________ transportation and accommodations so that the client can focus on enjoying the trip.

7. belonging to the period before written history

The museum has a fascinating new exhibit that explains how scientists identify and classify the bones of ______________ animals.

8. to have authority over, oversee

Tomorrow is the first opportunity our principal will have to ______________ at the community school board meeting.

Synonyms

Select the two words or expressions that are most nearly the same in meaning.

1. a. billow	b. surge	c. confer	d. induce
2. a. maneuver	b. liberate	c. manipulate	d. engulf
3. a. keepsake	b. memento	c. pacifist	d. oracle
4. a. outright	b. sheepish	c. ravenous	d. famished
5. a. relish	b. supplement	c. gloat	d. infuriate
6. a. accommodate	b. pry	c. empower	d. authorize
7. a. replenish	b. saunter	c. balk	d. amble
8. a. titanic	b. stealthy	c. meteoric	d. immense
9. a. contemporary	b. compliant	c. submissive	d. rigorous
10. a. waylay	b. stupefy	c. compress	d. compact
11. a. numb	b. limber	c. nimble	d. celestial
12. a. fidelity	b. consequence	c. allegiance	d. synopsis
13. a. deluge	b. cascade	c. queue	d. enigma
14. a. prowl	b. besiege	c. immerse	d. douse
15. a. tally	b. confront	c. vacate	d. encounter

Antonyms

Select the two words that are most nearly opposite in meaning.

16. a. detract	b. enumerate	c. append	d. confiscate
17. a. optional	b. acute	c. taut	d. bumbling
18. a. giddy	b. maximum	c. minimum	d. mortal
19. a. jovial	b. glum	c. immobile	d. smug
20. a. depict	b. acquit	c. wither	d. thrive
21. a. deter	b. cringe	c. motivate	d. bluster
22. a. pessimist	b. optimist	c. responsive	d. incalculable
23. a. dole	b. vow	c. prevaricate	d. ruffle
24. a. replica	b. innovation	c. sham	d. trait
25. a. retrieve	b. denounce	c. idolize	d. expend

Analogies

Select the item that best completes the comparison.

26. chain saw is to **topple** as
- **a.** pickax is to irk
- **b.** bulldozer is to befuddle
- **c.** trowel is to scan
- **d.** fungus is to blight

27. exalt is to **higher** as
- **a.** deem is to higher
- **b.** debase is to lower
- **c.** lag is to higher
- **d.** persevere is to lower

28. inhabitant is to **settled** as
- **a.** orphan is to disinterested
- **b.** citizen is to abominable
- **c.** homebody is to gory
- **d.** vagabond is to wandering

29. thankful is to **ingratitude** as
- **a.** unrepentant is to remorse
- **b.** ambiguous is to uncertainty
- **c.** belligerent is to strife
- **d.** eternal is to duration

30. inept is to **bungle** as
- **a.** sensitive is to strand
- **b.** aggressive is to pacify
- **c.** frugal is to conserve
- **d.** amiable is to insult

31. fear is to **intimidate** as
- **a.** dirt is to scour
- **b.** force is to quash
- **c.** trust is to discredit
- **d.** argument is to verge

32. serene is to **stormy** as
- **a.** boisterous is to quiet
- **b.** petty is to trifling
- **c.** martial is to warlike
- **d.** global is to universal

33. vegetable is to **perishable** as
- **a.** argument is to logical
- **b.** pet is to gullible
- **c.** iron is to durable
- **d.** clown is to sinister

Two-Word Completions

To complete the sentences, select the best word pair from among the choices given.

34. The league's referees have begun ____________ stricter rules about the use of ____________ signals during a game.
- **a.** foiling . . . resourceful
- **b.** commemorating . . . burly
- **c.** designating . . . wholesome
- **d.** implementing . . . illicit

35. Taking the ____________ to make friends with new students at school can really help them ____________ the changes happening in their lives.
- **a.** initiative . . . cope with
- **b.** terrain . . . abstain from
- **c.** onset . . . repent
- **d.** illusion . . . tarry

36. Doesn't it make you a(n) ____________ to expect that she pay you back right away when it often takes you a month to ____________ someone?
- **a.** sage . . . constrain
- **b.** hypocrite . . . reimburse
- **c.** nonconformist . . . prosecute
- **d.** atrocity . . . refurbish

37. It is a bad idea to ____________ breakfast in the morning, because you will probably find yourself ____________ and tired later in the day.
- **a.** cede . . . inflammatory
- **b.** rummage through . . . sulky
- **c.** skimp on . . . sluggish
- **d.** dissect . . . strapping

Supplying Words in Context

To complete each sentence, select the best word from among the choices given. Not all words in the word bank will be used. You may modify the word form as necessary.

arid	**devastate**	**prevail**	**retaliate**
beacon	**encompass**	**puncture**	**sabotage**
culprit	**facet**	**refute**	**subordinate**
debut	**maze**	**rendezvous**	**variable**

38. Now that the two candidates have finished their long, hard campaigns, it is up to the voters to say which one will ____________________.

39. My long-awaited ____________________ with Eileen turned out to be a disappointment when she got sick and could not make it.

40. I am grateful to my parents, who have always ____________________ their own interests and desires to the well-being of their children.

41. I cannot believe that these repeated breakdowns of the machinery are no more than "accidents"; I suspect ____________________.

42. His arguments were so soundly based and so well presented that no one could ____________________ them.

43. Only a tiny ____________________ in the skin showed where the doctor had made the injection.

delude	**epic**	**instantaneous**	**sleuth**
dispatch	**far-fetched**	**misrepresent**	**taskmaster**
dumbfounded	**fray**	**pantomime**	**unerring**
eerie	**groundless**	**pathetic**	**valiant**

44. What a(n) ____________________ feeling it gave us to listen to ghost stories as we sat around the flickering campfire!

45. In the days of silent movies, actors and actresses had to express ideas and emotions by means of ____________________.

46. Coach Robinson is a strict ____________________, who expects instant obedience and 100 percent effort from all his players.

47. We have learned by experience that she is so shrewd that her judgments of people are almost ____________________.

48. You are just ____________________ yourself if you think you can do well in school without regular, systematic study.

49. The story of the men who first climbed to the top of Mount Everest is a(n) ____________________ of human courage and strength.

Word Associations

*Select the word or expression that best completes the meaning of the sentence or answers the question, with particular reference to the meaning of the word in **boldface** type.*

50. A school course dealing with **vocations** will help you
a. become a "math shark"
b. develop your speaking ability
c. plan for a career
d. become a good dancer

51. A person who **abducts** another will probably
a. be arrested for kidnapping
b. receive a prize
c. go to the hospital
d. get picked for a team

52. If you receive news that is **disquieting** you will probably be
a. upset
b. pleased
c. delighted
d. calm

53. Which of the following would be a **chastening** experience?
a. spending the day at the beach
b. doing poorly on this exam
c. winning a scholarship
d. going to a party

54. A person who is wearing **manacles** is probably a
a. teacher
b. judge
c. model
d. prisoner

55. A study program might properly be called **intensive** if it
a. is open to everyone
b. is a lot of fun
c. will help you get a summer job
d. calls for hours of hard work

56. A basketball player who lacks **stamina** would be likely to
a. tire quickly
b. miss foul shots
c. show a lack of team spirit
d. argue with the referee

57. You would seek **sanctuary** if you were
a. rich
b. in the dark
c. being pursued
d. hungry

58. A person who **reminisces** a great deal might be criticized for
a. using foul language
b. borrowing money
c. living in the past
d. insulting other people

59. A student who is lost in a **reverie**
a. is daydreaming
b. is well prepared for final exams
c. has taken a wrong turn
d. has a toothache

60. You will **affirm** your mastery of the words taught in this book if you
a. never use them in class
b. score 100% on this Final Test
c. spell them incorrectly
d. forget what they mean

61. A habit that is deeply **ingrained** is
a. easy to get rid of
b. of no great importance
c. a bad one
d. hard to change

Choosing the Right Meaning

Read each sentence carefully. Then select the item that best completes the statement below the sentence.

62. As punishment for failing the exam, his father **restricted** his after-school activities.

The word **restricted** most nearly means

a. widened **b.** guided **c.** ended **d.** limited

63. The teacher corrected the **misapprehension** that the rule "*I* before *E* except after *C*" applies in all cases.

The word **misapprehension** most nearly means

a. misunderstanding **b.** plan **c.** formula **d.** examination

64. After our ill-fated first meeting, I had many **misgivings** about the new team member, but I've found I like her very much after taking time to get to know her.

The word **misgivings** most nearly means

a. presents **b.** victories **c.** doubts **d.** setbacks

65. The report provided the **data** I needed to finish my research paper.

The word **data** most nearly means

a. money b. information **c.** equipment **d.** assistance

66. He spent so much time **dawdling** over which movie to see that by the time he made a decision, both films had already started.

The word **dawdling** most nearly means

a. working **b.** fighting **c.** napping **d.** loafing

67. Her dream is to turn her talent as a skilled **mimic** into a career as an actress.

The word **mimic** most nearly means

a. politician **b.** athlete **c.** imitator **d.** speaker

68. Although she usually acted meek, during tough times she showed more **grit** than anyone else.

The word **grit** most nearly means

a. courage **b.** judgment **c.** restlessness **d.** fear

69. The **inevitable** result of procrastination is a lot of stress the night before an exam.

The word **inevitable** most nearly means

a. unexpected **b.** regrettable **c.** unavoidable **d.** sudden

70. Those who had been following the case closely thought the "not guilty" verdict a **parody** of justice.

The word **parody** most nearly means

a. example **b.** mockery **c.** fear **d.** cause

WORD LIST

The following is a list of all the words taught in the Units of this book. The number after each entry indicates the page on which the word is defined.

INDEX